Progressive Intolerance

Last Stop Before Hitler

Juleon Schins

Progressive Intolerance:

Last Stop Before Hitler

ISBN 978-1-64550-498-6 (Paperback)

Contents

This book is part of a 2019 decalogue consisting of

- Sign of Times: Music Anthology and Lyric Analysis
- Hollywood Misogyny
- Beginners' Guide to the FED:
  Why it is Unique on our Planet
- The Kennedy Kurse: Four Obvious Konnektions
- Manichaeism and Satanic Child Abuse
- Progressive Intolerance: Last Stop Before Hitler
- Patriotic Ingenuousness
- Deism versus Theism:
  2-7 in the Scientific Arena of the 20th Century
- Feminine Feminist:
  A Missing Link Eluding Discovery
- The Snake: Three Millennia of Anti-Semitism

Dedicated to the Left,
which I warmly appreciate,
whence fatherly admonish

INTRODUCTION
Terminology

In order not to hurt people unnecessarily, I will coin my own definitions of the four basic concepts “politically left”, “politically right”, “morally progressive” and “morally conservative”. Whoever feels “morally progressive”, but does not fit into my definition, does not fall under the conclusions drawn in this booklet. The same holds for any other of the four mentioned concepts.

I.1 Progressive versus Conservative

Throughout this booklet I consider the concepts “progressive” and “conservative” ONLY in a moral sense. They do NOT refer to anything beyond that moral sense. The “morally progressive” firmly *believes* that morality is defined by the law. The “morally conservative” firmly *believes* that morality is defined by human nature, whatever the latter concept may mean. From the very definitions it is obvious that progressives all agree about what is good and bad, while among conservatives many different opinions exist: As many as there exist different opinions concerning the definition of "human nature".

A conservative way to state the same idea is the following: the progressive position concerning provoked abortion is a democratic matter like the choice to give precedence to traffic coming from the right. Both issues may change in time in congruence with the opinion of the democratic majority.

Conservatives agree with progressives concerning traffic laws. They do not agree on provoked abortion, because they *believe* that is not a democratic majority issue. They *believe* that the laws cannot but *reflect* the truth contained in the concept of "human nature". They also *believe* that human nature is defined not so much by our common genetic heritage, but by the nature of the human soul. They *believe* that if humanity had no soul, but bonobo's had, humanity would populate wild life reserves and zoos, while the bonobo's would build churches, government buildings, palaces of justice, police and secret service bureaus.

Whether a tax payer sleeps or not, he remains a person with fundamental rights. I assure you that a wake baby or fetus (at the moment of provoked abortion) expresses his or her feelings much more explicitly than any sleeping adult. Hence, as a conservative, I consider the progressive's opinion on morality as a contradiction in terms.

I.2 Roots of Obscurantism

Take another example of that in order intrinsic stupidity. In Roman times it was obvious that a free Roman citizen could dispose of his slaves as he wished. I consider this behavior as leftist. Why? *Because the law allowed him to.* Any contemporary leftist, supposedly reincarnated a Roman citizen, would not hesitate to slowly roast a slave to death. Obviously, the same leftist would feel highly offended when reincarnated as a Roman slave, but alas, what can society do when the law has been established democratically? Slaves are no people, as the Romans thought. This overt lie has been corrected by the three centuries of Christians offering their lives in the Colosseum. *In not a single other culture such a heroic feat ever occurred.* After 18 centuries, some idiotic obscurantists tried to put the clock back to ancient Roman times. The idiots called their movement "Enlightenment", in order to fool the weak of mind. In this booklet, I will refer to Enlightenment as Obscurantism.

A well-known product of Obscurantism is the anti-Darwinian interpretation of Darwinism. Darwin was a scientist, and he always referred to his brilliant insight as a property of the human body. He never meant it to apply to the human soul. This satanist interpretation of Darwinism was exactly what Obscurantism needed to get Hitler democratically elected. What did all German progressives do, collectively? They chose Hitler, and they stood behind him throughout WW II. They did have moral problems with Hitler's massacre of Jews, Catholic priests, and other social outcasts, but somehow they did not manage to express these moral problems. They had been indoctrinated too long with the Obscurantist notion of morality.

I.3 Jewish Origin of Conservatism

Conservatism was born in the Ancient Jewish society. In the time of the Christ, Sadducees were progressive, Scribes and Pharisees conservative, and the illiterate people filled the gap between the two extremes. A straightforward sign of the Sadducees' progressivity was their throwing away all of the Jewish Bible but its first five books, called the Pentateuch. Jesus, a conservative, ridiculed them by pointing out their plain inconsistency: the Pentateuch mentions "the God of Abraham, Isaac, and Jacob". Jesus remarked, "Well, what do you think? Does God reign over dead, or over living?". The Sadducees felt so embarrassed, that from that moment on, they did not dare to ask a single other question on the interpretation of Holy Scripture. They swallowed their deep humiliation and planned for a horrible revenge.

I.4 Obscurantism in the 20th Century

After the terror attack on Charlie Hebdo, the French comic journal with the famous jokes of Le Charbonnier, one of the lethal victims of that attack, French President

François Hollande emotionally declared that, in spite of all appearances, the initiative of this act of terror was NOT with the Muslims, but with "ces illuminés", these "illuminated", which is, translated in this book's terminology, "these obscurantists".

Progressivity has an intrinsic problem of inconsistency. Whenever a small terror group manipulates society into believing the acceptability of an immoral law, illiterate progressives vote in favor of that law, not knowing that they are being abused. Once the law is in place, and people understand their being deceived, there is no turning back, because the same small terror group will not allow that. Hence, *I do not consider any progressive as immoral, but highly moral, though at the time highly vulnerable to immoral mafias.*

Likewise, were the Lutheran Germans in the Weimar Republic. They were eminently just and righteous people, who fell in a trap prepared by Obscurantism. It took a German-written Papal Letter to make the Catholics understand that Hitler was an Obscurantist, backed by enormous capital from Obscurantism.

Let it be clear to all American progressives: in the Weimar Republic, you would all have voted exactly like German progressives.

I.5 Obscurantism in the 21st Century

A distinctive feature of contemporary Obscurantism is that whatever right-wing party is always called "fascist" by the left wing. It is immediately provided, by all extant progressive parties, with a "cordon sanitaire". That is supposed to mean: "these people are infected with an as lethal as contagious disease".

The illiterate left lacks the brains to understand the intrinsic contradiction of their stand. Their proud preaches of "progressive tolerance" only refers to those who think like they do. That is not tolerance, but incest.

Real tolerance is giving up a tiny bit of one's majority democratic rights in favor of more freedom for a large minority.

In the German Wehrmacht (not to be mistaken for Nazi's) the officials used to say to the privates: "überlass das Denken den Pferden!", or "leave the thinking to the horses".

I.6 Left and Right

In this booklet I *define* the terms left and right to refer to proponents of a care-taking Nation, and of a free market, respectively. That is to say, the left strives at building a huge administration, which busies itself with the administration of *spending money* on whatever is needed to realize their Utopia, even at the cost of taking over parental responsibility with respect to the education of their own children.

On the other hand, the right needs a government *only for three main tasks:*

- the juridical chase on illegal cartels that monopolize the free market
- dictating the high-school exams and overseeing the emission of licenses
- organizing the national defense

This endeavor coincides with the Catholic 19th century principle of "subsidiarity", coined in the context of the social defense of the rights of factory employees: *The moral obligation to solve political problems on the lowest scale possible.* In Europe the very opposite occurs: Brussels extends its prescriptions to the height of sidewalks.

While an army can only be organized on a national level, a school can be organized on the level of a suburb. The government does not need to specify what matter will be taught in the 12th week at day 3, hour 4. The government only needs to come up with an exam that tests the children's ability on the field of language, arts, and sciences. Why ask questions on Darwinism, as long as the American people are deeply divided on this issue? *The mere effort to do so measures one's intolerance.*

The very opposite of "subsidiarity" is "centralization of power". The ideal of left-wing centralization was the reign of the French Louis XIV (the "Sun King"), while the right-wing ideal is the chaos of late Medieval sovereign North-Italian cities. The latter invented the stock market, by te way.

Given that the couple conservative-progressive is defined morally, and that of right-left politically, one would expect all four combinations to occur: conservative right, conservative left, progressive right, and progressive left. However, that is not at all the case.

Throughout the booklet quotes are written in a different font as compared to my own text.

CHAPTER 1

Fascism, Nazism, Communism

The masterpiece of German marketing was having people believe that Hitler was an Austrian, and Mozart a German. The masterpiece of left-wing politics was having believe that fascism and nazism are right-wing phenomena. The syllogism is quite simple: Hitler and Mussolini committed racist genocide, that is politically incorrect, left-wing politics is politically correct, hence they came from the right wing.

Reality is quite the opposite.

1.1 Nazism

The term "Nazi" is a four-letter short for the German adjective "**na**tionalso**zi**alistisch". That adjective is but one term of a German Party called NSDAP, a short for "**N**ational**S**ozialistische **D**eutsche **A**rbeiter**P**artei". Translated to English, this means literally "National Socialist German Laborers' Party" The name leaves no doubt that this party is a left-wing party. Hitler headed this party at the moment the Chancellor requested him to form a government. Hitler's original voters either came from the left or the extreme left. Who thinks that Hitler was an extreme right-wing phenomenon, should go back to high school and take a history lesson.

Hitler was awarded a medal for courage shown during WW I. He was too eccentric, however, to be promoted in the army. He always remained a lowest level official. That is a second proof of Hitler coming from the left: right-wing Putsches are always decisions made by either generals (like Videla) or coronels (like Gadhafi). Hence, the methods of Hitler's Gestapo (**Ge**heime **Sta**ats**po**lizei, or Secret National Police) are *identical* to those of the communist Stasi (**Sta**ats**si**cherheitsdienst, or Bureau of National security).[1]

---

1 See "The Snake: 2400 years of Anti-Semitism", by Yitzhak Rosenthal (2019)

1.2 Fascism

Benito Mussolini was, from 1900 to 1914, member of the Italian socialist party.[2] Moreover, he was both journalist and founder of outspoken left-wing magazines like "L'Avvenire del Lavoratore",[3] "Avanti!",[4] and "Utopia". Clearly, Mussolini's fascism is exactly as left-wing as nazism and communism. With Mussolini it was even more obvious, as he never had an army profile. He was an Italian citizen with extreme left-wing ambitions. In order to seize power Mussolini did have to fight other left-wing parties, but in many-party systems like in European countries, such is rather rule than exception. Left-wing parties are competitors for leftist votes, in much the same way as right-wing parties are competitors for right-wing votes.

As Mussolini never rose to nationally recognized Italian leadership, and never massively killed his fellow Italians (apart from sending Italian soldiers to Russia), he does not make it to the list of mass-killers of history.

On the other hand, nazism and communism do carry the responsibility for mass executions on their own

2 The socialist party sacked him in 1914 because of his Great-Italian ambitions
3 Translated, "the future of the laborer"
4 Translated "Forward!": the socialist magazine of Milan

citizens (apart from waging inhuman wars), and this in *total absence of any civil war.*[5]

Compared to left-wing assassinations, right-wing assassinations (by army leaders like Gaddafi, Videla, Pinochet and Franco) do not sum up to a single percent of the left-wing ones. The crying mothers are simply paid by left-wing resources in order to divert the attention from historical reality. Too bad, however, that this counting exercise requires some historical knowledge. That is the weak point of left-wing intelligence: it considers that history has to *confirm* the left-wing ideal. If it does not do so, the historical facts *have to be manipulated*, else the absolute truth of the left-wing world view would be damaged. And that is a mortal sin in the Church of Political Left.

1.3 The Fate of Dictatorial Systems

History shows that right-wing dictators give up their power in favor of democracy, as soon as their country does not face the danger of an imminent civil war, or of imminent left-wing dictatorship. On the other hand, left-wing dictatorships either never end, or end in a

5 That is, merely based upon an ideal, a vision, of how society should look like

tremendous blood bath. The 20th and 21st centuries are replete with examples:

Stalin's Russia
Fidel Castro's Cuba
Chávez' Venezuela
Pol-Pot's Cambodia
Ho-Chi-Minh's Vietnam
Pathet's Laos
Mao's China

These are all self-declared Marxist-Leninist dictatorships: A synonym for killing fields.

1.4 Stalinism and Maoism

Ukraine's farming system used to provide the whole of Europe with its fantastic grain production. Stalin's conscience problem, however, was the income difference between rich landowners and poor laborers, or farmers-on-rent. Hence he decided to wipe out the whole population, both land owners and laborers, because the former had failed to socialize their wealth, and the latter had failed to seize it by force. That was the immediate end of Ukraine's grain production, and Stalin's first deportation of a whole country's population to northern

Siberia, where people had no future but dying of undercooling. Stalin's five-year plan alone required more deaths than the all deaths of WW II summed up, at both sides: Military and Civil at the time.

Just like Stalin reduced Hitler to a goblin, Mao did so to Stalin. He emitted a decree, according to which all Chinese were to give up their metal for the sake of Chinese glory. Where Hitler killed tens, Stalin killed hundreds, and Mao thousands of millions.

1.5 Right-Wing Dictatorial Systems

The main difference between left and right dictatorial systems is that left-wing dictators come forth from political leaders, while right-wing dictators from army leaders. Usually the army sympathizes with a right-wing dictator, while it abhors of a left-wing dictator. An excellent example of the latter was Hitler's continuous quarrel with his Wehrmacht generals and coronels.

This is very hard to understand for leftists, because it is an historical fact: soldiers think like all other ordinary people. They proceed from them; they are part of them. Consequently, right-wing dictators are much more appreciated by the ordinary people than left-wing dictators. This was the case for Libyan coronel Muammar Ghaddafi, Argentinian general Jorge Videla, Chilean general Augusto Pinochet, and Spanish general Francisco

Franco. They all lost their reputation *after giving up their power in favor of democracy, merely as a consequence of heavy brainwashing investment by the left.*

Libyans literally *adored* Ghaddafi. And which was Ghaddafi's biggest crime? He owned a lot of gold. He owned so much of it, that he publicly declared that the Libyan gold-backed currency would in no time replace the Northern African (French) Franc. Neither Nicolas Sarkozy liked the idea, nor did Hillary Clinton, both puppets of extreme left-wing mafias. So they made a deal. *Hillary's death squads would slaughter the Lybian population and kill Ghaddafi, while France and the US would publish the slaughter photographs as due to Ghaddafi.* How exactly they divided Ghaddafi's gold is not known, but fact is that today's North-African currency is still the Franc.

Meanwhile, Clinton ordered her death squads to continue their march onto Iraq, in order to fund ISIS and provide it with the newest military technology. The Muslim enlisted fighters were commanded to hit some "so-called" Jewish colonists. This gave them the conviction they were indeed a Muslim organization. They did not know, and still do not know, that they were fully financed by the Clinton Foundation, and led by the Israeli Mossad. All assumedly Muslim terrorism in Europe therefore boils down to a mere execution of the Mossad's directives,[6] the latter being fully controlled by the EZ mafia.

1.6 Left-Progressive Intolerance

The intolerance of left progressivity is again a historical fact, and as such incomprehensible to the political left. It has an ideal of such intrinsic beauty (equality of income for all citizens, except the divine leaders), that this ideal must be true, by mere religious dogma. Any historical evidence against the beauty of this ideal *must necessarily be* the result of right-wing manipulation.

Since political left-wing ideals are self-evident, all people who do not embrace them must necessarily be anti-social scum, not even worth prison meat. This is not the result of *learning from the past experiences,* but simply a *belief in the main dogma of the Church of the Political Left.*

Too bad, that the term "tolerance" refers to the majority's free choice to offering up *some majority rights* in favor of the largest minority. As mentioned in the introduction, majority "tolerance" towards the majority is mere incest. The Leftist Church never understood this.

6 This was more than obvious in England, where Scotland Yard and Mossad quarreled publicly over the authorship of the 2005 terror attack on the London subways.

On the other hand, all right wing dictators use to give way to democracies. This is clearly the case with Argentinian general Jorge Videla, Chilean general Augusto Pinochet, and Spanish general Francisco Franco. Videla paid for his military coup with death in a prison, inflicted onto him by a blindly rabid, democratic left. The man may have many murders on his conscience, but nobody can assess how many ulterior murders he avoided by saving his country a civil war.[7]

Have you ever seen this happen in a left-wing dictatorship? I wager my very own that Venezuelan Nicolás Maduro rather kills all Venezuelans than taking the risk of imprisonment.

The transition from dictatorship to democracy is an exclusive property of the right wing. It specifically did NOT apply to Lenin's Russia, Mao's China, Pol Pot's Cambodia, Ho-Chi-Minh's Vietnam, nor to Fidel Castro's Cuba. Under Fidel's brother Raúl, Cuba has turned into a deep state of corrupt army officials.

---

7 The mere fact that general Videla freely appeared for a tribunal, already proves his clean conscience.

CHAPTER 2

Emotion and Sentiment

2.1 Progressive Psychopathology

The right-wing progressive psychopathology was born in the late 19th century, when Africa was systematically left out of business by global companies like Nestlé. They were able to block African products on the monopolized market, there was no law prohibiting them to do so, whence they did it: morality was no issue. Africa was once and forever forced to deliver their cocoa to Nestlé for production costs. The right-wing conscience indicator fell to zero Kelvin. The right-wing progressives needed mental compensation to appease their oppressed consciences. Hence they invested 1% of their profits into window dressing. They became the glorious poverty fighters for all people over the globe. This immediately caught the fancy of left-wing progressives, who had their conscience problems, too.[8]

2.2 The Netherlands

The Netherlands have illustrated history with the invention of a theology which declared the black race as an animal. Hence the South-African word *apartheid,* which is a Dutch neologism for separation of mankind and bestiality. The root being "apart", it is clearly of Germanic origin, as is the final part of the word, "heid", translated "hood" (like in "parenthood"). The Dutch two main provinces, Northern and Southern Holland, were the spiritual ancestors of that theology, together with the other four sea-bound provinces Utrecht, Zeeland, Friesland, and Groningen. What can one expect from a country that made its greatest profits abroad, in what my ancestors called "wingewesten", translated "provinces of profit"?

The easiest way to get rich is to steal. That is why the progressive psychopathology is so infectious. It infected half of my country, to wit, the north-western part above "the rivers": The Rhine (flowing in from Germany) and the Meuse (flowing in from Belgium).

---

8 Albeit not from mistreating the African continent as a whole

The Southern part would later be infected by collective apathy. That was the glorious achievement of a single Dutch Cardinal, Bernard Alfrink. In September 2018 an influential Dutch newspaper reported that Alfrink had several times relocated pedophile priests in new parishes after proven sexual abuse of children, *at least for four priests*. Obviously, such practices earned him the highest Royal and Knight decorations:

Knight Great Cross, Order of Orange-Nassau (1963)
Knight Great Cross, Order of the Dutch Lion (1974)
Bailiff of Honor Great Cross Sovereign Military Hospital, Order of Saint John of Jerusalem, Rhodes, and Malta
Knight Great Cross, Order of the Holy Sepulcher of Jerusalem
Grand Official, Order of the Crown of Oak (Luxemburg)
Grand Prior of the Dutch Commandeers of the Holy Sepulcher of Jerusalem

---

This says as much of our rotten Knight Orders, as it does about the thoroughly rotten Dutch Royal House, which is well documented to have co-financed Hitler's Nazi regime. And what shall we say about the below eminently "Catholic" Universities that elected Bernard Cardinal Alfrink for their honorary doctorates:

Katholieke Universiteit Leuven, Belgium (1961, Theology)
University of Notre Dame, IN, USA (1965, Law)
Villanova University, PA, USA (1973, Education)
University of Yale, CT, USA (1976, Theology)
Katholieke Universiteit Nijmegen, NL (1976, Theology)

This not so holy Cardinal used to reprimand his priests by calling them publicly by their surnames, and asking them: "you here, too?" Probably nothing but a consequence of his own traumatic experience during priesthood when interrogated about his presence at all parties in the diocese. Once he received the following answer:[9]

> Sure, Your Excellency. If Your Excellency would kindly submit, I was born here.

2.3 France

Examples of Dutch right-wing politicians who plead for the reduction of immigration are Janmaat, Fortuyn, and Wilders. The eminently tolerant left immediately tore them to pieces, as they could no longer bear their painfully crying consciences.[10]

---

9 https://nl.wikipedia.org/wiki/Bernardus_Alfrink
10 Pim Fortuyn was assassinated by a left-wing mercenary, whom nobody knows the whereabouts, carefully hidden by the leftist mafia.

The French have their Protestant Slave Trading Companies, too, in Nantes and Bordeaux. However, Catholicism always had a majority over Protestantism. That is the only reason why Marine Le Pen receives less deadly blows than Dutch Catholic politicians defending their cultural identity. But EZ will never allow her to rule, even at the cost of coming up with an EZ puppet like Emmanuel Macron, banker of Jacob Rothschild. This geriatrophile did not make it to Presidency thanks to the good looks of his wife, nor to his long experience in politics, but only to the financial mafia designated EZ in the present decalogue.

2.4 Italy

In Italy the strong woman goes by the name of Giorgia Meloni. I transcribed her speech in Verona, at the congress for the family, in "Feminine Feminist". Unlike the progressives, who hate their own culture (an accumulation of lies, murders and deceit), conservatives like Meloni, Fortuyn, and Le Pen love it (because of the many virtues that built it). Italy has suffered an unimaginable immigration of Northern Africans, that it has neither the funds nor the necessary infrastructure to provide with job, food and roof. The immigrants cannot help it either, but they have to fight for survival, and can only do so by stealing. This I do not consider a sin, by the way. The sin lies *exclusively* with the progressive right, which caused Africa to stall as an economic slave continent for at least three centuries.

2.5 Spain

Exactly the same thing is happening to Spain. This time the conservatives unite in a party called VOX, which is Latin for “voice”, apart from being some Spanish acronym. The last thing I saw on Spanish television, before I returned from holidays to the Netherlands, is how Spanish progressives mistreat that party. A spokesman of VOX had dared to point out that a group violation of an 18-year old Spanish girl was the work of *Maghrebis*, Spanish for import Moroccans. The two left-progressive anchor-women went hysterical:

> VOX is racist, we don't need any protection, and certainly not of men, who are the cause of our misfortunes.

My dear anchorwomen: possibly *you two* do not need men’s help, but the sevenfold-violated 18-year old girl was in dire need of male help. So what is that supposed to mean: “we don’t need help of men?” Are you talking for yourselves or for the Spanish female population? Do you really mean that *all men indistinctly* are potential group violators? Then why do you clothe like whores? Is that to attract other lesbians, or because *you were told by your male managing directors* to prove your point by exhibiting your genitals?

Just like the Netherlands, France, and Italy, Spain has already shown not be able to cope with political corruption, nor with keeping their own population from systematic suicide by large-scale infertility programs, provoked abortion, abuse of substance and alcohol.[11] Meanwhile, progressives *all over the place* keep preaching that more and more Muslims should be imported.

The latter choice is actually smart, for once. That such an import destroys the Spanish culture is of no concern to progressives, as they have none but a cynic sympathy for self-extinction. *The essential idea is that the suicided progressive voters have to be substituted by living ones, even if they are culturally stuck in the 8th century.* At least, that is where I would historically place the golden age of chopping off hands and feet for petty thefts, mostly due to children dying of hunger. "Who then lives, then cares", is the motto of children-less progressivity. Yes, sure. Progressives do merit a collective Darwin's Award.

---

11 One of the recent responsibilities of the Dutch police is to control the chemical purity of ecstasy, usually abused of in disco's. This is a typical retrograde "progressive" solution to a moral problem. It is solved by granting that everybody gets his cut: The National Taxes, the National Police, and all associated producers of ecstasy. Under the ultra-hypocritical pretense of executing the law on consumption safety.

2.6 England

As far as "racism" is concerned, we heard that before. Progressive love to chant "racists, Nazis, Fascists" in choir. Eric Clapton was crucified by a retrograde English progressivity for pleading for a "white England". It is somewhat blunt, I admit, but do not mistake a musician for a politician. Clapton simply used a cheap image to point out the obvious: That among Muslims, the percentage of males who think of western women as a collection of freely disposable whores, is ten to one hundred times larger than among (ex-)Christians. This is not because male Muslims are *per se* more violent than (ex-)Christians, but because in their home village they are used to seeing women in burkas. What does an English progressive expect from such people, when confronted with our putrid television porno, and its "willful actresses"?

Not so much, probably. Progressives do not have the brains to understand the very concept of "culture". British progressivity feels it should follow mainland Europe in this nonsense, and take up boatloads of Muslims who profoundly abhor of progressivity. No wonder Muslim fathers shut up their girls at home (ordinary practice among Semites), and wait for an honest, virtuous, imported Muslim to marry her. When a Muslim girl allows that to happen, she becomes her husband's slave. No wonder, again, that Muslim women are trying to escape their retrograde culture by every means possible.

Meanwhile, progressives keep asking themselves why (apart from France) Muslims not only do not integrate, but actively oppose cultural integration.[12] A conservative is much more pragmatic: first try to cure your own population's collective suicide, and once that is solved, you may try to help out other people. *One simply cannot give what one does not have oneself.*

---

12 I propose we dedicate another award to progressivity, for the invention and consistent practical application of negative IQ.

CHAPTER 3
Terror

3.1 Terror and Progressivity

Terror is an exclusively progressive achievement. There does not exist such a thing as "conservative terror". This may be a mere question of definition. In my dictionary, *terror is defined as a consistent series of secret attacks on the lives of one's co-nationals, with the goal of forcing them into a given political position.*

When conservatives are confronted with terror, they hit back, and start a full-scale open war. That is not terror. That is *war against terror*. The differences are:

- terror requires secrecy, while war is open
- terror demands innocent lives, while in an openly declared war there are no innocent soldiers;
- terror implies a loss of freedom, while *war against terror* searches the conquest of freedom.

One may easily check the history of whatever nation. I did so already in the two books of this decalogue, "the snake" and "patriotic ingenuousness". The results of that investigation are astonishing: Since 2400 BC, all terror is systematically orchestrated by EZ, a Jewish-American progressive mafia. EZ's tactics are to reign by spreading discord wherever one can:

- Get Athens to fight Sparta (2400 BC);
- Get Catholics to fight Protestants, simply by placing explosives at both sides;
- Split up countries in a fratricide war, like the Spanish civil war of 1936-1939. That war literally began with communists burning down convents. These communists were definitely NOT Spanish, as not a single Spanish in his or her right mind would spontaneously do something like that, even if the hierarchy had been in bed with rich aristocrats for ages;
- Get US Democrats to fight US Republicans. The ferocious hatred between the two is clearly fratricidal, and cannot but come from outside. The 9/11 terror attack on the New York twin towers was an obvious example of EZ orchestration;
- Get France and Germany to fight twice in a single century. Many do not see this, but it is rather obvious that Hitler was nothing but a puppet financed by EZ. Their only goal in WW II was to steal German-Jewish savings deposited in Rothschild's banks.

To name but a few.

3.2 Jared Kushner

The older generation readership knows this of course, but the younger possibly not: 666 is the number of a Fifth Avenue high riser in downtown New York, for which Jared Kushner, President Trump's son in law, bade $ 1800 million in 2007, an amount that is at least twice the price for similar buildings at different numbers.

This is nothing but a manifestation of Jared's fixation on kabbalah. Short after Jared's bankrupt, Anbang bought it for $ 2850 million. Surprise, surprise: today the building is in the hands of the "Kushner clan". Obviously, a twenty-year old has not yet earned $ 1800 million, so he cannot have been anything else but a dispensable puppet in his clan. Too bad for President, the essentials of Jared's loans to cover the $ 1800 million, came from Banks in China and Russia. Follow the money, and you know immediately where Trump's information concerning democrat election strategy came from.

Is that morally wrong? Not on the right-wing progressive scale, which has been set by Nixon's Watergate scandal, but obviously on the conservative scale. Whoever thinks that democrats after Nixon were cleaner than Nixon himself, is a dreamer.

Let me introduce Timothy L. O'Brien to the readership: executive editor of "Bloomberg Opinion", full-job journalist and ex-editor for the New York Times, the Wall Street Journal, the Huffington Post and the Talk magazine. With these credentials, someone more opposed to Trump's ideals is hardly thinkable. In the following article, he heavily hits Jared Kushner.[13] I do not claim this article to tell the full truth, but at least a high degree does.

Senators, Please Ask Jared Kushner About 666 Fifth Avenue

A Chinese financier has pulled out of a bailout for Trump's son-in-law. Now let's talk about his meetings with a Russian bank. In a happy moment in the otherwise cloudy world of the Trump family and the flood of financial conflicts they've carted into Washington, a major Chinese investor has decided not to pour billions of dollars into a Manhattan skyscraper owned by the Jared Kushner clan.

Had this deal gone forward —the effect would have been to bail Kushner out of a huge, misbegotten investment while letting his family take home at least $400 million and retain a minority ownership stake in the building— it would have compromised President Donald Trump's diplomacy with China.

The background: Anbang, an insurer and prolific deal-maker close to China's government, had considered investing $4 billion in 666 Fifth Avenue. Kushner had overpaid for the building in 2007, when he bought it with the help of bank

13 Bloomberg LP, March 29th, 2017

loans for $1.8 billion. The financial crisis ensued, occupancy rates plummeted and Kushner had to be rescued by outside investors to keep the troubled building afloat. Anbang's investment would have valued the building at a handsome $2.85 billion, and also refinanced about $1.15 billion in debt. The possibility of a transaction brought scrutiny from two Bloomberg news reporters, Caleb Melby and David Kocieniewski, as well as from Congress and the New York Times. I discussed it in a column here two weeks ago. And for good reason: Kushner is a senior White House adviser who has Trump's ear on foreign policy. The math of Trump's 36-year-old son-in-law being saved from a reckless investment by China presented all sorts of conflicts of interest and the potential for disastrous policy moves by the White House.

So Anbang is now gone and all has been made right? Well, no. Kushner's family still owns a building that needs a financial lifeline, so 666 Fifth Avenue presents something that Congress may want to examine more closely when Jared Kushner meets with the Senate Intelligence Committee as part of an inquiry into possible collusion between Trump's campaign team and Russia during the 2016 presidential election. The Federal Bureau of Investigation is also investigating the Trump-Russia connection, its director, James Comey, confirmed during a congressional hearing last week. There has been no suggestion that Kushner is part of the FBI probe, but the Senate's decision to question him makes him, as the Times pointed out when it broke the story of Kushner's upcoming testimony, "the closest person to the president to be called upon in any of the investigations, and the only one currently serving in the White House." Kushner's meetings with Russian bankers during the presidential transition last fall and winter apparently help explain why the Senate is interested in speaking with him. The timeline matters. Kushner began talking with Chinese investors about 666 Fifth Avenue last summer, around the time that Trump locked up the Republican nomination. Then he spearheaded more serious talks that took place in New York about a week after his father-in-law was elected in November.

According to the Times, Kushner met with Russia's ambassador to the U.S., Sergey Kislyak, in early December as part of what appeared to be normal presidential transition meetings. A second Kislyak meeting with a Kushner deputy followed in December, as well as another, brokered by Kislyak, between Kushner and the head of a Russian bank, Vnesheconombank. The U.S. had imposed financial sanctions on that bank because of Russian President Vladimir Putin's military incursions in Ukraine and annexation of Crimea. Vnesheconombank has close ties to the Kremlin and its chief executive, Sergey Gorkov, attended a training academy for members of Russia's security and intelligence services. A Trump spokeswoman described Kushner's meetings with the Russians as routine, which they may have been given his role at the time as Trump's liaison to foreign powers. But given how important 666 Fifth Avenue was for Kushner at the time, it's also possible that he saw the Russians as potential investors alongside the Chinese. Or as financial backups should the Chinese walk away from a deal. The Times, citing a government source, said that the Senate plans to ask Kushner if financial help for 666 Fifth was part of his chats with Gorkov and Vnesheconombank.

Kushner's responses to questions about Russian and Chinese financing for his family's building may clarify what inspired him to negotiate so diligently with foreign lenders at a time when he surely understood the negotiating value of having his father-in-law on the cusp of assuming power in the White House.

His appearance in the Senate will also offer a chance to quiz him about the intersection of personal financial dealings and public policymaking. That's an issue that remains troubling because Kushner, and his wife Ivanka Trump, and the president himself, have avoided adequately separating themselves from their private business interests even as they wield power.

3.3 The Middle East

What is going on here? Does an extreme left-wing progressive attack an extreme right-wing progressive? It appears so, from outside. However, one should take utmost care with media in general: Hollywood,[14] New York Times, Washington Post, and all European subsidiaries[15] are fully owned by Rothschild's banking empire. That empire is not another huge bank in some country anymore. It is a system of thousands of banks all over the world, which directly depend on EZ, that is to say, to a mafia presently presided by Jacob Rothschild. Together, these banks have about ten times the financial strength of the USA. Moreover, EZ determines American financial policy by means of the Federal Reserve System,[16] which is as anti-constitutional as one can possibly imagine. It should not come as a surprise that Rothschild owns the full American debt, either.[17] Nor should the "lies" by subsequent Democrat and Republic US Presidents concerning the Vietnam war surprise American citizens. Obviously, it is not up to American

14 See "Sign of Times: A Music Anthology with Lyrics Analysis" (2019) and "Hollywood's Misogyny" (2019) in this decalogue

15 All influential European journals merely copy-paste what Washington Post and New York Times (EZ's main outlets) write about President Trump and US foreign policy, as Rothschild's financial mafia owns the former, too.

16 See "A Beginners' Guide to the FED: Why it is Unique on Our Planet" (2019) from this decalogue

17 The US National Debt outgrew the US BNP a few years ago

Presidents to determine the foreign policy. That is already in EZ's hands, since many decennia. This equally holds for secret ops of the CIA (like 2001/9/11).[18] What American knows of a single American President (but possibly JFK) who ever criticized the Israeli illegal expansion policy by means of occupation *kibbutz's*?[19] How funny! So many Presidents, from the left as well as from the right, *all coincide in their Middle Eastern politics. They even coincide in hiding the Israeli attempt to sink an American Strategic Reconnaissance Vessel, the USS Liberty, in June 8th, 1967, near the Sinai Peninsula?* Meanwhile, apart from Israel, in the Middle East all countries but Iran have fallen into chaos: Lebanon, Syria, Iraq, Jordan, Saudi Arabia, Egypt, and all small oil-producing countries.

As sure as a German bunker, this has little to do with oil: It suffices to look at the US oil-selling policy. Thanks to President Trump, Iran still stands today. On the day he fulfills his two terms, Iran will be officially declared a national enemy, with exactly the same armaments that The Obama Administration adduced for Iraq, in which not a single genocidal weapon had been found by an official NATO delegation?

The older generation readership might remember that Iran's ex-President Mahmoud Ahmadinejad (he served

---

18 See "Patriotic Ingenuousness" (2019) in this decalogue

19 Except Jack Kennedy, and the nearly-assassinated Ronald Reagan. JFK's capital sin was EO 11,110. For more detail, see "The Kennedy Kurse" (2019).

from 2005 through 2013) accused the US government of the 9/11 terror attack. This was twice stupid. First, the government was not at all implied, apart from evidently Vice President Dick Cheney,[20] and possibly Secretary of Defense Donald Rumsfeld, given the latter's perfect timing of a $ 2300 billion gap in DoD transactions:[21]

> The technology revolution has transformed organizations across the private sector, but not ours, not fully, not yet. We are, as they say, tangled in our anchor chain. Our financial systems are decades old. According to some estimates, we cannot track $2.3 trillion in transactions. We cannot share information from floor to floor in this building because it's stored on dozens of technological systems that are inaccessible or incompatible.

The reason given by Rumsfeld is utterly nonsensical. I do not even think of making my point here.

---

20 On Infoplease webpage "https://www.infoplease.com/us/government/executive-branch/cabinet-members-of-george-w-bush" Dick Cheney's photograph does not even appear. Apparently, EZ has already started to obliterate him from history. On 9/11, while President G.W. Bush was hiding in some unknown bunker, Vice President Dick Cheney exercised full Presidential power in the White House. *As is clear from Secretary of Transportation (2001-20060) Norman Yoshio Mineta's testimony, Cheney was responsible for keeping all aircraft on the ground, while the drones were reportedly approaching the Pentagon and the Twin Towers.*

21 Monday September 10th, 2001: *The day before 9/11*

Now back to Iran's ex-President Mahmoud Ahmadinejad. As we already mentioned, he was not smart when accusing the US government of planning 9/11, first, because it did not. Neither did the American people, who rightly consider the Middle-Eastern punishments of homosexuals outrageous and unhuman, as they consider Muslim heavy-bearded religious leaders throwing around fatwa's at everyone who dares to propose an innovation to their 8th century law book, *Quran's Sharia.*

The second reason he should not do so, is his total lack of military intelligence. If the Iranian Secrete Services are not able to explain the already mentioned Israeli brute attack on the USS Liberty in 1967, President Mahmoud Ahmadinejad had better think it over twice before saying things that only contribute to his popularity within Iran.

The USS Liberty was US's newest espionage vessel, replete with the newest technological inventions. Israel does not allow foreign espionage, whence the USS Liberty was predestined to return to the US a spook. Israel's combined Secret Forces bombarded the vessel during a full week, leaving behind an empty vessel that did nothing but floating. The necessary amount of floating to reach the Libyan coast. It was repaired and painted anew. The survivors were received in the US as heroes. James Ennes was one of them. Unlike all his colleagues, he did not settle for a cheap silence: The official briefing to the American people only mentioned "a skirmish", due to a slight "miscommunication" with Israel. Poor Ennes did not believe his own ears nor eyes. According to him, "all military radio stations bordering the Mediterranean Sea had been receiving SOS-signals of USS Liberty", so he decided to write a book about what had happened. His book has never been read in the US, because of EZ's full control of mass media. Both the American Marine and the American Congress declared only minor flaws, and all major flaws ended up, systematically, in the cover-up bin.[22] James Ennes never understood that the orders to attack the USS Liberty came from the same person who controls the US media. Probably he thought of JFK as assassinated by a lone wolf, too. RIP. Ennes was a courageous progressive.

3.4 Modern Slavery

As EZ already tried in the 18th century, to wit, to re-introduce slavery, it is still trying in the 21st, though not by blunt imposition, *but rather by collective suicidal free choice.* Both conservatism and progressivity hardly understand what is going on. The single most important divergence between conservatism and progressivity is that, while conservatism smells something has to be completely wrong, progressivity understands nothing at all nor smells any danger.

22 See "Patriotic Ingenuousness" (2019) in this decalogue

Even though I fiercely attack progressivity in this booklet, I am not at all personally against any particular person with progressive ideals. Quite to the contrary, I love any progressive person as much as I love any conservative: As a true Child of God. The reason for my fierce attacks on progressivity is only one: its ideal is a lie. I do not hold any single progressive person accountable, nor all of them together, for defending a lie. I rather pity them for their failing to understand that progressivity is a lie. Every negation of an absolute moral order is a lie, by definition. EZ abuses of that lie to make people feel more comfortable, by relieving them of their bad consciences,[23] and by offering more bearable lives, prey to the abuse of alcohol and reality-softening substances.

What progressivity does not grasp, is that this mentality is exactly what EZ tries to spread all over the globe. Once the majority of people on our planet believe in their dream-world, they have willfully sunk to the very level of slaves. Deprived of all virtues, such slaves will not be able to fight any battle beyond gaming level. EZ will simply steam-roll over our emptied cultures. EZ is smart enough to understand that vices only lead to weakness, whence their own are strongly admonished NOT to follow the main stream amorality. EZ's obvious prime enemy is the Catholic Church.[24]

---

23 loaded with provoked abortions

24 Remember obscurantist Voltaire: "écrasez l'infâme". In free translation: "kill the Catholic Church".

EPILOGUE
The Empty Quadrant

As promised in the introduction, I would come back on the question why not all four cross-species exist, between the two moral categories "progressive" and "conservative" on one hand, and the two political categories "left" and "right", as defined in the introduction. Indeed, we mentioned both right-wing and left-wing progressives, as well as their interaction in history. We also mentioned right-wing conservatives. Apparently, the only category not mentioned in this booklet is that of the left-wing conservatives. I do not mean to affirm that this category contains really nobody, but that whatever people might exist in that category never made any impact. In short, this category is FAPP[25] empty.

The obvious question is why: Why would there be no politically relevant people that are left-wing and conservative? Or, in terms of the very definitions: Why

---

25 "for all practical purposes", as John Bell used to say in his treatises on the quantum mechanics of two entangled particles

would there be no people who believe both in morality as defined by human nature (as opposed to human majority choice) and in the nation as an economically care-taking institute?[26]

Does the impossibility derive from one of the two principles (left wing or conservative), or does it derive from both? From a conservative perspective the reason is quite obvious: It derives from conservatism. An economically care-taking nation is much too liable to take care of everything, religion and ideals included. Hence, conservatives are essentially opposed to nations that do not respect the Catholic notion of subsidiarity.

Whatever centralizing system, albeit conservative in name, is horrifying to any conservative. That should equally apply to conservative political action: It cannot be possible that two different persons share views on the solution to a given social problem, only for their being conservatives.

On the other hand, I do not see a solution to the FAPP-absence of left-wing conservatives from the left-wing point of view. Why should one's being in favor of a care-taking nation necessarily be amoral, in the sense of considering morality as a national democratic choice? Is "taking care" in radical opposition to accepting the notion of a human nature, as fixed as are one's genes, and therefore not liable to democratic election? To a

26 The first-century Church was a prototype society that was both conservative and left-wing. However, that Church opposed the ambition to ever make it to a nation. Hence, it does not qualify.

conservative this is mere inconsistency. Apparently, inconsistency is at the very heart of progressivity.

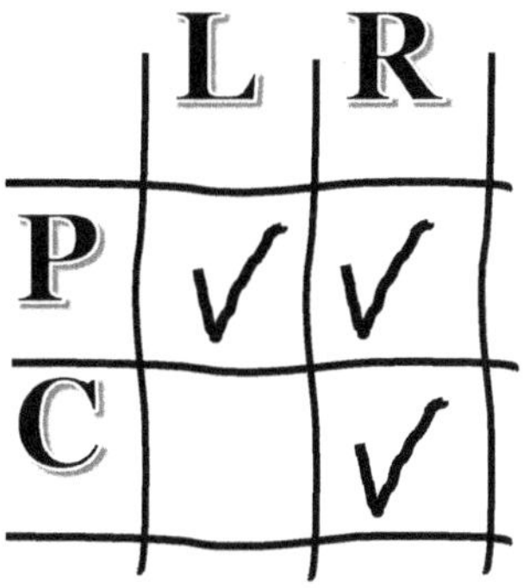

The only person I know, who possibly could claim to be a left-wing conservative, is French President François Hollande.

Appendix 1
The Zionist Protocols

The two appendices included in this book were originally meant for "The Snake", part of this same political decalogue. However, "The Snake" got too thick, whence I decided to publish its two appendices as an ebook on my publisher's website. Since the material treated in the present book is very intertwined with that of "The Snake", the two appendices are published here.

A1.1 Introduction

Victor E. Marsden, the author of the following translation of the famous "Protocols of the Meetings of the Learned Elders of Zion" was himself a victim of the Revolution.[27] He had lived for many years in Russia and was married to

---

27 All text in this Appendix is reproduced from http://www.biblebelievers.org.au/przion1.htm

a Russian lady. Among his other activities in Russia he had been for a number of years a Russian Correspondent of the *Morning Post*, a position he occupied when the Revolution broke out, and his vivid descriptions of events in Russia will still be in the recollection of many of the readers of that Journal. Naturally, he was singled out for the anger of the Soviet. On the day that Captain Cromie was murdered by Jews, Victor Marsden was arrested and thrown into the Peter-Paul Prison, expecting every day to have his name called out for execution. This, however, he escaped, and eventually he was allowed to return to England very much of a wreck in bodily health. However, he recovered under treatment and the devoted care of his wife and friends. One of the first things he undertook, as soon as he was able, was this translation of the Protocols. Mr. Marsden was eminently well qualified for the work. His intimate acquaintance with Russia, Russian life and the Russian language on the one hand, and his mastery of a terse literary English style on the other, placed him in a position of advantage, which few others could claim. The consequence is that we have in his version an eminently readable work, and though the subject-matter is somewhat formless, Mr. Marsden's literary touch reveals the thread running through the twenty-four Protocols.

It may be said with truth that this work was carried out at the cost of Mr. Marsden's own life's blood. He told the writer of this Preface that he could not stand more than an hour at a time of his work on it in the British Museum, as the diabolical spirit of the matter which he was obliged to turn into English made him positively ill.

Mr. Marsden's connection with the *Morning Post* was not severed by his return to England, and he was well enough to accept the post of special correspondent of that journal in the suite of H.R.H., the Prince of Wales on his Empire tour. From this he returned with the Prince, apparently in much better health, but within a few days of his landing he was taken suddenly ill, and died after a very brief illness. May this work be his crowning monument! In it he has performed an immense service to the English-speaking world, and there can be little doubt that it will take its place in the first rank of the English versions of "the protocols of the Meetings of the learned elders of Zion."

Of the Protocols themselves, little need be said in the way of introduction. The book in which they are embodied was first published in the year 1897 by Philip Stepanov for private circulation among his intimate friends. The first time Nilus published them was in 1901 in a book called *The Great Within the Small* and reprinted in 1905. A copy of this is in the British Museum bearing the date of its reception, August 10, 1906. All copies that were known to exist in Russia were destroyed in the Kerensky regime, and under his successors, the possession of a copy by anyone in Soviet land was a crime sufficient to ensure the owner being shot on sight. The fact is in itself sufficient proof of the genuineness of the Protocols. The Jewish journals, of course, say that they are a forgery, leaving it to be understood that Professor Nilus, who embodied them in a work of his own, had concocted them for his own purposes.

This is a secret which has not been revealed. They are the Hidden Hand. They are not the "Board of Deputies" (the Jewish Parliament in England) or the "Universal Israelite Alliance" which sits in Paris. But the late Walter Rathenau of the Allgemeiner Electrizitätsgesellschaft has thrown a little light on the subject and doubtless he was in possession of their names, being, in all likelihood, one of the chief leaders himself. Writing in the *Wiener Freie Presse*, December 24, 1912, he said:

> "Three hundred men, each of whom knows all the others, govern the fate of the European continent, and they elect their successors from their entourage."

In the year 1844, on the eve of the Jewish Revolution of 1848, Benjamin Disraeli, whose real name was Israel, and who was a "damped," or baptized Jew, published his novel, *Coningsby*, in which occurs this ominous passage:

> "The world is governed by very different personages from what is imagined by those who are not behind the scenes."

And he went on to show that these personages were all Jews. Now that Providence has brought to the light of day these secret Protocols all men may clearly see the hidden personages specified by Disraeli at work "behind the scenes" of all the Governments. This revelation entails on all peoples the grave responsibility of examining and revising *au fond* their attitude towards the Race and Nation which boasts of its survival over all Empires.

There are two words in this translation which are unusual, the word "Agentur" and "political" used as a substantive, Agentur appears to be a word adopted from the original and it means the whole body of agents and agencies made use of by the Elders, whether members of the tribe or their Gentile tools. By "the Political" Mr. Marsden means, not exactly the "body politic" but the entire machinery of politics.

A1.2 The symbolic snake of Zionism

Protocol III opens with a reference to the Symbolic Snake of Judaism. In his Epilogue to the 1905 Edition of the Protocols, Nilus gives the following interesting account of this symbol:

> "According to the records of secret Jewish Zionism, Solomon and other Jewish learned men already, in 929BC, thought out a scheme in theory for a peaceful conquest of the whole universe by Zion. As history developed, this scheme was worked out in detail and completed by men who were subsequently initiated in this question. These learned men decided by peaceful means to conquer the world for Zion with the slyness of

the Symbolic Snake, whose head was to represent those who have been initiated into the plans of the Jewish administration, and the body of the Snake to represent the Jewish people—the administration was always kept secret, even from the Jewish nation itself. As this Snake penetrated into the hearts of the nations which it encountered. it undermined and devoured all the non-Jewish power of these States. It is foretold that the Snake has still to finish its work, strictly adhering to the designed plan, until the course which it has to run is closed by the return of its head to Zion and until, by this means, the Snake has completed its round of Europe and has encircled it—and until, by dint of enchaining Europe, it has encompassed the whole world. This it is to accomplish by using every endeavor to subdue the other countries by an economical conquest. The return of the head of the Snake to Zion can only be accomplished after the power of all the Sovereigns of Europe has been laid low, that is to say, when by means of economic crises and wholesale destruction effected everywhere, there shall have been brought about a spiritual demoralization and a moral corruption, chiefly with the assistance of Jewish women masquerading as French, Italians, etc. These are the surest spreaders of licentiousness into the lives of the leading men at the heads of nations."

Its first stage in Europe was in 429BC in Greece, where, about the time of Pericles, the Snake first started eating into the power of that country. The second stage was in Rome in the time of Augustus, about 69BC. The third in Madrid in the time of Charles V, in 1552. The fourth in Paris about 1790, in the time of Louis XVI. The fifth in London from 1814 onwards. The sixth in Berlin in 1871 after the Franco-Prussian war. The seventh in St. Petersburg, over which is drawn the head of the Snake under the date of 1881.

All these States which the Snake traversed have had the foundations of their constitutions shaken, Germany, with its apparent power, forming no exception to the rule. In economic conditions, England and Germany are spared, but only till the conquest of Russia is accomplished by the Snake, on which at present [i.e., 1905] all its efforts are concentrated. The further course of the Snake is not shown on this map, *but arrows indicate its next movement towards Moscow, Kiev and Odessa.* It is now well known to us to what extent the latter cities form the centers of the militant Jewish race. Constantinople is shown as the last stage of the Snake's course before it reaches Jerusalem.

The term Goy(im) means Gentile(s) or non-Jew(s). It is used throughout the protocols, and retained (i.e. left untranslated) by Mr. Marsden.

A1.3 Contents

Protocol 1: The Basic Doctrine

1. .Putting aside fine phrases we shall speak of the significance of each thought: by comparisons and deductions we shall throw light upon surrounding facts.
2. What I am about to set forth, then, is our system from the two points of view, that of ourselves and that of the Goyim.
3. It must be noted that men with bad instincts are more in number than the good, and therefore the best results in governing them are attained by violence and terrorisation, and not by academic discussions. Every man aims at power, everyone would like to become a dictator if only he could, and rare indeed are the men who would not be willing to sacrifice the welfare of all for the sake of securing their own welfare.
4. What has restrained the beasts of prey who are called men? What has served for their guidance hitherto?
5. In the beginnings of the structure of society, they were subjected to brutal and blind force; afterwards - to Law, which is the same force, only disguised. I draw the conclusion that by the law of nature, right lies in force.
6. Political freedom is an idea but not a fact. This idea one must know how to apply whenever it appears necessary with this bait of an idea to attract the masses of the people to one's party for the purpose of crushing another who is in authority. This task is rendered easier if the opponent has himself been infected with the idea of freedom, so-called liberalism, and, for the sake of an idea, is willing to

yield some of his power. It is precisely here that the triumph of our theory appears; the slackened reins of government are immediately, by the law of life, caught up and gathered together by a new hand, because the blind might of the nation cannot for one single day exist without guidance, and the new authority merely fits into the place of the old already weakened by liberalism.

7. In our day the power which has replaced that of the rulers who were liberal is the power of Gold. Time was when Faith ruled. The idea of freedom is impossible of realization because no one knows how to use it with moderation. It is enough to hand over a people to self-government for a certain length of time for that people to be turned into a disorganized mob. From that moment on we get internecine strife which soon develops into battles between classes, in the midst of which States burn down and their importance is reduced to that of a heap of ashes.

8. Whether a State exhausts itself in its own convulsions, whether its internal discord brings it under the power of external foes - in any case it can be accounted irretrievably lost: it is in our power. The despotism of Capital, which is entirely in our hands, reaches out to it a straw that the State, willy-nilly, must take hold of: if not - it goes to the bottom.

9. Should anyone of a liberal mind say that such reflections as the above are immoral, I would put the following questions: If every State has two foes and if in regard to the external foe it is allowed and not considered immoral to use every manner and art of conflict, as for

example to keep the enemy in ignorance of plans of attack and defense, to attack him by night or in superior numbers, then in what way can the same means in regard to a worse foe, the destroyer of the structure of society and the commonwealth, be called immoral and not permissible?

10. Is it possible for any sound logical mind to hope with any success to guide crowds by the aid of reasonable counsels and arguments, when any objection or contradiction, senseless though it may be, can be made and when such objection may find more favor with the people, whose powers of reasoning are superficial? Men in masses and the men of the masses, being guided solely by petty passions, paltry beliefs, traditions and sentimental theorems, fall a prey to party dissension, which hinders any kind of agreement even on the basis of a perfectly reasonable argument. Every resolution of a crowd depends upon a chance or packed majority, which, in its ignorance of political secrets, puts forth some ridiculous resolution that lays in the administration a seed of anarchy.

11. The political has nothing in common with the moral. The ruler who is governed by the moral is not a skilled politician, and is therefore unstable on his throne. He who wishes to rule must have recourse both to cunning and to make-believe. Great national qualities, like frankness and honesty, are vices in politics, for they bring down rulers from their thrones more effectively and more certainly than the most powerful enemy. Such qualities must be the

attributes of the kingdoms of the Goyim, but we must in no wise be guided by them.

12. Our right lies in force. The word "right" is an abstract thought and proved by nothing. The word means no more than: Give me what I want in order that thereby I may have a proof that I am stronger than you.

13. Where does right begin? Where does it end?

14. In any State in which there is a bad organization of authority, an impersonality of laws and of the rulers who have lost their personality amid the flood of rights ever multiplying out of liberalism, I find a new right - to attack by the right of the strong, and to scatter to the winds all existing forces of order and regulation, to reconstruct all institutions and to become the sovereign lord of those who have left to us the rights of their power by laying them down voluntarily in their liberalism.

15. Our power in the present tottering condition of all forms of power will be more invincible than any other, because it will remain invisible until the moment when it has gained such strength that no cunning can any longer undermine it.

16. Out of the temporary evil we are now compelled to commit will emerge the good of an unshakable rule, which will restore the regular course of the machinery of the national life, brought to naught by liberalism. The result justifies the means. Let us, however, in our plans, direct our attention not so much to what is good and moral as to what is necessary and useful.

17. Before us is a plan in which is laid down strategically the line from which we cannot deviate without running the risk of seeing the labor of many centuries brought to naught.
18. In order to elaborate satisfactory forms of action it is necessary to have regard to the rascality, the slackness, the instability of the mob, its lack of capacity to understand and respect the conditions of its own life, or its own welfare. It must be understood that the might of a mob is blind, senseless and un-reasoning force ever at the mercy of a suggestion from any side. The blind cannot lead the blind without bringing them into the abyss; consequently, members of the mob, upstarts from the people even though they should be as a genius for wisdom, yet having no understanding of the political, cannot come forward as leaders of the mob without bringing the whole nation to ruin.
19. Only one trained from childhood for independent rule can have understanding of the words that can be made up of the political alphabet.
20. A people left to itself, i.e., to upstarts from its midst, brings itself to ruin by party dissensions excited by the pursuit of power and honors and the disorders arising therefrom. Is it possible for the masses of the people calmly and without petty jealousies to form judgment, to deal with the affairs of the country, which cannot be mixed up with personal interest? Can they defend themselves from an external foe? It is unthinkable; for a plan broken up into as many parts as there are heads in

the mob, loses all homogeneity, and thereby becomes unintelligible and impossible of execution.

21. It is only with a despotic ruler that plans can be elaborated extensively and clearly in such a way as to distribute the whole properly among the several parts of the machinery of the State: from this the conclusion is inevitable that a satisfactory form of government for any country is one that concentrates in the hands of one responsible person. Without an absolute despotism there can be no existence for civilization which is carried on not by the masses but by their guide, whosoever that person may be. The mob is savage, and displays its savagery at every opportunity. The moment the mob seizes freedom in its hands it quickly turns to anarchy, which in itself is the highest degree of savagery.

22. Behold the alcoholic animals, bemused with drink, the right to an immoderate use of which comes along with freedom. It is not for us and ours to walk that road. The peoples of the Goyim are bemused with alcoholic liquors; their youth has grown ingenuous on classicism and from early immorality, into which it has been inducted by our special agents - by tutors, lackeys, governesses in the houses of the wealthy, by clerks and others, by our women in the places of dissipation frequented by the Goyim. In the number of these last I count also the so-called "society ladies," voluntary followers of the others in corruption and luxury.

23. Our countersign is - Force and Make-believe. Only force conquers in political affairs, especially if it be

concealed in the talents essential to statesmen. Violence must be the principle, and cunning and make-believe the rule for governments which do not want to lay down their crowns at the feet of agents of some new power. This evil is the one and only means to attain the end, the good. Therefore, we must not stop at bribery, deceit and treachery when they should serve towards the attainment of our end. In politics one must know how to seize the property of others without hesitation if by it we secure submission and sovereignty.

24. Our State, marching along the path of peaceful conquest, has the right to replace the horrors of war by less noticeable and more satisfactory sentences of death, necessary to maintain the terror which tends to produce blind submission. Just but merciless severity is the greatest factor of strength in the State: not only for the sake of gain but also in the name of duty, for the sake of victory, we must keep to the program of violence and make-believe. The doctrine of squaring accounts is precisely as strong as the means of which it makes use. Therefore, it is not so much by the means themselves as by the doctrine of severity that we shall triumph and bring all governments into subjection to our super-government. It is enough for them to know that we are too merciless for all disobedience to cease.

25. Far back in ancient times we were the first to cry among the masses of the people the words "Liberty, Equality, Fraternity," words many times repeated since these days by ingenuous poll-parrots who, from all sides

around, flew down upon these baits and with them carried away the well-being of the world, true freedom of the individual, formerly so well guarded against the pressure of the mob. The would-be wise men of the Goyim, the intellectuals, could not make anything out of the uttered words in their abstractedness; did not see that in nature there is no equality, cannot be freedom: that Nature herself has established inequality of minds, of characters, and capacities, just as immutably as she has established subordination to her laws: never stopped to think that the mob is a blind thing, that upstarts elected from among it to bear rule are, in regard to the political, the same blind men as the mob itself, that the adept, though he be a fool, can yet rule, whereas the non-adept, even if he were a genius, understands nothing in the political - to all those things the Goyim paid no regard; yet all the time it was based upon these things that dynastic rule rested: the father passed on to the son a knowledge of the course of political affairs in such wise that none should know it but members of the dynasty and none could betray it to the governed. As time went on, the meaning of the dynastic transference of the true position of affairs in the political was lost, and this aided the success of our cause.

26. In all comers of the earth the words "Liberty, Equality, Fraternity," brought to our ranks, thanks to our blind agents, whole legions who bore our banners with enthusiasm. And all the time these words were canker-worms at work boring into the well-being of the Goyim, putting an end everywhere to peace, quiet, solidarity and

destroying all the foundations of the Goy States. As you will see later, this helped us to our triumph: it gave us the possibility, among other things, of getting into our hands the master card - the destruction of the privileges, or in other words of the very existence of the aristocracy of the Goyim, that class which was the only defense peoples and countries had against us. On the ruins of the natural and genealogical aristocracy of the Goyim we have set up the aristocracy of our educated class headed by the aristocracy of money. The qualifications for this aristocracy we have established in wealth, which is dependent upon us, and in knowledge, for which our learned elders provide the motive force.

27. Our triumph has been rendered easier by the fact that in our relations with the men, whom we wanted, we have always worked upon the most sensitive chords of the human mind, upon the cash account, upon the cupidity, upon the insatiability for material needs of man; and each one of these human weaknesses, taken alone, is sufficient to paralyze initiative, for it hands over the will of men to the disposition of him who has bought their activities.

28. The abstraction of freedom has enabled us to persuade the mob in all countries that their government is nothing but the steward of the people who are the owners of the country, and that the steward may be replaced like a worn-out glove.

29. It is this possibility of replacing the representatives of the people which has placed at our disposal, and, as it were, given us the power of appointment.

Protocol 2: Economic Wars

1. It is indispensable for our purpose that wars, so far as possible, should not result in territorial gains: war will thus be brought on to the economic ground, where the nations will not fail to perceive in the assistance we give the strength of our predominance, and this state of things will put both sides at the mercy of our international Agentur; which possesses millions of eyes ever on the watch and unhampered by any limitations whatsoever. Our international rights will then wipe out national rights, in the proper sense of right, and will rule the nations precisely as the civil law of States rules the relations of their subjects among themselves.

2. The administrators, whom we shall choose from among the public, with strict regard to their capacities for servile obedience, will not be persons trained in the arts of government, and will therefore easily become pawns in our game in the hands of men of learning and genius who will be their advisers, specialists bred and reared from early childhood to rule the affairs of the whole world. As is well known to you, these specialists of ours have been drawing to fit them for rule the information they need from our political plans from the lessons of history, from observations made of the events of every moment as it passes. The Goyim are not guided by practical use of unprejudiced historical observation, but by theoretical routine without any critical regard for consequent results. We need not, therefore, take any account of them - let

them amuse themselves until the hour strikes, or live on hopes of new forms of enterprising pastime, or on the memories of all they have enjoyed. For them let that play the principal part which we have persuaded them to accept as the dictates of science (theory). It is with this object in view that we are constantly, by means of our press, arousing a blind confidence in these theories. The intellectuals of the Goyim will puff themselves up with their knowledges and without any logical verification of them will put into effect all the information available from science, which our Agentur specialists have cunningly pieced together for the purpose of educating their minds in the direction we want.

3. Do not suppose for a moment that these statements are empty words: think carefully of the successes we arranged for Darwinism (Evolution), Marxism (Communism), Nietzsche-ism (Socialism). To us Jews, at any rate, it should be plain to see what a disintegrating importance these directives have had upon the minds of the Goyim.

4. It is indispensable for us to take account of the thoughts, characters, tendencies of the nations in order to avoid making slips in the political and in the direction of administrative affairs. The triumph of our system of which the component parts of the machinery may be variously disposed according to the temperament of the peoples met on our way, will fail of success if the practical application of it be not based upon a summing up of the lessons of the past in the light of the present.

5. In the hands of the States of to-day there is a great force that creates the movement of thought in the people, and that is the Press. The part played by the Press is to keep pointing out requirements supposed to be indispensable, to give voice to the complaints of the people, to express and to create discontent. It is in the Press that the triumph of freedom of speech finds its incarnation. But the Goyim States have not known how to make use of this force; and it has fallen into our hands. Through the Press we have gained the power to influence while remaining ourselves in the shade; thanks to the Press we have got the gold in our hands, notwithstanding that we have had to gather it out of the oceans of blood and tears. But it has paid us, though we have sacrificed many of our people. Each victim on our side is worth in the sight of God a thousand Goyim.

Protocol 3: Methods of Conquest

1. To-day I may tell you that our goal is now only a few steps off. There remains a small space to cross and the whole long path we have trodden is ready now to close its cycle of the Symbolic Snake, by which we symbolize our people. When this ring closes, all the States of Europe will be locked in its coil as in a powerful vice.

2. The constitution scales of these days will shortly break down, for we have established them with a certain lack of

accurate balance in order that they may oscillate incessantly until they wear through the pivot on which they turn. The Goyim are under the impression that they have welded them sufficiently strong and they have all along kept on expecting that the scales would come into equilibrium. But the pivots - the kings on their thrones - are hemmed in by their representatives, who play the fool, distraught with their own uncontrolled and irresponsible power. This power they owe to the terror which has been breathed into the palaces. As they have no means of getting at their people, into their very midst, the kings on their thrones are no longer able to come to terms with them and so strengthen themselves against seekers after power. We have made a gulf between the far-seeing Sovereign Power and the blind force of the people so that both have lost all meaning, for like the blind man and his stick, both are powerless apart.

3. In order to incite seekers after power to a misuse of power we have set all forces in opposition one to another, breaking up their liberal tendencies towards independence. To this end we have stirred up every form of enterprise, we have armed all parties, we have set up authority as a target for every ambition. Of States we have made gladiatorial arenas where a lot of confused issues contend ... A little more, and disorders and bankruptcy will be universal ...

4. Babblers, inexhaustible, have turned into oratorical contests the sittings of Parliament and Administrative Boards. Bold journalists and unscrupulous pamphleteers

daily fall upon executive officials. Abuses of power will put the final touch in preparing all institutions for their overthrow and everything will fly skyward under the blows of the maddened mob.

5. All people are chained down to heavy toil by poverty more firmly than ever. They were chained by slavery and serfdom; from these, one way and another, they might free themselves. These could be settled with, but from want they will never get away. We have included in the constitution such rights as to the masses appear fictitious and not actual rights. All these so-called "People's Rights" can exist only in idea, an idea which can never be realized in practical life. What is it to the proletariat laborer, bowed double over his heavy toil, crushed by his lot in life, if talkers get the right to babble, if journalists get the right to scribble any nonsense side by side with good stuff, once the proletariat has no other profit out of the constitution save only those pitiful crumbs which we fling them from our table in return for their voting in favor of what we dictate, in favor of the men we place in power, the servants of our Agentur ... Republican rights for a poor man are no more than a bitter piece of irony, for the necessity he is under of toiling almost all day gives him no present use of them, but the other hand robs him of all guarantee of regular and certain earnings by making him dependent on strikes by his comrades or lockouts by his masters.

6. The people, under our guidance, have annihilated the aristocracy, who were their one and only defense and foster-mother for the sake of their own advantage which

is inseparably bound up with the well-being of the people. Nowadays, with the destruction of the aristocracy, the people have fallen into the grips of merciless money-grinding scoundrels who have laid a pitiless and cruel yoke upon the necks of the workers.

7. We appear on the scene as alleged saviors of the worker from this oppression when we propose to him to enter the ranks of our fighting forces - Socialists, Anarchists, Communists - to whom we always give support in accordance with an alleged brotherly rule (of the solidarity of all humanity) of our social masonry. The aristocracy, which enjoyed by law the labor of the workers, was interested in seeing that the workers were well fed, healthy, and strong. We are interested in just the opposite - in the diminution, the killing out of the Goyim. Our power is in the chronic shortness of food and physical weakness of the worker because by all that this implies he is made the slave of our will, and he will not find in his own authorities either strength or energy to set against our will. Hunger creates the right of capital to rule the worker more surely than it was given to the aristocracy by the legal authority of kings.

8. By want and the envy and hatred which it engenders we shall move the mobs and with their hands we shall wipe out all those who hinder us on our way.

9. When the hour strikes for our sovereign lord of all the world to be crowned it is these same hands which will sweep away everything that might be a hindrance thereto

10. The Goyim have lost the habit of thinking unless prompted by the suggestions of our specialists. Therefore they do not see the urgent necessity of what we, when our kingdom comes, shall adopt at once, namely this, that it is essential to teach in national schools one simple, true piece of knowledge, the basis of all knowledge - the knowledge of the structure of human life, of social existence, which requires division of labor, and, consequently, the division of men into classes and conditions. It is essential for all to know that owing to difference in the objects of human activity there cannot be any equality, that he, who by any act of his compromises a whole class, cannot be equally responsible before the law with him who affects no one but only his own honor. The true knowledge of the structure of society, into the secrets of which we do not admit the Goyim, would demonstrate to all men that the positions and work must be kept within a certain circle, that they may not become a source of human suffering, arising from an education which does not correspond with the work which individuals are called upon to do. After a thorough study of this knowledge, the peoples will voluntarily submit to authority and accept such position as is appointed them in the State. In the present state of knowledge and the direction we have given to its development of the people, blindly believing things in print - cherishes - thanks to promptings intended to mislead and to its own ignorance - a blind hatred towards all conditions which it considers

above itself, for it has no understanding of the meaning of class and condition.

11. This hatred will be still further magnified by the effects of an economic crises, which will stop dealing on the exchanges and bring industry to a standstill. We shall create by all the secret subterranean methods open to us and with the aid of gold, which is all in our hands, a universal economic crisis whereby we shall throw upon the streets whole mobs of workers simultaneously in all the countries of Europe. These mobs will rush delightedly to shed the blood of those whom, in the simplicity of their ignorance, they have envied from their cradles, and whose property they will then be able to loot.

12. "Ours" they will not touch, because the moment of attack will be known to us and we shall take measures to protect our own.

13. We have demonstrated that progress will bring all the Goyim to the sovereignty of reason. Our despotism will be precisely that; for it will know how, by wise severities, to pacify all unrest, to cauterize liberalism out of all institutions.

14. When the populace has seen that all sorts of concessions and indulgences are yielded it in the name of freedom it has imagined itself to be sovereign lord and has stormed its way to power, but, naturally like every other blind man, it has come upon a host of stumbling blocks. It has rushed to find a guide, it has never had the sense to return to the former state and it has laid down its plenipotentiary powers at our feet. Remember the French

Revolution, to which it was we [the Philadelphes, i.e. the French branch of the Illuminati] who gave the name of “Great": the secrets of its preparations are well known to us for it was wholly the work of our hands.

15. Ever since that time we have been leading the peoples from one disenchantment to another, so that in the end they should turn also from us in favor of that king-despot of the blood of Zion, whom we are preparing for the world.

16. At the present day we are, as an international force, invincible, because if attacked by some we are supported by other States. It is the bottomless rascality of the Goyim peoples, who crawl on their bellies to force, but are merciless towards weakness, unsparing to faults and indulgent to crimes, unwilling to bear the contradictions of a free social system but patient unto martyrdom under the violence of a bold despotism - it is those qualities which are aiding us to independence. From the premier-dictators of the present day, the Goyim peoples suffer patiently and bear such abuses as for the least of them they would have beheaded twenty kings.

17. What is the explanation of this phenomenon, this curious inconsequence of the masses of the peoples in their attitude towards what would appear to be events of the same order?

18. It is explained by the fact that these dictators whisper to the peoples through their agents that through these abuses they are inflicting injury on the States with the highest purpose - to secure the welfare of the peoples, the international brotherhood of them all, their solidarity and

equality of rights. Naturally they do not tell the peoples that this unification must be accomplished only under our sovereign rule.

19. And thus the people condemn the upright and acquit the guilty, persuaded ever more and more that it can do whatsoever it wishes. Thanks to this state of things, the people are destroying every kind of stability and creating disorders at every step.

20. The word "freedom" brings out the communities of men to fight against every kind of force, against every kind of authority even against God and the laws of nature. For this reason we, when we come into our kingdom, shall have to erase this word from the lexicon of life as implying a principle of brute force which turns mobs into bloodthirsty beasts.

21. These beasts, it is true, fall asleep again every time when they have drunk their fill of blood, and at such time can easily be riveted into their chains. But if they be not given blood they will not sleep and continue to struggle.

Protocol 4: Materialism Replaces Religion

1. Every republic passes through several stages. The first of these is comprised in the early days of mad raging by the blind mob, tossed hither and thither, right and left: the second is demagogy from which is born anarchy, and

that leads inevitably to despotism - not any longer legal and overt, and therefore responsible despotism, but to unseen and secretly hidden, yet nevertheless sensibly felt despotism in the hands of some secret organization or other, whose acts are the more unscrupulous inasmuch as it works behind a screen, behind the backs of all sorts of agents, the changing of whom not only does not injuriously affect but actually aids the secret force by saving it, thanks to continual changes, from the necessity of expanding its resources on the rewarding of long services.

2. Who and what is in a position to overthrow an invisible force? And this is precisely what our force is. Gentile masonry blindly serves as a screen for us and our objects, but the plan of action of our force, even its very abiding-place, remains for the whole people an unknown mystery.

3. But even freedom might be harmless and have its place in the State economy without injury to the well-being of the peoples if it rested upon the foundation of faith in God, upon the brotherhood of humanity, unconnected with the conception of equality, which is negatived by the very laws of creation, for they have established subordination. With such a faith as this a people might be governed by a wardship of parishes, and would walk contentedly and humbly under the guiding hand of its spiritual pastor submitting to the dispositions of God upon earth. This is the reason why it is indispensable for us to undermine all faith, to tear out of the mind of the "Goyim" the very principle of god-head and the spirit, and

to put in its place arithmetical calculations and material needs.

4. In order to give the Goyim no time to think and take note, their minds must be diverted towards industry and trade. Thus, all the nations will be swallowed up in the pursuit of gain and in the race for it will not take note of their common foe. But again, in order that freedom may once for all disintegrate and ruin the communities of the Goyim, we must put industry on a speculative basis: the result of this will be that what is withdrawn from the land by industry will slip through the hands and pass into speculation, that is, to our classes.

5. The intensified struggle for superiority and shocks delivered to economic life will create, nay, have already created, disenchanted, cold and heartless communities. Such communities will foster a strong aversion towards the higher political and towards religion. Their only guide is gain, that is Gold, which they will erect into a veritable cult, for the sake of those material delights which it can give. Then will the hour strike when, not for the sake of attaining the good, not even to win wealth, but solely out of hatred towards the privileged, the lower classes of the Goyim will follow our lead against our rivals for power, the intellectuals of the Goyim.

Protocol 5: Despotism and Modern Progress

1. What form of administrative rule can be given to communities in which corruption has penetrated everywhere, communities where riches are attained only by the clever surprise tactics of semi-swindling tricks; where looseness reigns: where morality is maintained by penal measures and harsh laws but not by voluntarily accepted principles: where the feelings towards faith and country are obligated by cosmopolitan convictions? What form of rule is to be given to these communities if not that despotism which I shall describe to you later? We shall create an intensified centralization of government in order to grip in our hands all the forces of the community. We shall regulate mechanically all the actions of the political life of our subjects by new laws. These laws will withdraw one by one all the indulgences and liberties which have been permitted by the Goyim, and our kingdom will be distinguished by a despotism of such magnificent proportions as to be at any moment and in every place in a position to wipe out any Goyim who oppose us by deed or word.

2. We shall be told that such a despotism as I speak of is not consistent with the progress of these days, but I will prove to you that it is.

3. In the times when the peoples looked upon kings on their thrones as on a pure manifestation of the will of God, they submitted without a murmur to the despotic power

of kings: but from the day when we insinuated into their minds the conception of their own rights they began to regard the occupants of thrones as mere ordinary mortals. The holy unction of the Lord's Anointed has fallen from the heads of kings in the eyes of the people, and when we also robbed them of their faith in God the might of power was flung upon the streets into the place of public proprietorship and was seized by us.

4. Moreover, the art of directing masses and individuals by means of cleverly manipulated theory and verbiage, by regulations of life in common and all sorts of other quirks, in all which the Goyim understand nothing, belongs likewise to the specialists of our administrative brain. Reared on analysis, observation, on delicacies of fine calculation, in this species of skill we have no rivals, any more than we have either in the drawing up of plans of political actions and solidarity. In this respect the Jesuits alone might have compared with us, but we have contrived to discredit them in the eyes of the unthinking mob as an overt organization, while we ourselves all the while have kept our secret organization in the shade. However, it is probably all the same to the world who is its sovereign lord, whether the head of Catholicism or our despot of the blood of Zion! But to us, the Chosen People, it is very far from being a matter of indifference.

5. For a time perhaps we might be successfully dealt with by a coalition of the "goyim" of all the world: but from this danger we are secured by the discord existing among them whose roots are so deeply seated that they can never

now be plucked up. We have set one against another the personal and national reckonings of the Goyim, religious and race hatreds, which we have fostered into a huge growth in the course of the past twenty centuries. This is the reason why there is not one State which would anywhere receive support if it were to raise its arm, for every one of them must bear in mind that any agreement against us would be unprofitable to itself. We are too strong - there is no evading our power. The nations cannot come to even an inconsiderable private agreement without our secretly having a hand in it.

6. Per me reges regnant. "It is through me that Kings reign." And it was said by the prophets that we were chosen by God Himself to rule over the whole earth. God has endowed us with genius that we may be equal to our task. Were genius in the opposite camp it would still struggle against us, but even so, a newcomer is no match for the old-established settler: the struggle would be merciless between us, such a fight as the world has never seen. Aye, and the genius on their side would have arrived too late. All the wheels of the machinery of all States go by the force of the engine, which is in our hands, and that engine of the machinery of States is - Gold. The science of political economy invented by our learned elders has for long past been giving royal prestige to capital.

7. Capital, if it is to co-operate untrammeled, must be free to establish a monopoly of industry and trade: this is already being put in execution by an unseen hand in all quarters of the world. This freedom will give political

force to those engaged in industry, and that will help to oppress the people. Nowadays it is more important to disarm the peoples than to lead them into war: more important to use for our advantage the passions which have burst into flames than to quench their fire: more important to eradicate them. The principle object of our directorate consists in this: to debilitate the public mind by criticism; to lead it away from serious reflections calculated to arouse resistance; to distract the forces of the mind towards a sham fight of empty eloquence.

8. In all ages the people of the world, equally with individuals, have accepted words for deeds, for they are content with a show and rarely pause to note, in the public arena, whether promises are followed by performance. Therefore we shall establish show institutions which will give eloquent proof of their benefit to progress.

9. We shall assume to ourselves the liberal physiognomy of all parties, of all directions, and we shall give that physiognomy a voice in orators who will speak so much that they will exhaust the patience of their hearers and produce an abhorrence of oratory.

10. In order to put public opinion into our hands we must bring it into a state of bewilderment by giving expression from all sides to so many contradictory opinions and for such length of time as will suffice to make the "Goyim" lose their heads in the labyrinth and come to see that the best thing is to have no opinion of any kind in matters political, which it is not given to the public to understand,

because they are understood only by him who guides the public. This is the first secret.

11. The second secret requisite for the success of our government is comprised in the following: To multiply to such an extent national failings, habits, passions, conditions of civil life, that it will be impossible for anyone to know where he is in the resulting chaos, so that the people in consequence will fail to understand one another. This measure will also serve us in another way, namely, to sow discord in all parties, to dislocate all collective forces which are still unwilling to submit to us, and to discourage any kind of personal initiative which might in any degree hinder our affair. There is nothing more dangerous than personal initiative: if it has genius behind it, such initiative can do more than can be done by millions of people among whom we have sown discord. We must so direct the education of the Goyim communities that whenever they come upon a matter requiring initiative they may drop their hands in despairing impotence. The strain which results from freedom of actions saps the forces when it meets with the freedom of another. From this collision arise grave moral shocks, disenchantments, failures. By all these means we shall so wear down the "goyim" that they will be compelled to offer us international power of a nature that by its position will enable us without any violence gradually to absorb all the state forces of the world and to form a super-government. In place of the rulers of to-day we shall set up a bogey which will be called the Super-

Government Administration. Its hands will reach out in all directions like nippers and its organization will be of such colossal dimensions that it cannot fail to subdue all the nations of the world.

Protocol 6: Take-Over Technique

1. We shall soon begin to establish huge monopolies, reservoirs of colossal riches, upon which even large fortunes of the Goyim will depend to such an extent that they will go to the bottom together with the credit of the States on the day after the political smash ...

2. You gentlemen here present who are economists, just strike an estimate of the significance of this combination! ...

3. In every possible way we must develop the significance of our Super-Government by representing it as the Protector and Benefactor of all those who voluntarily submit to us.

4. The aristocracy of the Goyim as a political force, is dead - We need not take it into account; but as landed proprietors they can still be harmful to us from the fact that they are self-sufficing in the resources upon which they live. It is essential therefore for us at whatever cost to deprive them of their land. This object will be best attained by increasing the burdens upon landed property - in loading lands with debts. These measures will check

land-holding and keep it in a state of humble and unconditional submission.

5. The aristocrats of the Goyim, being hereditarily incapable of contenting themselves with little, will rapidly burn up and fizzle out.

6. At the same time we must intensively patronize trade and industry, but, first and foremost, speculation, the part played by which is to provide a counterpoise to industry: the absence of speculative industry will multiply capital in private hands and will serve to restore agriculture by freeing the land from indebtedness to the land banks. What we want is that industry should drain off from the land both labor and capital and by means of speculation transfer into our hands all the money of the world, and thereby throw all the Goyim into the ranks of the proletariat. Then the Goyim will bow down before us, if for no other reason but to get the right to exist.

7. To complete the ruin of the industry of the Goyim we shall bring to the assistance of speculation the luxury which we have developed among the Goyim, that greedy demand for luxury which is swallowing up everything. We shall raise the rate of wages which, however, will not bring any advantage to the workers, for, at the same time, we shall produce a rise in prices of the first necessaries of life, alleging that it arises from the decline of agriculture and cattle-breeding: we shall further undermine artfully and deeply sources of production, by accustoming the workers to anarchy and to drunkenness and side by side therewith

taking all measure to extirpate from the face of the earth all the educated forces of the "Goyim."
8. In order that the true meaning of things may not strike the "goyim" before the proper time we shall mask it under an alleged ardent desire to serve the working classes and the great principles of political economy about which our economic theories are carrying on an energetic propaganda.

Protocol 7: World-Wide Wars

1. The intensification of armaments, the increase of police forces - are all essential for the completion of the aforementioned plans. What we have to get at is that there should be in all the States of the world, besides ourselves, only the masses of the proletariat, a few millionaires devoted to our interests, police and soldiers.
2. Throughout all Europe, and by means of relations with Europe, in other continents also, we must create ferments, discords and hostility. Therein we gain a double advantage. In the first place we keep in check all countries, for they will know that we have the power whenever we like to create disorders or to restore order. All these countries are accustomed to see in us an indispensable force of coercion. In the second place, by our intrigues we shall tangle up all the threads which we have stretched into the cabinets of all States by means of

the political, by economic treaties, or loan obligations. In order to succeed in this we must use great cunning and penetration during negotiations and agreements, but, as regards what is called the "official language," we shall keep to the opposite tactics and assume the mask of honesty and complacency. In this way the peoples and governments of the Goyim, whom we have taught to look only at the outside whatever we present to their notice, will still continue to accept us as the benefactors and saviours of the human race.

3. We must be in a position to respond to every act of opposition by war with the neighbors of that country which dares to oppose us: but if these neighbors should also venture to stand collectively together against us, then we must offer resistance by a universal war.

4. The principal factor of success in the political is the secrecy of its undertakings: the word should not agree with the deeds of the diplomat.

5. We must compel the governments of the Goyim to take action in the direction favored by our widely conceived plan, already approaching the desired consummation, by what we shall represent as public opinion, secretly promoted by us through the means of that so-called "Great Power" - the press, which, with a few exceptions that may be disregarded, is already entirely in our hands.

6. In a word, to sum up our system of keeping the governments of the goyim in Europe in check, we shall show our strength to one of them by terrorist attempts and to all, if we allow the possibility of a general rising

against us, we shall respond with the guns of America or China or Japan. (The Russo-Japanese War of 1904-1905; Japan; Iraq and Afghanistan - Ed.).

Protocol 8: Provisional Government

1. We must arm ourselves with all the weapons which our opponents might employ against us. We must search out in the very finest shades of expression and the knotty points of the lexicon of law justification for those cases where we shall have to pronounce judgments that might appear abnormally audacious and unjust, for it is important that these resolutions should be set forth in expressions that shall seem to be the most exalted moral principles cast into legal form. Our directorate must surround itself with all these forces of civilization among which it will have to work. It will surround itself with publicists, practical jurists, administrators, diplomats and, finally, with persons prepared by a special super-educational training in our special schools. These persons will have consonance of all the secrets of the social structure, they will know all the languages that can be made up by political alphabets and words; they will be made acquainted with the whole underside of human nature, with all its sensitive chords on which they will have to play. These chords are the cast of mind of the Goyim, their tendencies, short-comings, vices and

qualities, the particularities of classes and conditions. Needless to say that the talented assistants of authority, of whom I speak, will be taken not from among the Goyim, who are accustomed to perform their administrative work without giving themselves the trouble to think what its aim is, and never consider what it is needed for. The administrators of the Goyim sign papers without reading them, and they serve either for mercenary reasons or from ambition.

2. We shall surround our government with a whole world of economists. That is the reason why economic sciences form the principal subject of the teaching given to the Jews. Around us again will be a whole constellation of bankers, industrialists, capitalists and - the main thing - millionaires, because in substance everything will be settled by the question of figures.

3. For a time, until there will no longer be any risk in entrusting responsible posts in our State to our brother-Jews, we shall put them in the hands of persons whose past and reputation are such that between them and the people lies an abyss, persons who, in case of disobedience to our instructions, must face criminal charges or disappear - this in order to make them defend our interests to their last gasp.

Protocol 9: Re-Education

1. In applying our principles let attention be paid to the character of the people in whose country you live and act; a general, identical application of them, until such time as the people shall have been re-educated to our pattern, cannot have success. But by approaching their application cautiously you will see that not a decade will pass before the most stubborn character will change and we shall add a new people to the ranks of those already subdued by us.
2. The words of the liberal, which are in effect the words of our masonic watchword, namely, "Liberty, Equality, Fraternity," will, when we come into our kingdom, be changed by us into words no longer of a watchword, but only an expression of idealism, namely, into "The right of liberty, the duty of equality, the ideal of brotherhood." That is how we shall put it, - and so we shall catch the bull by the horns ... de facto we have already wiped out every kind of rule except our own, although de jure there still remain a good many of them. Nowadays, if any States raise a protest against us it is only pro forma at our discretion and by our direction, for their anti-Semitism is indispensable to us for the management of our lesser brethren. I will not enter into further explanations, for this matter has formed the subject of repeated discussions amongst us. (Anti-Semitism is a mechanism devised and controlled by World Jewry).
3. For us there are not checks to limit the range of our activity. Our Super-Government subsists in extra-legal

conditions which are described in the accepted terminology by the energetic and forcible word - Dictatorship. I am in a position to tell you with a clear conscience that at the proper time we, the law-givers, shall execute judgment and sentence, we shall slay and we shall spare, we, as head of all our troops, are mounted on the steed of the leader. We rule by force of will, because in our hands are the fragments of a once powerful party, now vanquished by us. And the weapons in our hands are limitless ambitions, burning greediness, merciless vengeance, hatreds and malice.

4. It is from us that the all-engulfing terror proceeds. We have in our service persons of all opinions, of all doctrines, restoring monarchists, demagogues, socialists, communists, and utopian dreamers of every kind. We have harnessed them all to the task: each one of them on his own account is boring away at the last remnants of authority, is striving to overthrow all established form of order. By these acts all States are in torture; they exhort to tranquility, are ready to sacrifice everything for peace: but we will not give them peace until they openly acknowledge our international super-government, and with submissiveness.

5. The people have raised a howl about the necessity of settling the question of Socialism by way of an international agreement. Division into fractional parties has given them into our hands, for, in order to carry on a contested struggle one must have money, and the money is all in our hands.

6. We might have reason to apprehend a union between the "clear-sighted" force of the Goy kings on their thrones and the "blind" force of the Goy mobs, but we have taken all the needful measure against any such possibility: between the one and the other force we have erected a bulwark in the shape of a mutual terror between them. In this way the blind force of the people remains our support and we, and we only, shall provide them with a leader and, of course, direct them along the road that leads to our goal.
7. In order that the hand of the blind mob may not free itself from our guiding hand, we must every now and then enter into close communion with it, if not actually in person, at any rate through some of the most trusted of our brethren. When we are acknowledged as the only authority we shall discuss with the people personally on the market, places, and we shall instruct them on questings of the political in such wise as may turn them in the direction that suits us.
8. Who is going to verify what is taught in the village schools? But what an envoy of the government or a king on his throne himself may say cannot but become immediately known to the whole State, for it will be spread abroad by the voice of the people.
9. In order to annihilate the institutions of the Goyim before it is time we have touched them with craft and delicacy, and have taken hold of the ends of the springs which move their mechanism. These springs lay in a strict but just sense of order; we have replaced them by the

chaotic license of liberalism. We have got our hands into the administration of the law, into the conduct of elections, into the press, into liberty of the person, but principally into education and training as being the cornerstones of a free existence.

10. We have fooled, bemused and corrupted the youth of the "goyim" by rearing them in principles and theories which are known to us to be false although it is that they have been inculcated.

11. Above the existing laws without substantially altering them, and by merely twisting them into contradictions of interpretations, we have erected something grandiose in the way of results. These results found expression in the fact that the interpretations masked the law: afterwards they entirely hid them from the eyes of the governments owing to the impossibility of making anything out of the tangled web of legislation.

12. This is the origin of the theory of course of arbitration.

13. You may say that the Goyim will rise upon us, arms in hand, if they guess what is going on before the time comes; but in the West we have against this a manoeuvre of such appalling terror that the very stoutest hearts quail - the undergrounds, metropolitans, those subterranean corridors which, before the time comes, will be driven under all the capitals and from whence those capitals will be blown into the air with all their organizations and archives.

Protocol 10: Preparing for Power

1. To-day I begin with a repetition of what I said before, and I beg you to bear in mind that governments and people are content in the political with outside appearances. And how, indeed, are the Goyim to perceive the underlying meaning of things when their representatives give the best of their energies to enjoying themselves? For our policy it is of the greatest importance to take cognizance of this detail; it will be of assistance to us when we come to consider the division of authority of property, of the dwelling, of taxation (the idea of concealed taxes), of the reflex force of the laws. All these questions are such as ought not to be touched upon directly and openly before the people. In cases where it is indispensable to touch upon them they must not be categorically named, it must merely be declared without detailed exposition that the principles of contemporary law are acknowledged by us. The reason of keeping silence in this respect is that by not naming a principle we leave ourselves freedom of action, to drop this or that out of it without attracting notice; if they were all categorically named they would all appear to have been already given.

2. The mob cherishes a special affection and respect for the geniuses of political power and accepts all their deeds of violence with the admiring response: "rascally, well, yes, it is rascally, but it's clever! ... a trick, if you like, but how craftily played, how magnificently done, what impudent audacity!" ...

3. We count upon attracting all nations to the task of erecting the new fundamental structure, the project for which has been drawn up by us. This is why, before everything, it is indispensable for us to arm ourselves and to store up in ourselves that absolutely reckless audacity and irresistible might of the spirit which in the person of our active workers will break down all hindrances on our way.

4. When we have accomplished our Coup d'État we shall say then to the various peoples: "everything has gone terribly badly, all have been worn out with suffering. We are destroying the causes of your torment—nationalities, frontiers, differences of coinages. You are at liberty, of course, to pronounce sentence upon us, but can it possibly be a just one if it is confirmed by you before you make any trial of what we are offering you." ... Then will the mob exalt us and bear us up in their hands in a unanimous triumph of hopes and expectations. Voting, which we have made the instrument which will set us on the throne of the world by teaching even the very smallest units of members of the human race to vote by means of meetings and agreements by groups, will then have served its purposes and will play its part then for the last time by a unanimity of desire to make close acquaintance with us before condemning us.

5. To secure this we must have everybody vote without distinction of classes and qualifications, in order to establish an absolute majority, which cannot be got from the educated propertied classes. In this way, by

inculcating in all a sense of self-importance, we shall destroy among the Goyim the importance of the family and its educational value and remove the possibility of individual minds splitting off, for the mob, handled by us, will not let them come to the front nor even give them a hearing; it is accustomed to listen to us only who pay it for obedience and attention. In this way we shall create a blind, mighty force which will never be in a position to move in any direction without the guidance of our agents set at its head by us as leaders of the mob. The people will submit to this regime because it will know that upon these leaders will depend its earnings, gratifications and the receipt of all kinds of benefits.

6. A scheme of government should come ready made from one brain, because it will never be clinched firmly if it is allowed to be split into fractional parts in the minds of many. It is allowable, therefore, for us to have cognizance of the scheme of action but not to discuss it lest we disturb its artfulness, the interdependence of its component parts, the practical force of the secret meaning of each clause. To discuss and make alterations in a labor of this kind by means of numerous voting is to impress upon it the stamp of all ratiocinations and misunderstandings which have failed to penetrate the depth and nexus of its plottings. We want our schemes to be forcible and suitably concocted. Therefore we ought not to fling the work of genius of our guide to the fangs of the mob or even of a select company.

7. These schemes will not turn existing institutions upside down just yet. They will only effect changes in their economy and consequently in the whole combined movement of their progress, which will thus be directed along the paths laid down in our schemes.

8. Under various names there exists in all countries approximately one and the same thing. Representation, Ministry, Senate, State Council, Legislative and Executive Corps. I need not explain to you the mechanism of the relation of these institutions to one another, because you are aware of all that; only take note of the fact that each of the above-named institutions corresponds to some important function of the State, and I would beg you to remark that the word "important" I apply not to the institution but to the function, consequently it is not the institutions which are important but their functions. These institutions have divided up among themselves all the functions of government—administrative, legislative, executive, wherefore they have come to operate as do the organs in the human body. If we injure one part in the machinery of State, the State falls sick, like a human body, and ... will die.

9. When we introduced into the State organism the poison of Liberalism its whole political complexion underwent a change. States have been seized with a mortal illness—blood poisoning. All that remains is to await the end of their death agony.

10. Liberalism produced Constitutional States, which took the place of what was the only safeguard of the Goyim,

namely, Despotism; and a constitution, as you well know, is nothing else but a school of discords, misunderstandings, quarrels, disagreements, fruitless party agitations, party whims—in a word, a school of everything that serves to destroy the personality of State activity. The tribune of the "talkeries" has, no less effectively than the press, condemned the rulers to inactivity and impotence, and thereby rendered them useless and superfluous, for which reason indeed they have been in many countries deposed. Then it was that the era of republics become possible of realization; and then it was that we replaced the ruler by a caricature of a government—by a president, taken from the mob, from the midst of our puppet creatures, or slaves. This was the foundation of the mine which we have laid under the Goy people, I should rather say, under the Goy peoples.

11. In the near future we shall establish the responsibility of presidents.

12. By that time we shall be in a position to disregard forms in carrying through matters for which our impersonal puppet will be responsible. What do we care if the ranks of those striving for power should be thinned, if there should arise a deadlock from the impossibility of finding presidents, a deadlock which will finally disorganize the country? ...

13. In order that our scheme may produce this result we shall arrange elections in favor of such presidents as have in their past some dark, undiscovered stain, some "Panama" or other—then they will be trustworthy agents

for the accomplishment of our plans out of fear of revelations and from the natural desire of everyone who has attained power, namely, the retention of the privileges, advantages and honor connected with the office of president. The chamber of deputies will provide cover for, will protect, will elect presidents, but we shall take from it the right to propose new, or make changes in existing laws, for this right will be given by us to the responsible president, a puppet in our hands. Naturally, the authority of the presidents will then become a target for every possible form of attack, but we shall provide him with a means of self-defense in the right of an appeal to the people, for the decision of the people over the heads of their representatives, that is to say, an appeal to that same blind slave of ours—the majority of the mob. Independently of this we shall invest the president with the right of declaring a state of war. We shall justify this last right on the ground that the president as chief of the whole army of the country must have it at his disposal, in case of need for the defense of the new republican constitution, the right to defend which will belong to him as the responsible representative of this constitution.

14. It is easy to understand that in these conditions the key of the shrine will lie in our hands, and no one outside ourselves will any longer direct the force of legislation.

15. Besides this we shall, with the introduction of the new republican constitution, take from the Chamber the right of interpolation on government measures, on the pretext of preserving political secrecy, and, further, we shall by

the new constitution reduce the number of representatives to a minimum, thereby proportionately reducing political passions and the passion for politics. If, however, they should, which is hardly to be expected, burst into flame, even in this minimum, we shall nullify them by a stirring appeal and a reference to the majority of the whole people ... Upon the president will depend the appointment of presidents and vice-presidents of the Chamber and the Senate. Instead of constant sessions of Parliaments we shall reduce their sittings to a few months. Moreover, the president, as chief of the executive power, will have the right to summon and dissolve Parliament, and, in the latter case, to prolong the time for the appointment of a new parliamentary assembly. But in order that the consequences of all these acts which in substance are illegal, should not, prematurely for our plans, fall upon the responsibility established by us of the president, we shall instigate ministers and other officials of the higher administration about the president to evade his dispositions by taking measures of their own, for doing which they will be made the scapegoats in his place ... This part we especially recommend to be given to be played by the Senate, the Council of State, or the Council of Ministers, but not to an individual official.

16. The president will, at our discretion, interpret the sense of such of the existing laws as admit of various interpretation; he will further annul them when we indicate to him the necessity to do so, besides this, he will have the right to propose temporary laws, and even new

departures in the government constitutional working, the pretext both for the one and the other being the requirements for the supreme welfare of the State. (Presidential Decrees such as F.D.R. employed to debase the US dollar and steal the gold and to place the U.S. under a permanent State of Emergency and War against its own citizens?)

17. By such measure we shall obtain the power of destroying little by little, step by step, all that at the outset when we enter on our rights, we are compelled to introduce into the constitutions of States to prepare for the transition to an imperceptible abolition of every kind of constitution, and then the time is come to turn every form of government into our despotism.

18. The recognition of our despot may also come before the destruction of the constitution; the moment for this recognition will come when the peoples, utterly wearied by the irregularities and incompetence—a matter which we shall arrange for—of their rulers, will clamor: "Away with them and give us one king over all the earth who will unite us and annihilate the causes of disorders—frontiers, nationalities, religions, State debts—who will give us peace and quiet which we cannot find under our rulers and representatives."

19. But you yourselves perfectly well know that to produce the possibility of the expression of such wishes by all the nations it is indispensable to trouble in all countries the people's relations with their governments so as to utterly exhaust humanity with dissension, hatred, struggle, envy

and even by the use of torture, by starvation, by the inoculation of diseases, by want, so that the "goyim" see no other issue than to take refuge in our complete sovereignty in money and in all else.

20. But if we give the nations of the world a breathing space the moment we long for is hardly likely ever to arrive.

Protocol 11: The Totalitarian State

1. The State Council has been, as it were, the emphatic expression of the authority of the ruler: it will be, as the "show" part of the Legislative Corps, what may be called the editorial committee of the laws and decrees of the ruler. 2. This, then, is the program of the new constitution. We shall make Law, Right and Justice (1) in the guise of proposals to the Legislative Corps, (2) by decrees of the president under the guise of general regulations, of orders of the Senate and of resolutions of the State Council in the guise of ministerial orders, (3) and in case a suitable occasion should arise—in the form of a revolution in the State.

3. Having established approximately the modus agendi we will occupy ourselves with details of those combinations by which we have still to complete the revolution in the course of the machinery of State in the direction already indicated. By these combinations I

mean the freedom of the Press, the right of association, freedom of conscience, the voting principle, and many another that must disappear forever from the memory of man, or undergo a radical alteration the day after the promulgation of the new constitution. It is only at the moment that we shall be able at once to announce all our orders, for, afterwards, every noticeable alteration will be dangerous, for the following reasons: if this alteration be brought in with harsh severity and in a sense of severity and limitations, it may lead to a feeling of despair caused by fear of new alterations in the same direction; if, on the other hand, it be brought in a sense of further indulgences it will be said that we have recognized our own wrong-doing and this will destroy the prestige of the infallibility of our authority, or else it will be said that we have become alarmed and are compelled to show a yielding disposition, for which we shall get no thanks because it will be supposed to be compulsory ... Both the one and the other are injurious to the prestige of the new constitution. What we want is that from the first moment of its promulgation, while the peoples of the world are still stunned by the accomplished fact of the revolution, still in a condition of terror and uncertainty, they should recognize once for all that we are so strong, so inexpugnable, so super-abundantly filled with power, that in no case shall we take any account of them, and so far from paying any attention to their opinions or wishes, we are ready and able to crush with irresistible power all expression or manifestation thereof at every moment and in every place, that we have seized at once everything we wanted and shall in no case divide our power with them ... Then in fear and trembling they will close their eyes to everything, and be content to await what will be the end of it all.

4. The Goyim are a flock of sheep, and we are their wolves. And you know what happens when the wolves get hold of the flock? ....

5. There is another reason also why they will close their eyes: for we shall keep promising them to give back all the liberties we have taken away as soon as we have quelled the enemies of peace and tamed all parties ....

6. It is not worth to say anything about how long a time they will be kept waiting for this return of their liberties ....

7. For what purpose then have we invented this whole policy and insinuated it into the minds of the Goy without giving them any chance to examine its underlying meaning? For what, indeed, if not in order to obtain in a roundabout way what is for our scattered tribe unattainable by the direct road? It is this which has served as the basis for our organization of secret masonry which is not known to, and aims which are not even so much as suspected by, these "Goy" cattle, attracted by us into the "show" army of masonic lodges in order to throw dust in the eyes of their fellows.

8. God has granted to us, His Chosen People, the gift of the dispersion, and in this which appears in all eyes to be our weakness, has come forth all our strength, which has

now brought us to the threshold of sovereignty over all the world.

9. There now remains not much more for us to build up upon the foundation we have laid.

Protocol 12: Control of the Press

1. The word "freedom," which can be interpreted in various ways, is defined by us as follows –

2. Freedom is the right to do what which the law allows. This interpretation of the word will at the proper time be of service to us, because all freedom will thus be in our hands, since the laws will abolish or create only that which is desirable for us according to the aforesaid program.

3. We shall deal with the press in the following way: what is the part played by the press to-day? It serves to excite and inflame those passions which are needed for our purpose or else it serves selfish ends of parties. It is often vapid, unjust, mendacious, and the majority of the public have not the slightest idea what ends the press really serves. We shall saddle and bridle it with a tight curb: we shall do the same also with all productions of the printing press, for where would be the sense of getting rid of the attacks of the press if we remain targets for pamphlets and books? The produce of publicity, which nowadays is a source of heavy expense owing to the necessity of censoring it, will be turned by us into a very lucrative

source of income to our State: we shall lay on it a special stamp tax and require deposits of caution-money before permitting the establishment of any organ of the press or of printing offices; these will then have to guarantee our government against any kind of attack on the part of the press. For any attempt to attack us, if such still be possible, we shall inflict fines without mercy. Such measures as stamp tax, deposit of caution-money and fines secured by these deposits, will bring in a huge income to the government. It is true that party organs might not spare money for the sake of publicity, but these we shall shut up at the second attack upon us. No one shall with impunity lay a finger on the aureole of our government infallibility. The pretext for stopping any publication will be the alleged plea that it is agitating the public mind without occasion or justification. I beg you to note that among those making attacks upon us will also be organs established by us, but they will attack exclusively points that we have pre-determined to alter.

4. Not a single announcement will reach the public without our control. Even now this is already being attained by us inasmuch as all news items are received by a few agencies, in whose offices they are focused from all parts of the world. These agencies will then be already entirely ours and will give publicity only to what we dictate to them.

5. If already now we have contrived to possess ourselves of the minds of the Goy communities to such an extent the they all come near looking upon the events of the world

through the colored glasses of those spectacles we are setting astride their noses; if already now there is not a single State where there exist for us any barriers to admittance into what Goy ingenuousness calls State secrets: what will our positions be then, when we shall be acknowledged supreme lords of the world in the person of our king of all the world ....

6. Let us turn again to the future of the printing press. Every one desirous of being a publisher, librarian, or printer, will be obliged to provide himself with the diploma instituted therefore, which, in case of any fault, will be immediately impounded. With such measures the instrument of thought will become an educative means on the hands of our government, which will no longer allow the mass of the nation to be led astray in by-ways and fantasies about the blessings of progress. Is there any one of us who does not know that these phantom blessings are the direct roads to foolish imaginings which give birth to anarchical relations of men among themselves and towards authority, because progress, or rather the idea of progress, has introduced the conception of every kind of emancipation, but has failed to establish its limits .... All the so-called liberals are anarchists, if not in fact, at any rate in thought. Every one of them in hunting after phantoms of freedom, and falling exclusively into license, that is, into the anarchy of protest for the sake of protest....

7. We turn to the periodical press. We shall impose on it, as on all printed matter, stamp taxes per sheet and deposits of caution-money, and books of less than 30

sheets will pay double. We shall reckon them as pamphlets in order, on the one hand, to reduce the number of magazines, which are the worst form of printed poison, and, on the other, in order that this measure may force writers into such lengthy productions that they will be little read, especially as they will be costly. At the same time what we shall publish ourselves to influence mental development in the direction laid down for our profit will be cheap and will be read voraciously. The tax will bring vapid literary ambitions within bounds and the liability to penalties will make literary men dependent upon us. And if there should be any found who are desirous of writing against us, they will not find any person eager to print their productions. Before accepting any production for publication in print, the publisher or printer will have to apply to the authorities for permission to do so. Thus we shall know beforehand of all tricks preparing against us and shall nullify them by getting ahead with explanations on the subject treated.

8. Literature and journalism are two of the most important educative forces, and therefore our government will become proprietor of the majority of the journals. This will neutralize the injurious influence of the privately-owned press and will put us in possession of a tremendous influence upon the public mind .... If we give permits for ten journals, we shall ourselves found thirty, and so on in the same proportion. This, however, must in no wise be suspected by the public. For which reason all journals published by us will be of the most opposite, in

appearance, tendencies and opinions, thereby creating confidence in us and bringing over to us quite unsuspicious opponents, who will thus fall into our trap and be rendered harmless.

9. In the front rank will stand organs of an official character. They will always stand guard over our interests, and therefore their influence will be comparatively insignificant.

10. In the second rank will be the semi-official organs, whose part it will be to attack the tepid and indifferent.

11. In the third rank we shall set up our own, to all appearance, opposition, which, in at least one of its organs, will present what looks like the very antipodes to us. Our real opponents at heart will accept this simulated opposition as their own and will show us their cards.

12. All our newspapers will be of all possible complexions— aristocratic, republican, revolutionary, even anarchical—for so long, of course, as the constitution exists .... Like the Indian idol "Vishnu" they will have a hundred hands, and every one of them will have a finger on any one of the public opinions as required. When a pulse quickens these hands will lead opinion in the direction of our aims, for an excited patient loses all power of judgment and easily yields to suggestion. Those fools who will think they are repeating the opinion of a newspaper of their own camp will be repeating our opinion or any opinion that seems desirable for us. In the vain belief that they are following the organ of their party

they will, in fact, follow the flag which we hang out for them.

13. In order to direct our newspaper militia in this sense we must take special and minute care in organizing this matter. Under the title of central department of the press we shall institute literary gatherings at which our agents will without attracting attention issue the orders and watchwords of the day. By discussing and controverting, but always superficially, without touching the essence of the matter, our organs will carry on a sham fight fusillade with the official newspapers solely for the purpose of giving occasion for us to express ourselves more fully than could well be done from the outset in official announcements, whenever, of course, that is to our advantage.

14. These attacks upon us will also serve another purpose, namely, that our subjects will bc convinced to the existence of full freedom of speech and so give our agents an occasion to affirm that all organs which oppose us are empty babblers, since they are incapable of finding any substantial objections to our orders.

15. Methods of organization like these, imperceptible to the public eye but absolutely sure, are the best calculated to succeed in bringing the attention and the confidence of the public to the side of our government. Thanks to such methods we shall be in a position as from time to time may be required, to excite or to tranquillize the public mind on political questions, to persuade or to confuse, printing now truth, now lies, facts or their contradictions,

according as they may be well or ill received, always very cautiously feeling our ground before stepping upon it .... We shall have a sure triumph over our opponents since they will not have at their disposition organs of the press in which they can give full and final expression to their views owing to the aforesaid methods of dealing with the press. We shall not even need to refute them except very superficially.

16. Trial shots like these, fired by us in the third rank of our press, in case of need, will be energetically refuted by us in our semi-official organs.

17. Even nowadays, already, to take only the French press, there are forms which reveal masonic solidarity in acting on the watchword: all organs of the press are bound together by professional secrecy; like the augurs of old, not one of their numbers will give away the secret of his sources of information unless it be resolved to make announcement of them. Not one journalist will venture to betray this secret, for not one of them is ever admitted to practice literature unless his whole past has some disgraceful sore or other .... These sores would be immediately revealed. So long as they remain the secret of a few the prestige of the journalist attracts the majority of the country—the mob follow after him with enthusiasm.

18. Our calculations are especially extended to the provinces. It is indispensable for us to inflame there those hopes and impulses with which we could at any moment fall upon the capital, and we shall represent to the capitals that these expressions are the independent hopes and

impulses of the provinces. Naturally, the source of them will be always one and the same—ours. What we need is that, until such time as we are in the plenitude power, the capitals should find themselves stifled by the provincial opinion of the nations, i.e., of a majority arranged by our Agentur. What we need is that at the psychological moment the capitals should not be in a position to discuss an accomplished fact for the simple reason, if for no other, that it has been accepted by the public opinion of a majority in the provinces.

19. When we are in the period of the new regime transitional to that of our assumption of full sovereignty we must not admit any revelation by the press of any form of public dishonesty; it is necessary that the new regime should be thought to have so perfectly contended everybody that even criminality has disappeared ... Cases of the manifestation of criminality should remain known only to their victims and to chance witnesses—no more.

Protocol 13: Distractions

1. The need for daily bread forces the Goyim to keep silence and be our humble servants. Agents taken on to our press from among the Goyim will at our orders discuss anything which it is inconvenient for us to issue directly in official documents, and we meanwhile, quietly amid the din of the discussion so raised, shall simply take and carry

through such measures as we wish and then offer them to the public as an accomplished fact. No one will dare to demand the abrogation of a matter once settled, all the more so as it will be represented as an improvement ... And immediately the press will distract the current of thought towards, new questions, (have we not trained people always to be seeking something new?). Into the discussions of these new questions will throw themselves those of the brainless dispensers of fortunes who are not able even now to understand that they have not the remotest conception about the matters which they undertake to discuss. Questions of the political are unattainable for any save those who have guided it already for many ages, the creators.

2. From all this you will see that in securing the opinion of the mob we are only facilitating the working of our machinery, and you may remark that it is not for actions but for words issued by us on this or that question that we seem to seek approval. We are constantly making public declaration that we are guided in all our undertakings by the hope, joined to the conviction, that we are serving the common weal.

3. In order to distract people who may be too troublesome from discussions of questions of the political we are now putting forward what we allege to be new questions of the political, namely, questions of industry. In this sphere let them discuss themselves silly! The masses are agreed to remain inactive, to take a rest from what they supposed to be political (which we trained them to in order to use them

as a means of combating the Goy governments) only on condition of being found new employments, in which we are prescribing them something that looks like the same political object. In order that the masses themselves may not guess what they are about we further distract them with amusements, games, pastimes, passions, people's palaces .... soon we shall begin through the press to propose competitions in art, in sport in all kinds: these interests will finally distract their minds from questions in which we should find ourselves compelled to oppose them. Growing more and more unaccustomed to reflect and form any opinions of their own, people will begin to talk in the same tone as we because we alone shall be offering them new directions for thought ... of course through such persons as will not be suspected of solidarity with us.

4. The part played by the liberals, utopian dreamers, will be finally played out when our government is acknowledged. Till such time they will continue to do us good service. Therefore we shall continue to direct their minds to all sorts of vain conceptions of fantastic theories, new and apparently progressive: for have we not with complete success turned the brainless heads of the Goyim with progress, till there is not among the Goyim one mind able to perceive that under this word lies a departure from truth in all cases where it is not a question of material inventions, for truth is one, and in it there is no place for progress. Progress, like a fallacious idea, serves to obscure

truth so that none may know it except us, the Chosen of God, its guardians.

5. When, we come into our kingdom our orators will expound great problems which have turned humanity upside down in order to bring it at the end under our beneficent rule.

6. Who will ever suspect then that all these peoples were stage-managed by us according to a political plan which no one has so much as guessed at in the course of many centuries?

Protocol 14: Assault on Religion

1. When we come into our kingdom it will be undesirable for us that there should exist any other religion than ours of the One God with whom our destiny is bound up by our position as the Chosen People and through whom our same destiny is united with the destinies of the world. We must therefore sweep away all other forms of belief. If this gives birth to the atheists whom we see to-day, it will not, being only a transitional stage, interfere with our views, but will serve as a warning for those generations which will hearken to our preaching of the religion of Moses, that, by its stable and thoroughly elaborated system has brought all the peoples of the world into subjection to us. Therein we shall emphasize its mystical right, on which, as we shall say, all its educative power is based .... Then at

every possible opportunity we shall publish articles in which we shall make comparisons between our beneficent rule and those of past ages. The blessing of tranquility, though it be a tranquility forcibly brought about by centuries of agitation, will throw into higher relief the benefits to which we shall point. The errors of the Goyim governments will be depicted by us in the most vivid hues. We shall implant such an abhorrence of them that the peoples will prefer tranquility in a state of serfdom to those rights of vaunted freedom which have tortured humanity and exhausted the very sources of human existence, sources which have been exploited by a mob of rascally adventurers who know not what they do .... useless changes of forms of government to which we instigated the "Goyim" when we were undermining their state structures, will have so wearied the peoples by that time that they will prefer to suffer anything under us rather than run the risk of enduring again all the agitations and miseries they have gone through. [This "religion of Moses," the so-called "Oral Torah" or Babylonian Talmud, is the antithesis of Moses and the Prophets, Note of the Editor].

2. At the same time we shall not omit to emphasize the historical mistakes of the Goy governments which have tormented humanity for so many centuries by their lack of understanding of everything that constitutes the true good of humanity in their chase after fantastic schemes of social blessings, and have never noticed that these schemes kept on producing a worse and never a better

state of the universal relations which are the basis of human life ...

3. The whole force of our principles and methods will lie in the fact that we shall present them and expound them as a splendid contrast to the dead and decomposed old order of things in social life.

4. Our philosophers will discuss all the shortcomings of the various beliefs of the "Goyim," but no one will ever bring under discussion our faith from its true point of view since this will be fully learned by none save ours who will never dare to betray its secrets.

5. In countries known as progressive and enlightened we have created a senseless, filthy, abominable literature. For some time after our entrance to power we shall continue to encourage its existence in order to provide a telling relief by contrast to the speeches, party program, which will be distributed from exalted quarters of ours .... Our wise men, trained to become leaders of the Goyim, will compose speeches, projects, memoirs, articles, which will be used by us to influence the minds of the Goyim, directing them towards such understanding and forms of knowledge as have been determined by us.

Protocol 15: Ruthless Suppression

1. When we at last definitely come into our kingdom by the aid of Coups d'État prepared everywhere for one and

the same day, after definitely acknowledged we shall make it our task to see that against us such things as plots shall no longer exist. With this purpose we shall slay without mercy all who take arms to oppose our coming into our kingdom. Every kind of new institution of anything like a secret society will also be punished with death; those of them which are now in existence, are known to us, serve us and have served us, we shall disband and send into exile to continents far removed from Europe. In this way we shall proceed with those "goy" masons who know too much; such of these as we may for some reason spare will be kept in constant fear of exile. We shall promulgate a law making all former members of secret societies liable to exile from Europe as the center of rule.

2. Resolutions of our government will be final, without appeal.

3. In the Goy societies, in which we have planted and deeply rooted discord and Protestantism, the only possible way of restoring order is to employ merciless measures that prove the direct force of authority: no regard must be paid to the victims who fall, they suffer for the well-being of the future. The attainment of that well-being, even at the expense of sacrifices, is the duty of any kind of government that acknowledges as justification for its existence not only its privileges but its obligations. The principal guarantee of stability of rule is to confirm the aureole of power, and this aureole is attained only by such a majestic inflexibility of might as shall carry on its face

the emblems of inviolability from mystical causes - from the choice of God. Such was, until recent times, the Russian autocracy, the one and only serious foe we had in the world, without counting the Papacy. Bear in mind the example when Italy, drenched with blood, never touched a hair of the head of Sulla who had poured forth that blood: Sulla enjoyed an apotheosis for his might in him, but his intrepid return to Italy ringed him round with inviolability. The people do not lay a finger on him who hypnotizes them by his daring and strength of mind.

4. Meantime, however, until we come into our kingdom, we shall act in the contrary way: we shall create and multiply free masonic lodges in all the countries of the world, absorb into them all who may become or who are prominent in public activity, for these lodges we shall find our principal intelligence office and means of influence. All these lodges we shall bring under one central administration, known to us alone and to all others absolutely unknown, which will be composed of our learned elders. The lodges will have their representatives who will serve to screen the above-mentioned administration of Masonry and from whom will issue the watchword and program. In these lodges we shall tie together the knot which binds together all revolutionary and liberal elements. Their composition will be made up of all strata of society. The most secret political plots will be known to us and fall under our guiding hands on the very day of their conception. Among the members of these lodges will be almost all the agents of international and

national police since their service is for us irreplaceable in the respect that the police is in a position not only to use its own particular measures with the insubordinate, but also to screen our activities and provide pretexts for discontents, et cetera.

5. The class of people who most willingly enter into secret societies are those who live by their wits, careerists, and in general people, mostly light-minded, with whom we shall have no difficulty in dealing and in using to wind up the mechanism of the machine devised by us. If this world grows agitated the meaning of that will be that we have had to stir up in order to break up its too great solidarity. But if there should arise in its midst a plot, then at the head of that plot will be no other than one of our most trusted servants. It is natural that we and no other should lead Masonic activities, for we know where to we are leading, we know the final goal of every form of activity whereas the Goyim have knowledge of nothing, not even of the immediate effect of action; they put before themselves, usually, the momentary reckoning of the satisfaction of their self-opinion in the accomplishment of their thought without even remarking that the very conception never belonged to their initiative but to our instigation of their thought ...

6. The Goyim enter the lodges out of curiosity or in the hope by their means to get a nibble at the public pie, and some of them in order to obtain a hearing before the public for their impracticable and groundless fantasies: they thirst for the emotion of success and applause, of

which we are remarkably generous. And the reason why we give them this success is to make use of the high conceit of themselves to which it gives birth, for that insensibly disposes them to assimilate our suggestions without being on their guard against them in the fullness of their confidence that it is their own infallibility which is giving utterance to their own thoughts and that it is impossible for them to borrow those of others .... You cannot imagine to what extent the wisest of the Goyim can be brought to a state of unconscious naiveté in the presence of this condition of high conceit of themselves, and at the same time how easy it is to take the heart out of them by the slightest ill-success, though it be nothing more than the stoppage of the applause they had, and to reduce them to a slavish submission for the sake of winning a renewal of success .... by so much as ours disregard success if only they can carry through their plans, by so much the "goyim" are willing to sacrifice any plans only to have success. This psychology of theirs materially facilitates for us the task of setting them in the required direction. These tigers in appearance have the souls of sheep and the wind blows freely through their heads. We have set them on the hobby-horse of an idea about the absorption of individuality by the symbolic unit of collectivism .... They have never yet and they never will have the sense to reflect that this hobby-horse is a manifest violation of the most important law of nature, which has established from the very creation of the world one unit unlike another and precisely for the purpose of instituting individuality ....

7. If we have been able to bring them to such a pitch of ingenuous blindness is it not a proof, and an amazingly clear proof, of the degree to which the mind of the Goyim is undeveloped in comparison with our mind? This it is, mainly, which guarantees our success.

8. And how far-seeing were our learned elders in ancient times when they said that to attain a serious end it behooves not to stop at any means or to count the victims sacrificed for the sake of that end .... We have not counted the victims of the seed of the Goy cattle, though we have sacrificed many of our own, but for that we have now already given them such a position on the earth as they could not even have dreamed of. The comparatively small numbers of the victims from the number of ours have preserved our nationality from destruction.

9. Death is the inevitable end for all. It is better to bring that end nearer to those who hinder our affairs than to ourselves, to the founders of this affair. We execute masons in such wise that none save the brotherhood can ever have a suspicion of it, not even the victims themselves of our death sentence, they all die when required as if from a normal kind of illness ..... Knowing this, even the brotherhood in its turn dare not protest. By such methods we have plucked out of the midst of Masonry the very root of protest against our disposition. While preaching liberalism to the Goy we at the same time

keep our own people and our agents in a state of unquestioning submission.

10. Under our influence the execution of the laws of the Goyim has been reduced to a minimum. The prestige of the law has been exploded by the liberal interpretations introduced into this sphere. In the most important and fundamental affairs and questions, judges decide as we dictate to them, see matters in the light wherewith we enfold them for the administration of the Goyim, of course, through persons who are our tools though we do not appear to have anything in common with them - by newspaper opinion or by other means .... Even senators and the higher administration accept our counsels. The purely brute mind of the Goyim is incapable of use for analysis and observation, and still more for the foreseeing whither a certain manner of setting a question may tend.

11. In this difference in capacity for thought between the Goyim and ourselves may be clearly discerned the seal of our position as the Chosen People and of our higher quality of humanness, in contradistinction to the brute mind of the Goyim. Their eyes are open, but see nothing before them and do not invent (unless perhaps, material things). From this it is plain that nature herself has destined us to guide and rule the world.

12. When comes the time of our overt rule, the time to manifest its blessing, we shall remake all legislatures, all our laws will be brief, plain, stable, without any kind of interpretations, so that anyone will be in a position to know them perfectly. The main feature which will run

right through them is submission to orders, and this principle will be carried to a grandiose height. Every abuse will then disappear in consequence of the responsibility of all down to the lowest unit before the higher authority of the representative of power. Abuses of power subordinate to this last instance will be so mercilessly punished that none will be found anxious to try experiments with their own powers. We shall follow up jealously every action of the administration on which depends the smooth running of the machinery of the State, for slackness in this produces slackness everywhere; not a single case of illegality or abuse of power will be left without exemplary punishment.

13. Concealment of guilt, connivance between those in the service of the administration - all this kind of evil will disappear after the very first examples of severe punishment. The aureole of our power demands suitable, that is, cruel, punishments for the slightest infringement, for the sake of gain, of its supreme prestige. The sufferer, though his punishment may exceed his fault, will count as a soldier falling on the administrative field of battle in the interests of authority, principle and law, which do not permit that any of those who hold the reins of the public coach should turn aside from the public highway to their own private paths. For examples our judges will know that whenever they feel disposed to plume themselves on foolish clemency they are violating the law of justice which is instituted for the exemplary edification of men by penalties for lapses and not for display of the spiritual

qualities of the judges .... Such qualities it is proper to show in private life, but not in a public square which is the educational basis of human life.

14. Our legal staff will serve not beyond the age of 55, firstly because old men more obstinately hold to prejudiced opinions, and are less capable of submitting to new directions, and secondly because this will give us the possibility by this measure of securing elasticity in the changing of staff, which will thus the more easily bend under our pressure: he who wishes to keep his place will have to give blind obedience to deserve it. In general, our judges will be elected by us only from among those who thoroughly understand that the part they have to play is to punish and apply laws and not to dream about the manifestations of liberalism at the expense of the educational scheme of the State, as the Goyim in these days imagine it to be .... This method of shuffling the staff will serve also to explode any collective solidarity of those in the same service and will bind all to the interests of the government upon which their fate will depend. The young generation of judges will be trained in certain views regarding the inadmissibility of any abuses that might disturb the established order of our subjects among themselves.

15. In these days the judges of the Goyim create indulgences to every kind of crimes, not having a just understanding of their office, because the rulers of the present age in appointing judges to office take no care to inculcate in them a sense of duty and consciousness of the

matter which is demanded of them. As a brute beast lets out its young in search of prey, so do the Goyim give to them for what purpose such place was created. This is the reason why their governments are being ruined by their own forces through the acts of their own administration.

16. Let us borrow from the example of the results of these actions yet another lesson for our government.

17. We shall root out liberalism from all the important strategic posts of our government on which depends the training of subordinates for our State structure. Such posts will fall exclusively to those who have been trained by us for administrative rule. To the possible objection that the retirement of old servants will cost the Treasury heavily, I reply, firstly, they will be provided with some private service in place of what they lose, and, secondly, I have to remark that all the money in the world will be concentrated in our hands, consequently it is not our government that has to fear expense.

18. Our absolutism will in all things be logically consecutive and therefore in each one of its decrees our supreme will must be respected and unquestionably fulfilled: it will ignore all murmurs, all discontents of every kind and will destroy to the root every kind of manifestation of them in act by punishment of an exemplary character.

19. We shall abolish the right of appeal, which will be transferred exclusively to our disposal - to the cognizance of him who rules, for we must not allow the conception among the people of a thought that there could be such a

thing as a decision that is not right of judges set up by us. If, however, anything like this should occur, we shall ourselves quash the decision, but inflict therewith such exemplary punishment on the judge for lack of understanding of his duty and the purpose of his appointment as will prevent a repetition of such cases .... I repeat that it must be born in mind that we shall know every step of our administration which only needs to be closely watched for the people to be content with us, for it has the right to demand from a good government a good official.

20. Our government will have the appearance of a patriarchal paternal guardianship on the part of our ruler. Our own nation and our subjects will discern in his person a father caring for their every need, their every act, their every interrelation as subjects one with another, as well as their relations to the ruler. They will then be so thoroughly imbued with the thought that it is impossible for them to dispense with this submission and guidance, if they wish to live in peace and quiet, that they will acknowledge the autocracy of our ruler with a devotion bordering on "apotheosis," especially when they are convinced that those whom we set up do not put their own in place of authority, but only blindly execute his dictates. They will be rejoiced that we have regulated everything in their lives as is done by wise parents who desire to train children in the cause of duty and submission. For the peoples of the world in regard to the secrets of our polity are ever

through the ages only children under age, precisely as are also their governments.

21. As you see, I found our despotism on right and duty: the right to compel the execution of duty is the direct obligation of a government which is a father for its subjects. It has the right of the strong that it may use it for the benefit of directing humanity towards that order which is defined by nature, namely, submission. Everything in the world is in a state of submission, if not to man, then to circumstances or its own inner character, in all cases, to what is stronger. And so shall we be this something stronger for the sake of good.

22. We are obliged without hesitation to sacrifice individuals, who commit a breach of established order, for in the exemplary punishment of evil lies a great educational problem.

23. When the King of Israel sets upon his sacred head the crown offered him by Europe he will become patriarch of the world. The indispensable victims offered by him in consequence of their suitability will never reach the number of victims offered in the course of centuries by the mania of magnificence, the emulation between the Goy governments.

24. Our King will be in constant communion with the peoples, making to them from the tribune speeches which fame will in that same hour distribute over all the world.

Protocol 16 Brainwashing

1. In order to effect the destruction of all collective forces except ours we shall emasculate the first stage of collectivism - the universities, by re-educating them in a new direction. Their officials and professors will be prepared for their business by detailed secret programs of action from which they will not with immunity diverge, not by one iota. They will be appointed with especial precaution, and will be so placed as to be wholly dependent upon the government.
2. We shall exclude from the course of instruction State Law as also all that concerns the political question. These subjects will be taught to a few dozen of persons chosen for their pre-eminent capacities from among the number of the initiated. The universities must no longer send out from their halls milk sops concocting plans for a constitution, like a comedy or a tragedy, busying themselves with questions of policy in which even their own fathers never had any power of thought.
3. The ill-guided acquaintance of a large number of persons with questions of polity creates utopian dreamers and bad subjects, as you can see for yourselves from the example of the universal education in this direction of the Goyim. We must introduce into their education all those principles which have so brilliantly broken up their order. But when we are in power we shall remove every kind of disturbing subject from the course of education and shall make out of the youth obedient children of authority,

loving him who rules as the support and hope of peace and quiet.

4. Classicism as also any form of study of ancient history, in which there are more bad than good examples, we shall replace with the study of the program of the future. We shall erase from the memory of men all facts of previous centuries which are undesirable to us, and leave only those which depict all the errors of the government of the Goyim. The study of practical life, of the obligations of order, of the relations of people one to another, of avoiding bad and selfish examples, which spread the infection of evil, and similar questions of an educative nature, will stand in the forefront of the teaching program, which will be drawn up on a separate plan for each calling or state of life, in no wise generalizing the teaching. This treatment of the question has special importance.

5. Each state of life must be trained within strict limits corresponding to its destination and work in life. The occasional genius has always managed and always will manage to slip through into other states of life, but it is the most perfect folly for the sake of this rare occasional genius to let through into ranks foreign to them the untalented who thus rob of their places those who belong to those ranks by birth or employment. you know yourselves in what all this has ended for the "Goyim" who allowed this crying absurdity.

6. In order that he who rules may be seated firmly in the hearts and minds of his subjects it is necessary for the

time of his activity to instruct the whole nation in the schools and on the market places about this meaning and his acts and all his beneficent initiatives.
7. We shall abolish every kind of freedom of instruction. Learners of all ages have the right to assemble together with their parents in the educational establishments as it were in a club: during these assemblies, on holidays, teachers will read what will pass as free lectures on questions of human relations, of the laws of examples, of the philosophy of new theories not yet declared to the world. These theories will be raised by us to the stage of a dogma of faith as a traditional stage towards our faith. On the completion of this exposition of our program of action in the present and the future I will read you the principles of these theories.
8. In a word, knowing by the experience of many centuries that people live and are guided by ideas, that these ideas are imbibed by people only by the aid of education provided with equal success for all ages of growth, but of course by varying methods, we shall swallow up and confiscate to our own use the last scintilla of independence of thought, which we have for long past been directing towards subjects and ideas useful for us. The system of bridling thought is already at work in the so-called system of teaching by object lessons, the purpose of which is to turn the Goyim into unthinking submissive brutes waiting for things to be presented before their eyes in order to form an idea of them .... In

France, one of our best agents, Bourgeois, has already made public a new program of teaching by object lessons.

Protocol 17: Abuse of Authority

1. The practice of advocacy produces men cold, cruel, persistent, unprincipled, who in all cases take up an impersonal, purely legal standpoint. They have the inveterate habit to refer everything to its value for the defense and not to the public welfare of its results. They do not usually decline to undertake any defense whatever, they strive for an acquittal at all costs, caviling over every petty crux of jurisprudence and thereby they demoralize justice. For this reason we shall set this profession into narrow frames which will keep it inside this sphere of executive public service. Advocates, equally with judges, will be deprived of the right of communication with litigants; they will receive business only from the court and will study it by notes of report and documents, defending their clients after they have been interrogated in court on facts that have appeared. They will receive an honorarium without regard to the quality of the defense. This will render them mere reporters on law-business in the interests of justice and as counterpoise to the proctor who will be the reporter in the interests of prosecution; this will shorten business before the courts. In this way will be established a practice of honest unprejudiced

defense conducted not from personal interest but by conviction. This will also, by the way, remove the present practice of corrupt bargain between advocates to agree only to let that side win which pays most .....

2. We have long past taken care to discredit the priesthood of the "Goyim," and thereby to ruin their mission on earth which in these days might still be a great hindrance to us. Day by day its influence on the peoples of the world is falling lower. Freedom of conscience has been declared everywhere, so that now only years divide us from the moment of the complete wrecking of that Christian religion: as to other religions we shall have still less difficulty in dealing with them, but it would be premature to speak of this now. We shall set clericalism and clericals into such narrow frames as to make their influence move in retrogressive proportion to its former progress.

3. When the time comes finally to destroy the papal court the finger of an invisible hand will point the nations towards this court. When, however, the nations fling themselves upon it, we shall come forward in the guise of its defenders as if to save excessive bloodshed. By this diversion we shall penetrate to its very bowels and be sure we shall never come out again until we have gnawed through the entire strength of this place. (Karl Rothschild acted as "peacemaker" between the Vatican and her enemies, loaning the Vatican five million pounds in a period of difficulty. Gregory XVI conferred a Papal decoration on Kalman Rothschild since when Rothschilds have been "Guardians of the Vatican Treasury").

4. The king of the jews will be the real pope of the universe, the patriarch of the international church
5. But, in the meantime, while we are re-educating youth in new traditional religions and afterwards in ours, we shall not overtly lay a finger on existing churches, but we shall fight against them by criticism calculated to produce schism . . .
6. In general, then, our contemporary press will continue to convict State affairs, religions, incapacities of the Goyim, always using the most unprincipled expressions in order by every means to lower their prestige in the manner which can only be practiced by the genius of our gifted tribe.
7. Our kingdom will be an apologia of the divinity Vishnu, in whom is found its personification - in our hundred hands will be, one in each, the springs of the machinery of social life. We shall see everything without the aid of official police which, in that scope of its rights which we elaborated for the use of the Goyim, hinders governments from seeing. In our programs one-third of our subjects will keep the rest under observation from a sense of duty, on the principle of volunteer service to the State. It will then be no disgrace to be a spy and informer, but a merit: unfounded denunciations, however, will be cruelly punished that there may be no development of abuses of this right.
8. Our agents will be taken from the higher as well as the lower ranks of society, from among the administrative class who spend their time in amusements, editors,

printers and publishers, booksellers, clerks, and salesmen, workmen, coachmen, lackeys, et cetera. This body, having no rights and not being empowered to take any action on their own account, and consequently a police without any power, will only witness and report: verification of their reports and arrests will depend upon a responsible group of controllers of police affairs, while the actual act of arrest will be performed by the gendarmerie and the municipal police. Any person not denouncing anything seen or heard concerning questions of polity will also be charged with and made responsible for concealment, if it be proved that he is guilty of this crime.

9. Just as nowadays our brethren, are obliged at their own risk to denounce to the Kahal apostates of their own family or members who have been noticed doing anything in opposition to the Kahal, so in our kingdom over all the world it will be obligatory for all our subjects to observe the duty of service to the state in this direction.

10. Such an organization will extirpate abuses of authority, of force, of bribery, everything in fact which we by our counsels, by our theories of the superhuman rights of man, have introduced into the customs of the Goyim .... But how else were we to procure that increase of causes predisposing to disorders in the midst of their administration? .... Among the number of those methods one of the most important is—agents for the restoration of order, so placed as to have the opportunity in their disintegrating activity of developing and displaying their

evil inclinations—obstinate self-conceit, irresponsible exercise of authority, and, first and foremost, venality.

Protocol 18: Arrest of Opponents

1. When it becomes necessary for us to strengthen the strict measures of secret defense (the most fatal poison for the prestige of authority) we shall arrange a simulation of disorders or some manifestation of discontents finding expression through the co-operation of good speakers. Round these speakers will assemble all who are sympathetic to his utterances. This will give us the pretext for domiciliary prerequisites and surveillance on the part of our servants from among the number of the Goyim police ... 2. As the majority of conspirators act out of love for the game, for the sake of talking, so, until they commit some overt act we shall not lay a finger on them but only introduce into their midst observation elements .... It must be remembered that the prestige of authority is lessened if it frequently discovers conspiracies against itself: this implies a presumption of consciousness of weakness, or, what is still worse, of injustice. You are aware that we have broken the prestige of the Goy kings by frequent attempts upon their lives through our agents, blind sheep of our flock, who are easily moved by a few liberal phrases to crimes provided only they be painted in political colors. We have compelled the rulers to

acknowledge their weakness in advertising overt measures of secret defense and thereby we shall bring the promise of authority to destruction.

3. Our ruler will be secretly protected only by the most insignificant guard, because we shall not admit so much as a thought that there could exist against him any sedition with which he is not strong enough to contend and is compelled to hide from it.

4. If we should admit this thought, as the Goyim have done and are doing, we should ipso facto be signing a death sentence, if not for our ruler, at any rate for his dynasty, at no distant date.

5. According to strictly enforced outward appearances our ruler will employ his power only for the advantage of the nation and in no wise for his own or dynastic profits. Therefore, with the observance of this decorum, his authority will be respected and guarded by the subjects themselves, it will receive an apotheosis in the admission that with it is bound up the well-being of every citizen of the State, for upon it will depend all order in the common life of the pack.

6. Overt defense of the kind argues weakness in the organization of his strength. 7. Our ruler will always be among the people and be surrounded by a mob of apparently curious men and women, who will occupy the front ranks about him, to all appearance by chance, and will restrain the ranks of the rest out of respect as it will appear for good order. This will sow an example of restraint also in others. If a petitioner appears among the

people trying to hand a petition and forcing his way through the ranks, the first ranks must receive the petition and before the eyes of the petitioner pass it to the ruler, so that all may know that what is handed in reaches its destination, that consequently, there exists a control of the ruler himself. The aureole of power requires for his existence that the people may be able to say: "If the king knew of this," or: "the king will hear it." 8. With the establishment of official defense, the mystical prestige of authority disappears: given a certain audacity, and everyone counts himself master of it, the sedition-monger is conscious of his strength, and when occasion serves watches for the moment to make an attempt upon authority .... For the Goyim we have been preaching something else, but by that very fact we are enabled to see what measures of overt defense have brought them to

9. Criminals with us will be arrested at the first, more or less, well-grounded suspicion: it cannot be allowed that out of fear of a possible mistake an opportunity should be given of escape to persons suspected of a political lapse of crime, for in these matters we shall be literally merciless. If it is still possible, by stretching a point, to admit a reconsideration of the motive causes in simple crimes, there is no possibility of excuse for persons occupying themselves with questions in which nobody except the government can understand anything .... And it is not all governments that understand true policy.

Protocol 19: Rulers and People

1. If we do not permit any independent dabbling in the political we shall on the other hand encourage every kind of report or petition with proposals for the government to examine into all kinds of projects for the amelioration of the condition of the people; this will reveal to us the defects or else the fantasies of our subjects, to which we shall respond either by accomplishing them or by a wise rebuttal to prove the shortsightedness of one who judges wrongly.

2. Sedition-mongering is nothing more than the yapping of a lap-dog at an elephant. For a government well organized, not from the police but from the public point of view, the lap-dog yaps at the elephant in entire unconsciousness of its strength and importance. It needs no more than to take a good example to show the relative importance of both and the lap-dogs will cease to yap and will wag their tails the moment they set eyes on an elephant.

3. In order to destroy the prestige of heroism for political crime we shall send it for trial in the category of thieving, murder, and every kind of abominable and filthy crime. Public opinion will then confuse in its conception this category of crime with the disgrace attaching to every other and will brand it with the same contempt.

4. We have done our best, and I hope we have succeeded to obtain that the Goyim should not arrive at this means of contending with sedition. It was for this reason that

through the Press and in speeches, indirectly—in cleverly compiled school-books on history, we have advertised the martyrdom alleged to have been accredited by sedition-mongers for the idea of the commonweal. This advertisement has increased the contingent of liberals and has brought thousands of Goyim into the ranks of our livestock cattle.

Protocol 20: Financial Program

1. To-day we shall touch upon the financial program, which I put off to the end of my report as being the most difficult, the crowning and the decisive point of our plans. Before entering upon it I will remind you that I have already spoken before by way of a hint when I said that the sum total of our actions is settled by the question of figures.

2. When we come into our kingdom our autocratic government will avoid, from a principle of self-preservation, sensibly burdening the masses of the people with taxes, remembering that it plays the part of father and protector. But as State organization cost dear it is necessary nevertheless to obtain the funds required for it. It will, therefore, elaborate with particular precaution the question of equilibrium in this matter.

3. Our rule, in which the king will enjoy the legal fiction that everything in his State belongs to him (which may

easily be translated into fact), will be enabled to resort to the lawful confiscation of all sums of every kind for the regulation of their circulation in the State. From this follows that taxation will best be covered by a progressive tax on property. In this manner the dues will be paid without straitening or ruining anybody in the form of a percentage of the amount of property. The rich must be aware that it is their duty to place a part of their superfluities at the disposal of the State since the State guarantees them security of possession of the rest of their property and the right of honest gains, I say honest, for the control over property will do away with robbery on a legal basis.

4. This social reform must come from above, for the time is ripe for it—it is indispensable as a pledge of peace.

5. The tax upon the poor man is a seed of revolution and works to the detriment of the State which in hunting after the trifling is missing the big. Quite apart from this, a tax on capitalists diminishes the growth of wealth in private hands in which we have in these days concentrated it as a counterpoise to the government strength of the Goyim—their State finances.

6. A tax increasing in a percentage ratio to capital will give much larger revenue than the present individual or property tax, which is useful to us now for the sole reason that it excites trouble and discontent among the Goyim. (Now we know the purpose of the 16th Amendment!!)

7. The force upon which our king will rest consists in the equilibrium and the guarantee of peace, for the sake of

which things it is indispensable that the capitalists should yield up a portion of their incomes for the sake of the secure working of the machinery of the State. State needs must be paid by those who will not feel the burden and have enough to take from.

8. Such a measure will destroy the hatred of the poor man for the rich, in whom he will see a necessary financial support for the State, will see in him the organizer of peace and well-being since he will see that it is the rich man who is paying the necessary means to attain these things.

9. In order that payers of the educated classes should not too much distress themselves over the new payments they will have full accounts given them of the destination of those payments, with the exception of such sums as will be appropriated for the needs of the throne and the administrative institutions.

10. He who reigns will not have any properties of his own once all in the State represented his patrimony, or else the one would be in contradiction to the other; the fact of holding private means would destroy the right of property in the common possessions of all.

11. Relatives of him who reigns, his heirs excepted, who will be maintained by the resources of the State, must enter the ranks of servants of the State or must work to obtain the right to property; the privilege of royal blood must not serve for the spoiling of the treasury.

12. Purchase, receipt of money or inheritance will be subject to the payment of a stamp progressive tax. Any

transfer of property, whether money or other, without evidence of payment of this tax which will be strictly registered by names, will render the former holder liable to pay interest on the tax from the moment of transfer of these sums up to the discovery of his evasion of declaration of the transfer. Transfer documents must be presented weekly at the local treasury office with notifications of the name, surname and permanent place of residence of the former and the new holder of the property. This transfer with register of names must begin from a definite sum which exceeds the ordinary expenses of buying and selling necessaries, and these will be subject to payment only by a stamp impost of a definite percentage of the unit.

13. Just strike an estimate of how many times such taxes as these will cover the revenue of the Goyim States.

14. The State exchequer will have to maintain a definite complement of reserve sums, and all that is collected above that complement must be returned into circulation. On these sums will be organized public works. The initiative in works of this kind, proceeding from State sources, will bind the working class firmly to the interests of the State and to those who reign. From these same sums also a part will be set aside as rewards of inventiveness and productiveness.

15. On no account should so much as a single unit above the definite and freely estimated sums be retained in the State Treasuries, for money exists to be circulated and any kind of stagnation of money acts ruinously on the running

of the State machinery, for which it is the lubricant; a stagnation of the lubricant may stop the regular working of the mechanism.

16. The substitution of interest-bearing paper for a part of the token of exchange has produced exactly this stagnation. The consequences of this circumstance are already sufficiently noticeable.

17. A court of account will also be instituted by us, and in it the ruler will find at any moment a full accounting for State income and expenditure, with the exception of the current monthly account, not yet made up, and that of the preceding month, which will not yet have been delivered.

18. The one and only person who will have no interest in robbing the State is its owner, the ruler. This is why his personal control will remove the possibility of leakages or extravagances.

19. The representative function of the ruler at receptions for the sake of etiquette, which absorbs so much invaluable time, will be abolished in order that the ruler may have time for control and consideration. His power will not then be split up into fractional parts among time-serving favorites who surround the throne for its pomp and splendor, and are interested only in their own and not in the common interests of the State.

20. Economic crises have been produced by us for the Goyim by no other means than the withdrawal of money from circulation. Huge capitals have stagnated, withdrawing money from States, which were constantly obliged to apply to those same stagnant capitals for loans.

These loans burdened the finances of the State with the payment of interest and made them the bond slaves of these capitals .... The concentration of industry in the hands of capitalists out of the hands of small masters has drained away all the juices of the peoples and with them also the States .... (Editor's note: Now we know the purpose of the Federal Reserve Bank Corporation!!)

21. The present issue of money in general does not correspond with the requirements per head, and cannot therefore satisfy all the needs of the workers. The issue of money ought to correspond with the growth of population and thereby children also must absolutely be reckoned as consumers of currency from the day of their birth. The revision of issue is a material question for the whole world.

22. You are aware that the gold standard has been the ruin of the states which adopted it, for it has not been able to satisfy the demands for money, the more so that we have removed gold from circulation as far as possible.

23. With us the standard that must be introduced is the cost of working-man power, whether it be reckoned in paper or in wood. We shall make the issue of money in accordance with the normal requirements of each subject, adding to the quantity with every birth and subtracting with every death.

24. The accounts will be managed by each department (the French administrative division), each circle.

25. In order that there may be no delays in the paying out of money for State needs the sums and terms of such

payments will be fixed by decree of the ruler; this will do away with the protection by a ministry of one institution to the detriment of others.

26. The budgets of income and expenditure will be carried out side by side that they may not be obscured by distance one to another.

27. The reforms projected by us in the financial institutions and principles of the Goyim will be clothed by us in such forms as will alarm nobody. We shall point out the necessity of reforms in consequence of the disorderly darkness into which the Goyim by their irregularities have plunged the finances. The first irregularity, as we shall point out, consists in their beginning with drawing up a single budget which year after year grows owing to the following cause: this budget is dragged out to half the year, then they demand a budget to put things right, and this they expend in three months, after which they ask for a supplementary budget, and all this ends with a liquidation budget. But, as the budget of the following year is drawn up in accordance with the sum of the total addition, the annual departure from the normal reaches as much as 50 per cent in a year, and so the annual budget is trebled in ten years. Thanks to such methods, allowed by the carelessness of the Goy States, their treasuries are empty. The period of loans supervenes, and that has swallowed up remainders and brought all the Goy States to bankruptcy. (The United States was declared "bankrupt" at the Geneva Convention of 1929! [Editor's Note: see 31 USC 5112, 5118, and 5119).

28. You understand perfectly that economic arrangements of this kind, which have been suggested to the Goyim by us, cannot be carried on by us.

29. Every kind of loan proves infirmity in the State and a want of understanding of the rights of the State. Loans hang like a sword of Damocles over the heads of rulers, who, instead of taking from their subjects by a temporary tax, come begging with outstretched palm to our bankers. Foreign loans are leeches which there is no possibility of removing from the body of the State until they fall off of themselves or the State flings them off. But the Goy States do not tear them off; they go on in persisting in putting more on to themselves so that they must inevitably perish, drained by voluntary blood-letting.

30. What also indeed is, in substance, a loan, especially a foreign loan? A loan is—an issue of government bills of exchange containing a percentage obligation commensurate to the sum of the loan capital. If the loan bears a charge of 5 per cent, then in twenty years the State vainly pays away in interest a sum equal to the loan borrowed, in forty years it is paying a double sum, in sixty—treble, and all the while the debt remains an unpaid debt.

31. From this calculation it is obvious that with any form of taxation per head the State is baling out the last coppers of the poor taxpayers in order to settle accounts with wealthy foreigners, from whom it has borrowed money instead of collecting these coppers for its own needs without the additional interest.

32. So long as loans were internal the Goyim only shuffled their money from the pockets of the poor to those of the rich, but when we bought up the necessary persons in order to transfer loans into the external sphere, (Editor's Note: Woodrow Wilson and F.D. Roosevelt) all the wealth of States flowed into our cash-boxes and all the Goyim began to pay us the tribute of subjects.

33. If the superficiality of Goy kings on their thrones in regard to State affairs and the venality of ministers or the want of understanding of financial matters on the part of other ruling persons have made their countries debtors to our treasuries to amounts quite impossible to pay it has not been accomplished without, on our part, heavy expenditure of trouble and money.

34. Stagnation of money will not be allowed by us and therefore there will be no State interest-bearing paper, except a one per-cent series, so that there will be no payment of interest to leeches that suck all the strength out of the State. The right to issue interest-bearing paper will be given exclusively to industrial companies who find no difficulty in paying interest out of profits, whereas the State does not make interest on borrowed money like these companies, for the State borrows to spend and not to use in operations. (Editor's Note: Now we know why President Kennedy was assassinated in 1963 when he refused to borrow any more of the "Bank Notes" from the bankers of the Federal Reserve Bank and began circulating non-interest bearing "Notes" of the "United States of America"!!!).

35. Industrial paper will be bought also by the government which from being as now a payer of tribute by loan operations will be transformed into a lender of money at a profit. This measure will stop the stagnation of money, parasitic profits and idleness, all of which were useful for us among the Goyim so long as they were independent but are not desirable under our rule.
36. How clear is the undeveloped power of thought of the purely brute brains of the Goyim, as expressed in the fact that they have been borrowing from us with payment of interest without ever thinking that all the same these very moneys plus an addition for payment of interest must be got by them from their own State pockets in order to settle up with us. What could have been simpler than to take the money they wanted from their own people?
37. But it is a proof of the genius of our chosen mind that we have contrived to present the matter of loans to them in such a light that they have even seen in them an advantage for themselves.
38. Our accounts, which we shall present when the time comes, in the light of centuries of experience gained by experiments made by us on the Goy States, will be distinguished by clearness and definiteness and will show at a glance to all men the advantage of our innovations. They will put an end to those abuses to which we owe our mastery over the Goyim, but which cannot be allowed in our kingdom.
39. We shall so hedge about our system of accounting that neither the ruler nor the most insignificant public servant

will be in a position to divert even the smallest sum from its destination without detection or to direct it in another direction except that which will be once fixed in a definite plan of action. (*Editor's Note: Is this why a "private corporation," known as the "Internal Revenue Service," is in charge of collecting the "payments" of the "Income Taxes" and the IRS always deposits those "payments" to the Federal Reserve bank and never to the Treasury of the United States??*)

40. And without a definite plan it is impossible to rule. Marching along an undetermined road and with undetermined resources brings to ruin by the way heroes and demi-gods.

41. The Goy rulers, whom we once upon a time advised should be distracted from State occupations by representative receptions, observances of etiquette, entertainments, were only screens for our rule. [Editor's Note: Like the House of Windsor (Guelph) and the rest of the "Black Nobility"?]. The accounts of favorite courtiers who replaced them in the sphere of affairs were drawn up for them by our agents, and every time gave satisfaction to short-sighted minds by promises that in the future economies and improvements were foreseen .... Economies from what? From new taxes?—were questions that might have been but were not asked by those who read our accounts and projects.

42. You know to what they have been brought by this carelessness, to what pitch of financial disorder they have

arrived, notwithstanding the astonishing industry of their peoples ....

Protocol 21: Loans and Credit

1. To what I reported to you at the last meeting I shall now add a detailed explanation of internal loans. Of foreign loans I shall say nothing more, because they have fed us with the national moneys of the Goyim, but for our State there will be no foreigners, that is, nothing external.

2. We have taken advantage of the venality of administrators and slackness of rulers to get our moneys twice, thrice and more times over, by lending to the Goy governments moneys which were not at all needed by the States. Could anyone do the like in regard to us? .... Therefore, I shall only deal with the details of internal loans.

3. States announce that such a loan is to be concluded and open subscriptions for their own bills of exchange, that is, for their interest-bearing paper. That they may be within the reach of all the price is determined at from a hundred to a thousand; and a discount is made for the earliest subscribers. Next day by artificial means the price of them goes up, the alleged reason being that everyone is rushing to buy them. In a few days the treasury safes are, as they say, overflowing and there's more money than they can do with (why then take it?) The subscription, it is alleged,

covers many times over the issue total of the loan; in this lies the whole stage effect - look you, they say, what confidence is shown in the government's bills of exchange.

4. But when the comedy is played out there emerges the fact that a debit and an exceedingly burdensome debit has been created. For the payment of interest it becomes necessary to have recourse to new loans, which do not swallow up but only add to the capital debt. And when this credit is exhausted it becomes necessary by new taxes to cover, not the loan, but only the interest on it. These taxes are a debit employed to cover a debit .... [Editor's Note: Hence the cry to balance the budget!]

5. Later comes the time for conversions, but they diminish the payment of interest without covering the debt, and besides they cannot be made without the consent of the lenders; on announcing a conversion a proposal is made to return the money to those who are not willing to convert their paper. If everybody expressed his unwillingness and demanded his money back, the government would be hoist on their own petard and would be found insolvent and unable to pay the proposed sums. By good luck the subjects of the Goy governments, knowing nothing about financial affairs, have always preferred losses on exchange and diminution of interest to the risk of new investments of their moneys, and have thereby many a time enabled these governments to throw off their shoulders a debit of several millions.

6. Nowadays, with external loans, these tricks cannot be played by the Goyim for they know that we shall demand all our moneys back.
7. In this way in acknowledged bankruptcy will best prove to the various countries the absence of any means between the interests of the peoples and of those who rule them.
8. I beg you to concentrate your particular attention upon this point and upon the following: nowadays all internal loans are consolidated by so-called flying loans, that is, such as have terms of payment more or less near. These debts consist of moneys paid into the savings banks and reserve funds. If left for long at the disposition of a government these funds evaporate in the payment of interest on foreign loans, and are placed by the deposit of equivalent amount of rents.
9. And these last it is which patch up all the leaks in the State treasuries of the Goyim.
10. When we ascend the throne of the world all these financial and similar shifts, as being not in accord with our interests, will be swept away so as not to leave a trace, as also will be destroyed all money markets, since we shall not allow the prestige of our power to be shaken by fluctuations of prices set upon our values, which we shall announce by law at the price which represents their full worth without any possibility of lowering or raising. (Raising gives the pretext for lowering, which indeed was where we made a beginning in relation to the values of the Goyim).

11. We shall replace the money markets by grandiose government credit institutions, the object of which will be to fix the price of industrial values in accordance with government views. These institutions will be in a position to fling upon the market five hundred millions of industrial paper in one day, or to buy up for the same amount. In this way all industrial undertakings will come into dependence upon us. You may imagine for yourselves what immense power we shall thereby secure for ourselves ....

Protocol 22

Power of Gold

1 In all that has so far been reported by me to you, I have endeavored to depict with care the secret of what is coming, of what is past, and of what is going on now, rushing into the flood of the great events coming already in the near future, the secret of our relations to the Goyim and of financial operations. On this subject there remains still a little for me to add.

2. In our hands is the greatest power of our day - gold: in two days we can procure from our storehouses any quantity we may please.

3. Surely there is no need to seek further proof that our rule is predestined by God? Surely we shall not fail with such wealth to prove that all that evil which for so many centuries we have had to commit has served at the end of ends the cause of true well-being - the bringing of everything into order? Though it be even by the exercise

of some violence, yet all the same it will be established. (The motto of the Freemasons - “Out of Chaos, Order"). We shall contrive to prove that we are benefactors who have restored to the rent and mangled earth the true good and also freedom of the person, and therewith we shall enable it to be enjoyed in peace and quiet, with proper dignity of relations, on the condition, of course, of strict observance of the laws established by us. We shall make plain therewith that freedom does not consist in dissipation and in the right of unbridled license any more than the dignity and force of a man do not consist in the right of everyone to promulgate destructive principles in the nature of freedom of conscience, equality and the like, that freedom of the person in no wise consists in the right to agitate oneself and others by abominable speeches before disorderly mobs, and that true freedom consists in the inviolability of the person who honorably and strictly observes all the laws of life in common, that human dignity is wrapped up in consciousness of the rights and also of the absence of rights of each, and not wholly and solely in fantastic imaginings about the subject of one's ego.

4. One authority will be glorious because it will be all-powerful, will rule and guide, and not muddle along after leaders and orators shrieking themselves hoarse with senseless words which they call great principles and which are nothing else, to speak honestly, but utopian .... Our authority will be the crown of order, and in that is included the whole happiness of man. The aureole of this

authority will inspire a mystical bowing of the knee before it and a reverent fear before it of all the peoples. True force makes no terms with any right, not even with that of God: none dare come near to it so as to take so much as a span from it away.

Protocol 23: Instilling Obedience

1. That the peoples may become accustomed to obedience it is necessary to inculcate lessons of humility and therefore to reduce the production of articles of luxury. By this we shall improve morals which have been debased by emulation in the sphere of luxury. We shall re-establish small master production which will mean laying a mine under the privatc capital of manufactures. This is indispensable also for the reason that manufacturers on the grand scale often move, though not always consciously, the thoughts of the masses in directions against the government. A people of small masters knows nothing of unemployment and this binds him closely with existing order, and consequently with the firmness of authority. For us its part will have been played out the moment authority is transferred into our hands. Drunkenness also will be prohibited by law and punishable as a crime against the humanness of man who is turned into a brute under the influence of alcohol.

2. Subjects, I repeat once more, give blind obedience only to the strong hand which is absolutely independent of them, for in it they feel the sword of defense and support against social scourges .... What do they want with an angelic spirit in a king? What they have to see in him is the personification of force and power.
3. The supreme lord who will replace all now existing rulers, dragging in their existence among societies demoralized by us, societies that have denied even the authority of God, from whose midst breeds out on all sides the fire of anarchy, must first of all proceed to quench this all-devouring flame. Therefore he will be obliged to kill off those existing societies, though he should drench them with his own blood, that he may resurrect them again in the form of regularly organized troops fighting consciously with every kind of infection that may cover the body of the State with sores.
4. This Chosen One of God is chosen from above to demolish the senseless forces moved by instinct and not reason, by brutishness and not humanness. These forces now triumph in manifestations of robbery and every kind of violence under the mask of principles of freedom and rights. They have overthrown all forms of social order to erect on the ruins the throne of the King of the Jews; but their part will be played out the moment he enters into his kingdom. Then it will be necessary to sweep them away from his path, on which must be left no knot, no splinter.
5. Then will it be possible for us to say to the peoples of the world: "Give thanks to God and bow the knee before

him who bears on his front the seal of the predestination of man, to which God himself has led his star that none other but Him might free us from all the before-mentioned forces and evils".

Protocol 24: Qualities of the Ruler

1. I pass now to the method of confirming the dynastic roots of King David to the last strata of the earth.
2. This confirmation will first and foremost be included in that which to this day has rested the force of conservatism by our learned elders of the conduct of the affairs of the world, in the directing of the education of thought of all humanity.
3. Certain members of the seed of David will prepare the kings and their heirs, selecting not by right of heritage but by eminent capacities, inducting them into the most secret mysteries of the political, into schemes of government, but providing always that none may come to knowledge of the secrets. The object of this mode of action is that all may know that government cannot be entrusted to those who have not been inducted into the secret places of its art ....
4. To these persons only will be taught the practical application of the forenamed plans by comparison of the experiences of many centuries, all the observations on the politico-economic moves and social sciences - in a word,

all the spirit of laws which have been unshakably established by nature herself for the regulation of the relations of humanity.

5. Direct heirs will often be set aside from ascending the throne if in their time of training they exhibit frivolity, softness and other qualities that are the ruin of authority, which render them incapable of governing and in themselves dangerous for kingly office.

6. Only those who are unconditionally capable for firm, even if it be to cruelty, direct rule will receive the reins of rule from our learned elders.

7. In case of falling sick with weakness of will or other form of incapacity. kings must by law hand over the reins of rule to new and capable hands.

8. The king's plan of action for the current moment, and all the more so for the future, will be unknown, even to those who are called his closest counselors.

9. Only the king and the three who stood sponsor for him will know what is coming.

10. In the person of the king who with unbending will is master of himself and of humanity all will discern as it were fate with its mysterious ways. None will know what the king wishes to attain by his dispositions, and therefore none will dare to stand across an unknown path.

11. It is understood that the brain reservoir of the king must correspond in capacity to the plan of government it has to contain. It is for this reason that he will ascend the throne not otherwise than after examination of his mind by the aforesaid learned elders.

12. That the people may know and love their king, it is indispensable for him to converse in the market-places with his people. This ensures the necessary clinching of the two forces which are now divided one from another by us by the terror.
13. This terror was indispensable for us till the time comes for both these forces separately to fall under our influence.
14. The king of the Jews must not be at the mercy of his passions, and especially of sensuality: on no side of his character must he give brute instincts power over his mind. Sensuality worse than all else disorganizes the capacities of the mind and clearness of views, distracting the thoughts to the worst and most brutal side of human activity.
15. The prop of humanity in the person of the supreme lord of all the world of the holy seed of David must sacrifice to his people all personal inclinations.
16. Our supreme lord must be of an exemplary irreproachability.

Signed by the representative of Zion, of the 33rd Degree

APPENDIX 2
Henry Ford's "International Jew"

A2.1 Editor's Foreword

In an interview published in the New York World February 17, 1921, Mr. Henry Ford put the case for the "Protocols of Zion" tersely and convincingly. He said: "The only statement I care to make about the Protocols is that they fit in with what is going on. They are sixteen years old and they have fitted the world situation up to this time. They fit it now." He made this statement when Jewish leaders and the Jewish Press in America were fulminating against a series of articles printed in Ford's newspaper The Dearborn Independent during the years 1920 to 1922. After some years of pressure such as only organized Jewry can conceive or inflict, Henry Ford was made to apologize to Jewry in a letter addressed to Louis Marshall, then leader of the American Jewish Committee, dated June 30, 1927. Ford's apology was abject, but neither then, nor since did he ever deny the truth of the articles.

As clearly as the "Protocols of the Learned Elders of Zion" reveal a concerted plan of action, of intention and achievement, through centuries of world history, so the long series of articles in The Dearborn Independent expose the powerful concentration of forces organized by Jewish interests and the effects of Jewish influences in the United States from the time of the Civil War up to the uneasy years following the first world war. The scope of the original articles is wide, the analysis of the relentless march of Jewish ambition and the rapid acquisition of political power is deep and dispassionate. In their entirety they present a most thorough exposition of the range of Jewish influences in America over many decades; they provide adequate evidence of the motives that inspire such phenomena and the ultimate objective towards which Jewish policy is leading the world. In the 29 years that have passed since the publication of the series began, Jewish power in the United States has developed to a degree far out-distancing even the alarming proportions exposed at that time.

The Jewish "National State" of which we have heard so much deceptive talk elsewhere is already firmly established. De jure and de facto the United States of America can claim that title, though many American citizens may even yet be astonished and no doubt indignant to read the statement. But, examine the facts.

The Dearborn Independent articles fitted the American scene 30 years ago, they fit it now! The Jewish Question continues to mount the scale of public attention all over the civilized world, attracting ever a higher type of mind to the discussion of its significance. It cannot be encompassed within the range of a single volume.

This edited version seeks merely to give the gist of the four volumes in which the famous series of articles were printed under the title: The International Jew. Presenting the essential facts in easier sequence and condensed to about one-tenth of the original wordage, many contemporary illustrations have been eliminated, but the implications of the Jewish Question in America and the evidence of the impact of the Jewish idea on the lives of ordinary American citizens have been marshalled in a form readily assimilable by new readers, providing a useful digest for the informed. The way to a just solution of "the world's foremost problem" is clearly indicated. Truth is visible when honest men seek Her diligently. The reader, wherever he may be, to whatever nation he may belong, should seriously reflect upon the fact that the conditions long-operating in the United States and the conclusions which emerge from this investigation of the Jewish Question in that powerful country, can, in all probability, now be paralleled in his own land, his own city. If he should seek confirmation -- let him look around.

G. F. Green,

London, February, 1948.

A2.2 Preface: Henry Ford — the Man

Henry Ford was born on July 30, 1863, during the American Civil War, on a farm at Dearborn, near Detroit, Michigan. He was the son of William Ford, a prosperous farmer who was of Irish stock. His mother was of mixed Dutch and Scandinavian origin. At 17 he became an apprentice in a machine shop in Detroit, and he also kept a machine shop of his own and worked for a harvester company by repairing their portable farm engines. His mechanical genius showed itself in early youth, and in 1890, when he secured a post with the Detroit Edison Electric Company, he realized that the public were more interested in road vehicles than in tractors and he studied the principles of the gas engine to overcome the weight of steam engines. In 1887 he had built his first gas engine and kept on building more. His first gasoline "buggy" was given a public trial in 1893 at which it attained a speed of 25 miles an hour.

In 1903 he formed the Ford Motor Company with 12 shareholders and a capital of 100,000 dollars. In 1924 he was producing one thousand of the world-famous Ford motor-cars a day. In 1924 the annual production of the Ford works reached the towering peak of two million cars, trucks and tractors. The secret of his success lay in mass production methods, and high wages. Of humble origin himself he had a deep feeling for his employees, and worked out rough and ready principles in regard to labor which he constantly applied. One was to pay the highest possible wages, and in this he was a true reformer; another, to accept applicants for work without questions or references. Many European socialists were impressed by Ford's proof demonstration that Marx had been rendered obsolete by Ford and that capitalism could be rationalized and moralized. In 1918, Ford, who had been a supporter of President Wilson, had unsuccessfully run for the Senate, and there was some talk later -- it caused alarm among the professional politicians -- that he would run for the Presidency, but he announced that he would not stand against Coolidge. Ford made great endeavors, most of them impracticable, to negotiate peace between the warring nations of Europe in the first world war.

In 1920 he went into print and bought "The Dearborn Independent," a virile and very independent journal published in his home town. It was noted for its courageous and continuous examination of the Jewish Question in America, and for its objective views on true Americanism.

Ford was accused by many Jews, along with Deterding and Greuger, to be a financial backer of the Hitler movement in Germany. At the Nuremberg Tribunal, Baldur Von Shirach, Hitler Youth Leader, said he had become "Jew-wise" through reading Ford's books.

Ford was a resolute opponent of Roosevelt's policy of "controls" in industry and commerce, but in his later years his political and other public activities were few. He died aged 83, at Detroit, April 7, 1947. A famous American and one of the world's outstanding individuals.

In his book "My Life and Work," published in 1922, Henry Ford includes the following concerning the "International Jew" series of articles: "The work which we describe as Studies in the Jewish Question, and which is variously described by antagonists as "the Jewish campaign," "the attack on the Jews," "the anti-Semitic pogrom," and so forth, needs no explanation to those who have followed it. Its motives and purposes must be judged by the work itself. It is offered as a contribution to a question which deeply affects the country, a question which is racial at its source, and which concerns influences and ideals rather than persons. Our statements must be judged by candid readers who are intelligent enough to lay our words alongside life as they are able to observe it. If our word and their observation agree, the case is made. It is perfectly silly to begin to damn us before it has been shown that our statements are baseless or reckless. The first item to be considered is the truth of what we have set forth. And that is precisely the item which our critics choose to evade. Readers of our articles will see at once that we are not actuated by any kind of prejudice, except it may be a prejudice in favor of the principles which have made our civilization.

There had been observed in this country certain streams of influence which were causing a marked deterioration in our literature, amusements, and social conduct; business was departing from its old-time substantial soundness; a general letting-down of standards was felt everywhere. It was not the robust coarseness of the white man, the rude indelicacy, say, of Shakespeare's characters, but a nasty Orientalism which has insidiously affected every channel of expression — and to such an extent that it was time to challenge it. The fact that these influences are all traceable to one racial source is a fact to be reckoned with. Our work does not pretend to say that last word on the Jew in America. It says only the word which describes his present impress on that country. When that impress is changed, the report of it can be changed. Our opposition is only to ideas, false ideas which are sapping the moral stamina of the people. These ideas proceed from easily identified sources, they are promulgated by easily discoverable methods and they are controlled by mere exposure.

When people learn to identify the source and nature of these influences swirling around them, it is sufficient. Let the American people once understand that it is not natural degeneracy but calculated subversion that inflicts us, and they are safe. The explanation is the cure. This work was taken up without personal motives. When it reached a stage where we believed the American people could grasp the key, we let it rest for the time. Our enemies say that we began it for revenge and that we laid it down in fear. Time will show that our critics are merely dealing in evasion because they dare not tackle the main question."

A2.3 "The International Jew": Contents

Chapter 1: Jewish History in the US

The story of the Jews in America begins with Christopher Columbus. On August 2, 1492, more than 300,000 Jews were expelled from Spain and on August 3, the next day, Columbus set sail for the west, taking a group of Jews with him.

They were not, however, refugees, for the prophetic navigator's plans had aroused the sympathy of influential Jews for a long period previously. Columbus himself tells us that he consorted much with Jews. The first letter he wrote detailing his discoveries was to a Jew. Indeed, the eventful voyage itself which added to men's knowledge and wealth "the other half of the earth" was made possible by Jews. The pleasant story that it was Queen Isabella's jewels which financed the voyage has disappeared under cool research.

There were three Maranos or "secret Jews" who wielded great influence at the Spanish court: Luis de Santagel, who was an important merchant of Valencia and who was "farmer" of the royal taxes; his relative, Gabriel Sanchez, who was the royal treasurer; and their friend, the royal chamberlain, Juan Cabrero. These worked unceasingly on Queen Isabella's imagination, picturing to her the depletion of the royal treasury and the likelihood of Columbus discovering the fabulous gold of the Indies, until the Queen was ready to offer her jewels in pawn for the funds. But Santagel craved permission to advance the money himself, which he did, 17,000 ducats in all, about 5,000 pounds, perhaps equal to 40,000 pounds today.

Associated with Columbus in the voyage were at least five Jews: Luis de Torres, interpreter; Marco, the surgeon; Bernal, the physician; Alonzo de la Calle, and Gabriel Sanchez. Luis de Torres was the first man ashore, the first to discover the use of tobacco; he settled in Cuba and may be said to be the father of Jewish control of the tobacco business as it exists today.

Columbus' old patrons, Luis de Santagel and Gabriel Sanchez, received many privileges for the part they played in the work, but Columbus himself became the victim of a conspiracy fostered by Bernal, the ship's doctor, and suffered injustice and imprisonment as his reward.

From that beginning, Jews looked more and more to America as a fruitful field, and immigration set in strongly toward South America, principally Brazil. But because of military participation in a disagreement between the Brazilians and the Dutch, the Jews of Brazil found it necessary to emigrate, which they did in the direction of the Dutch colony of what is now New York. Peter Stuyvesant, the Dutch governor, did not entirely approve of their settling among his people and ordered them to leave, but the Jews had evidently taken the precaution to assure their being received if not welcomed, because upon revoking the order of Stuyvesant, the Directors gave as one of the reasons for the Jews being received, "the large amount of capital which they have invested in the shares of the Company."

Nevertheless they were forbidden to enter public service and to open retail shops, which had the effect of driving them into foreign trade in which they were soon exercising all but a monopoly because of their European connections.

This is only one of the thousand illustrations which can be given of the resourcefulness of the Jew. Forbid him in one direction he will excel in another. When he was forbidden to deal in new clothes, he sold old clothes - that was the beginning of the organized traffic in secondhand clothing. When he was forbidden to deal in merchandise, he dealt in waste - the Jew is the originator of the waste product business of the world; he was the originator of the salvage system; he found wealth in the debris of civilization. He taught people how to use old rags, how to clean old feathers, how to use gall nuts and rabbit skins. He has always had a taste for the furrier trade, which he now controls, and to him is due the multitude of common skins which now pass under various alluring trade names as furs of high origin.

Unwittingly, old Peter Stuyvesant (1610–1672) served as the last Dutch director-general of the colony of New Netherland from 1647 until it was ceded provisionally to the English in 1664, after which it was renamed New York. He was a major figure in the early history of New York City and his name has been given to various landmarks and points of interest throughout the city (e.g. Stuyvesant High School, Stuyvesant Town, Stuyvesant Plaza, Bedford–Stuyvesant neighborhood, etc.). Stuyvesant's accomplishments as director-general included a great expansion for the settlement of New Amsterdam beyond the southern tip of Manhattan. Among the projects built by Stuyvesant's administration were the protective wall on Wall Street, the canal that became Broad Street, and Broadway. Stuyvesant, himself a member of the Dutch Reformed Church, opposed religious pluralism and came into conflict with Lutherans, Jews, Roman Catholics and Quakers as they attempted to build places of worship in the city and practice their faiths. He compelled the Jews to make New York the principal port of America, and though a majority of New York Jews had fled to Philadelphia at the time of the American Revolution, most of them returned to New York at the earliest opportunity, instinct seeming to make them aware that, in New York was to be their principal paradise of gain. And so it has proved.

New York is the greatest center of Jewish population in the world. It is the gateway where the bulk of American imports and exports are taxed, and where practical all the business done in America pays tribute to the masters of money. The very land of the city is the holdings of the Jews.

No wonder that Jewish writers, viewing this unprecedented prosperity, this unchecked growth in wealth and power, exclaim enthusiastically that the United States is the Promised Land foretold by the prophets, and New York the New Jerusalem. Some have gone even further and described the peaks of the Rockies as "the mountains of Zion," and with reason, too, if the mining and coastal wealth of the Jews is considered.

In the time of George Washington there were about 4,000 Jews in the country, most of them well to do traders. They favored the American side and helped the revolutionary colonies out with loans at critical moments.

In fifty years the traceable increase in the Jewish population of the United States was more than 3,300,000. What it is today no man can estimate with any hope of accuracy.

To make a list of the lines of business controlled by the Jews of the United States would be to touch most of the vital industries of the country - those which are really vital, and those which cultivated habit have been made to seem vital. The theatrical business is exclusively Jewish: play-producing, booking, theater operation are all in the hands of Jews. This accounts for the fact that in almost every production today can be detected propaganda, sometimes glaringly commercial advertisement, sometimes direct political instruction.

The motion picture industry; the sugar industry; the tobacco industry; fifty per cent or more of the meat packing industry; over sixty per cent of the shoemaking industry; most of the musical purveying done in the country; jewelry; grain; cotton; oil; steel; magazine authorship; news distribution; the liquor business; the loan business; these, to name only the industries with national and international sweep, are in control of the

Jews of the United States, either alone or in association with Jews overseas.

The American people would be vastly surprised if they could see a line-up of some of the "American business men' who hold up our commercial prestige overseas. They are mostly Jews. This may throw a sidelight on the regard in which "American business methods" are held in some parts of the world. When many different races of people can carry on business under the name "American," and do it legally, too, it is not surprising that Americans do not recognize some of the descriptions of American methods which appear in the foreign Press. If the reputation of American business has suffered, it is because something other than American methods have been used under the American name.

Instances of Jewish prosperity in the United States are commonplace, but prosperity, the just reward of foresight and application, is not to be confounded with control. It would be impossible for any Gentile coalition under similar circumstances to attain the control which the Jews have won, for the reason that there is lacking in the Gentile a certain quality of working-togetherness, a certain conspiracy of objective, and the adhesiveness of intense racism, which characterizes the Jew. It is nothing to a Gentile that another man is a Gentile; it is next to everything to a Jew that the man at his door is another Jew.

The International Jewish plan to move their money market to the United States was what the American people did not want. We have the warning of history as to what this means. It has meant in turn that Spain, Venice, Germany or Great Britain received the blame or suspicion of the world for what the Jewish financiers have done. It is a most important consideration that most of the national animosities that exist today arose out of resentment against what Jewish money power did under the camouflage of national names.

"The British did this," "The Germans did this," when it was the International Jew who did it, the nations being but the marked spaces on his checker board. Today, around the world the blaming word is heard, "The United States did this. If it were not for the United States the world would be in a better shape. The Americans are a sordid, greedy, cruel people."

Why? Because the Jewish money power is centered here and is making money out of both our immunity and Europe's distress, playing one against the other; and because so many so-called "American business men" abroad today are not Americans at all - they are Jews.

Citizens wake up with a start to find that even the white nations are hardly allowed to see each other nowadays except through Jewish eyes. Great Britain and France seldom see a special American spokesman who is not a Jew. That may be the reason why they reciprocate by sending Jews to us, thinking perhaps that we prefer them.

Chapter 2: Angles of Jewish Influence

The Jewish Question exists wherever Jews appear, says Theodor Herzl, because they bring it with them. It is not their numbers that create the Question, for there is in almost every country a larger number of other aliens than of Jews. It is not their much-boasted ability, for it is now coming to be understood that, give the Jew an equal start and hold him to the rules of the game, and he is not smarter than anyone else; indeed, in one great class of Jews the zeal is quenched when opportunity for intrigue is removed.

The Jewish Question is not the number of Jews who reside here, not in the American's jealousy of the Jew's success, certainly not in any objection to the Jew's Mosaic religion; it is in something else, and that something else is the fact of Jewish influence on the life of the country where Jews dwell; in the United States it is the Jewish influence on American life.

That the Jews exert an influence, they themselves loudly proclaim. The Jews claim, indeed, that the fundamentals of the United States are Jewish and not Christian, and that the entire history of this country should be re-written to make proper acknowledgement of the prior glory due to Judah. If the question of influence rested entirely on the Jewish claim, there would be no occasion for doubt; they claim it all. But it is kindness to hold them to the facts; it is also more clearly explanatory of the conditions in our country.

If they insist that they "gave us our Bible" and "gave us our God" and "gave us our religion," as they do over and over again with nauseating superciliousness throughout all their polemic publications -- not a single one of these claims being true -- they must not grow impatient and profane while we complete the list of the real influences they have set at work in American life.

It is not the Jewish people but the Jewish idea, and the people only as vehicles of the idea, that is the point at issue. In this investigation of the Jewish Question, it is Jewish influence and the Jewish Idea that are being discovered and defined.

The Jews are propagandists. This was originally their mission. But they were to propagate the central tenet of their religion. This they failed to do. By failing in this they, according to their own Scriptures, failed everywhere They are now without a mission of blessing. Few of their leaders even claim a spiritual mission. But the mission idea is still with them in a degenerate form; it represents the grossest materialism of the day; it has become a means of sordid acquisition instead of a channel of service.

Labor and Jewry

The essence of the Jewish Idea in its influence on the labor world is the same as in all other departments -- the destruction of real values in favor of fictitious values. The Jewish philosophy of money is not to "make money," but to "get money." The distinction between these two is fundamental. That explains Jews being "financiers" instead of "captains of industry." It is the difference between "getting" and "making."

The creative, constructive type of mind has an affection for the thing it is doing. The non-Jewish worker formerly chose the work he liked best. He did not change employment easily, because there was a bond between him and the kind of work he had chosen. Nothing else was so attractive to him. He would rather draw a little less money and do what he liked to do, than a little more and do what irked him. The "maker" is always thus influenced by his liking.

Not so the "getter." It doesn't matter what he does, so long as the income is satisfactory. He has no illusions, sentiments or affections on the side of work. It is the "geld" that counts. He has no attachment for the things he makes, for he doesn't make any; he deals in the things which other men make and regards them solely on the side of their money-making value. "The joy of creative labor" is nothing to him, not even an intelligible saying.

Now, previous to the advent of Jewish socialistic and subversive ideas, the predominant thought in the labor world was to "make" things and thus "make" money. There was a pride among mechanics. Men who made things were a sturdy, honest race because they dealt with ideas of skill and quality, and their very characters were formed by the satisfaction of having performed useful functions in society. They were the Makers. And society was solid so long as they were solid. Men made shoes as exhibitions of their skill. Farmers raised crops for the inherent love of crops, not with reference to far-off money-markets. Everywhere the job was the main thing and the rest was incidental.

The only way to break down this strong safeguard of society -- a creative laboring class of sturdy character -- was to sow other ideas among it; and the most dangerous of all the ideas sown was that which substituted "get" for "make."

With the required manipulation of the money and food markets, enough pressure could be brought to bear on the ultimate consumers to give point to the idea of "get," and it was not long before the internal relations of American business were totally upset, with Jews at the head of the banking system, and Jews at the head of both the conservative and radical elements of the Labor Movement, and, most potent of all, the Jewish Idea sowed through the minds of workingmen. What Idea? The idea of "get" instead of "make."

The idea of "get" is a vicious, anti-social and destructive idea when held alone; but when held in company with "make" and as second in importance, it is legitimate and constructive. As soon as a man or a class is inoculated with the strictly Jewish idea of "getting" – ("getting mine"; "getting while the getting is good"; honestly if you can, dishonestly if you must –"but get it"– all of which are notes of this treasonable philosophy), the very cement of Duncan society loses its adhesiveness and begins to crumble. The great myth and fiction of Money has been forced into the place of real things, and the second step of the drama can thus be opened up.

Jewish influence on the thought of the working-men of the United States, as well as on the thought of business and professional men, has been bad, thoroughly bad. This is not manifested in a division between "capital" and "labor," for there are no such separate elements; there is only the executive and operating departments of American business. The real division is between the Jewish Idea of "get" and the Anglo-Saxon idea of "make," and at the present time the Jewish idea has been successful enough to have caused an upset.

All over the United States, in many branches of trade, Communist colleges are maintained, officered and taught by Jews. These so-called colleges exist in Chicago, Detroit, Cleveland, Rochester, Pittsburgh, New York, Philadelphia and other cities, the whole intent being to put all American labor on a "get" basis, which must prove the economic damnation of the country. That is the end sought, as in Russia.

Until Jews can show that the infiltration of foreign Jews and the Jewish Idea into the American labor movement has made for the betterment in character and estate, in citizenship and economic statesmanship, the charge of being an alien, destructive and treasonable influence will have to stand.

The Churches and Jewry

The last place the uninstructed observer would look for traces of Jewish influence is in the Christian Church, yet if he fails to look there he will miss much. If the libraries of our theological seminaries were equipped with complete files of Jewish literary effort during recent decades, and if the theological students were required to read these Jewish utterances there would be less silly talk and fewer "easy marks" for Jewish propaganda in the American pulpit. For the next 25 years every theological seminary should support a chair for the study of Modern Jewish influence and the Protocols. The fiction, that the Jews are an Old Testament people faithful to the Mosaic Law, would then be exploded, and timid Christians would no longer superstitiously hesitate to speak the truth about them because of that sadly misinterpreted text: "I will bless them that bless thee, and curse him that curseth thee."

There is a mission for the pulpit to liberate the Church from what the New Testament Scriptures call "the fear of the Jews." The pulpit has also the mission of liberating the Church from the error that Judah and Israel are synonymous. The reading of the Scriptures which confuse the tribe of Judah with Israel, and which interpret every mention of Israel as signifying the Jews, is at the root of more than one-half the confusion and division traceable in Christian doctrinal statements.

The Jews are not "The Chosen People," though practically the entire Church has succumbed to the propaganda which declares them to be so. The Jewish tinge of thought has of late years overspread many Christian statements, and the uninstructed clergy have proved more and more amenable to Jewish suggestion.

The flaccid condition of the Church, so much deplored by spokesmen who had regard for her inner life, was brought about not by "science," not by "scholarship," not by the "increase of light and learning" –for none of these things are antagonistic even to incomplete statements of truth– but by Jewish-German Higher Criticism. The defenders of the faith have fought long and valiantly against the inroads made by the so-called Higher Criticism, but were sadly incapacitated in their defense, because they did not see that its origin and purpose were Jewish. It was not Christian; it was not German; it was Jewish.

It is perfectly in keeping with the Jewish World Program that this destructive influence should be sent out under Jewish auspices, and it is perfectly in keeping with non-Jewish trustfulness to accept the thing without looking at its source. The Church is now victim of a second attack against her, in the rampant Socialism and Sovietism that have been thrust upon her in the name of flabby and unmoral theories of "brotherhood" and in an appeal to her "fairness." The church has been made to believe that she is a forum for discussion and not a high place for annunciation.

Jews have actually invaded, in person and in program, hundreds of American churches, with their subversive and impossible social ideals, and at last became so cocksure of their domination of the situation that they were met with the inevitable check.

Clergymen ought to know that seven-eighths of the economic mush they speak from the pulpit is prepared by Jewish professors of political economy and revolutionary leaders. They should be informed that economic thought has been so completely Judaized by means of a deliberate and masterly plan of camouflaged propaganda, that the mass-thought of the crowd (which is the thought mostly echoed in "popular" pulpits and editorials) is more Jewish than Jewry itself holds.

The Jew has got hold of the Church in doctrine, in liberalism, so-called, and in the feverish and feeble sociological diversions of many classes. If there is any place where a straight study of the Jewish Question should be made it is in the modern Church which is unconsciously giving allegiancc to a mass of Jewish propaganda. It is not reaction that is counselled here; it is progress along constructive paths, the paths of our forefathers, the Anglo-Saxons, who have to this day been the World-Builders, the Makers of cities and commerce and continents; and not the Jews who have never been builders or pioneers, who have never peopled the wilderness, but who move in upon the labors of other men. They are not to be blamed for not being Builders or Pioneers, perhaps; they are to be blamed for claiming all the rights of pioneers; but even then, perhaps, their blame ought not to be so great as the blame that rests upon the sons of the Anglo-Saxons for rejecting the straightforward

Building of their fathers, and taking up with the doubtful ideas of Judah.

Jewry In Schools And Colleges

Colleges are being constantly invaded by the Jewish Idea. The sons of the Anglo-Saxons are being attacked in their very heredity. The sons of the Builders, the Makers, are being subverted to the philosophy of the destroyers. Young men in the first exhilarating months of intellectual freedom are being seized with promissory doctrines, the source and consequences of which they do not see. There is a natural rebelliousness of youth, which promises progress; there is a natural venture to play free with ancient faiths; both of which are ebullitions of the spirit and significance of dawning mental virility. It is during the periods when these adolescent expansions are in process that the youth is captured by influences which deliberately lie in wait for him at the colleges. True, in after years a large proportion come to their senses sufficiently to be able "to sit on the fence and see themselves go by," and they come back to sanity. They find that "free-love" doctrines make exhilarating club topics, but that the Family -- the old-fashioned loyalty of one man and one woman to each other and their children -- is the basis not only of society, but of all personal character and progress. They find that Revolution, while a delightful subject for fiery debates and an excellent stimulant to the feeling of superman-likeness, is nevertheless not the process of progress.

The trouble with the colleges has progressed along precisely the same lines that have been described in connection with the churches. First, Jewish higher criticism in the destruction of young men's sense of respect for the ancient foundations; second, Jewish revolutionary social doctrines. The two always go together. They cannot live apart. They are the fulfillment of the Protocol's program to split non-Jewish society by means of ideas.

It is idle to attack the "radicalism" of college student -- these are the qualities of immaturity. But it is not idle to show that social radicalism ("radicalism" being a very good word very sadly misused) comes from a Jewish source. The central group of Red philosophers in every university is a Jewish group, with often enough a "Gentile front" in the shape of a deluded professor. Some of these professors are in the pay of outside Red organizations. There are Intercollegiate Socialist Societies, swarming with Jews and Jewish influences, and toting Jewish professors around the country, addressing fraternities under the patronage of the best civic and university auspices. Student lecture courses are fine pasture for this propaganda, the purpose being to give the students the thrill of believing that they are taking part in the beginning of a new great movement, comparable to the winning of Independence.

The revolutionary forces which head up in Jewry rely very heavily on the respectability which is given their movement by the adhesion of students and a few professors. It was so in Russia -- everyone knows what the name "student" eventually came to signify in that country. The Jewish Chautauqua, which works almost exclusively in colleges and universities, together with Bolshevism in art, science, religion, economics and sociology, are driving straight through the Anglo-Saxon traditions and landmarks of our race of students. These are ably assisted by professors and clergymen whose thinking has been dislocated and poisoned by Jewish subversive influences in theology and sociology.

What to do About It?

Simply identify the source and nature of the influence which has overrun our schools and universities. Let the students know that their choice is between the Anglo-Saxons and the Tribe of Judah. Let the students decide, in making up their allegiance, whether they will follow the Builders or those who seek to tear down. It is not a case for argument. The only absolute antidote to the Jewish influence is to call college students back to a pride of race. We often speak of the Fathers as if they were the few who happened to affix their signatures to a great document which marked a new era of liberty. The Fathers of our nation were the men of the Anglo-Saxon-Celtic race. The men who came from Europe with civilization in their blood and in their destiny. The men who crossed the Atlantic and set up civilization on a bleak and rock-bound coast; the men who drove north to Alaska and west to California; the men who opened up the tropics and subdued the arctics; the men who mastered the African veldt; the men who peopled Australia and seized the gates of the world at Suez, Gibraltar and Panama; men who have given form to every government and a livelihood to every people and an ideal to every century. They got neither their God nor their religion from Judah, nor yet their speech nor their creative genius -- they are the Ruling People. Chosen throughout the centuries to Master the world, by building it ever better and better, and not by breaking it down.

Into the camp of this race, among the sons of the rulers, comes a people that has no civilization to point to, no aspiring religion, no universal speech, no great achievement in any realm but the realm of "get," cast out of every land that gave them hospitality, and these people endeavor to tell the Sons of the Saxons what is needed to make the world what it ought to be!

If our sons follow this counsel of dark rebellion and destruction, it is because they do not know whose sons they are, of what race they are the scions. Let there be free speech to the limit in our universities and free intercourse of ideas, but let Jewish thoughts be labeled Jewish, and let our sons know the racial secret.

Name The Enemy!

The warning has already gone out through the colleges. The system of Jewish procedure is already fully known. How simple it is! First, you secularize the public schools – "secularize" is the precise word the Jews use for the process. You prepare the mind of the public school child by enforcing the rule that no mention shall ever be made to indicate that culture or patriotism is in any way connected with the deeper principles of the Anglo-Saxon religion. Keep it out, every sight and sound of it! Keep out also every word that will aid any child to identify the Jewish race. Then, when you have thus prepared the soil, you can go into the universities and colleges and enter upon the double program of pouring contempt on all the Anglo-Saxon landmarks, at the same time filling the void with Jewish revolutionary ideas.

The influence of the common people is driven out of the schools, where common people's influence can go; but Jewish influence is allowed to run rampant in the higher institutions where the common people's influence cannot go. Secularize the schools, and you can then Judaize the universities.

This is the "liberalism" which Jewish spokesmen so much applaud. In labor unions, in churches, in universities, it has tainted the principles of work, faith and society. The proof of it is written thickly over all Jewish activities and utterances. It is in exerting these very influences that Jewry convinces itself that it is fulfilling its "mission" to the world.

The capitalism attacked is non-Jewish capitalism; the orthodoxy attacked is Christian orthodoxy; the society attacked is the Anglo-Saxon form of society; all of which by their destruction would redound to the glory of Judaism.

The list could be extended – the influence of the Jewish idea on Anglo-Saxon sports and pleasure, on the Anglo-Saxon idea of patriotism, on the Anglo-Saxon conception of the learned professions; the influence of the Jewish idea runs down through every department of life.

"Well," one very badly deluded American editor, wrapped up in Jewish advertising contracts, was heard to say, "if the Jews can get away with it, then they have a right to." It is a variant of the "answer" of Jewish origin, which runs thus: "How can a paltry 3 million run the 100 million of the rest of us? Nonsense!"

Yes, let it be agreed; if the Jewish idea is the stronger, if the Jewish ability is the greater, let them conquer; let Anglo-Saxon principles and power go down in ruins before the Tribe of Judah. But first let the two ideas struggle under their own banners; let it be a fair struggle.

It is not a fair fight when in the movies, in the schools, in the Judaized churches, in the universities, the Anglo-Saxon idea is kept away from the Anglo-Saxons on the plea that it is "sectarian" or "clannish" or "obsolete" or something else, say, reaction.

It is not a fair fight when Jewish ideas are offered as Anglo-Saxon ideas, because offered under Anglo-Saxon auspices. Let the heritage of our Anglo-Saxon fathers have free course among their Anglo-Saxon sons, and the Jewish idea can never triumph over it, in the university forum or in the marts of trade. The Jewish idea never triumphs until first the people over whom it triumphs are denied the nurture of their native culture.

Judah has begun the struggle. Judah has made the invasion. Let it come. Let no man fear it. But let every man insist that the fight be fair. Let college students and leaders of thought know that the objective is the reign of the ideas and the race that have built all the civilization we see and that promises all the civilization of the future; let them also know that the attacking force is Jewish.

That is all that will be necessary. It is against this that the Jews protest. "You must not identify us," they say, "You must not use the 'Jew'." Why? Because unless the Jewish idea can creep in under the assumption of other than Jewish origin, it is doomed. Anglo-Saxon ideas dare proclaim themselves and their origin. A proper proclamation is all that is necessary today. Compel every invading idea to run up its flag!

Chapter 3: Victims or Persecutors?

From the earliest record of the Jews' contact with other nations, no long period of years has ever passed without the charge arising that the Jews constitute "a people within a people, a nation within a nation." When this charge is made today it is vehemently denied by men who pose as the defenders of their people, and the denial is more or less countenanced by all the Jews of every class. Yet there is nothing more clearly stated in Jewish teaching, nor more clearly indicated in Jewish life, than that the charge is true. But whether the truth should be used against the Jews is quite another question.

If the Jews are a nation, their nationality founded upon the double ground of race and religion, it is certainly outside the bounds of reason that they should be asked or expected to de-racialize, de-nationalize and "de-religionize" themselves; but neither is it to be expected that they should bitterly denounce those who state the facts. It is only on a basis of facts that a solution of any problem can come. Where the blame attaches is here: that the evident facts are denied, as if no one but the Jews themselves knew that there are such facts.

If the Jews are to be continuously a nation, as they teach, and if the condition of "a nation within a nation" becomes more and more intolerable, then the solution must come through one of two things: a separation of the "nation" from the rest of the nations, or an exaltation of the "nation" above the rest of the nations. There is a mass of evidence in Jewish writings that the leaders expect both of these conditions to come - a separate nation and a super-nation; indeed, the heart of Jewish teaching is that Jewry is a separate nation now, and on the way to becoming a super-nation. It is only those appointed to address the Gentiles who deny this: the real rabbinate of Judah does not deny.

Jews object to "Americanism"

In any investigation of the Jewish Question, the student is struck over and over again by the fact that what the Jews most complain of, they themselves began. They complain of what they call anti-Semitism; but it must be apparent to the dullest mind that there could never have been such a thing as anti-Semitism were there not first such a thing as Semitism. Then take the complaint about the Jews having to live in ghettos. The ghetto is a Jewish invention. In the beginning of the invasion of European cities, and centuries later of American cities, the Jews always lived by themselves because they wanted to; because they believed the presence of Gentiles contaminated them. Jewish writers, writing for Jews, freely admit this; but in writing for Gentiles, they refer to the ghetto as an illustration of Gentile cruelty. The idea of contamination originated with the Jews, it is an old oriental survival; it spread by suggestion to the Gentiles. So with this fact of the separate "nation"; it was the Jews who first recognized it, first insisted upon it and have always sought to realize that separateness both in thought and action.

More, the true and normal type of Jew believes that the influence of Americanism, or of any civilized Gentile state, is harmful to Judaism. That is a serious statement and no amount of Gentile assertion will be sufficient to confirm it. Indeed, it is such a statement as the Gentile mind could not have evolved, because the trend of Gentile feeling is all in the opposite direction, namely that Americanization is a good thing for the Jew. It is from authoritative Jewish sources we learn this fact, that what we call civilizing influences are looked upon as being at enmity with Judaism. It is not the Gentile who says that Jewish ideals, as ideals, are incompatible with the life of our country; it is the Jew who says so. It is he who inveighs against Americanism, not the American who inveighs against Judaism.

Americanism is yet unfinished, Judaism has been complete for centuries. While no American would think of pointing to any part of the country or to any group as representing the true and final type of Americanism, the Jews quite unhesitatingly point to parts of the world and to certain groups as representing the true type of Judaism. Where is the type to be found which Jewish writers recognize as the true one? The Jew of the ghetto is held up in Jewish treatises as the norm of Judaism. A famous rabbi of the synagogue of the Spanish and Portuguese Jews, on Central Park, New York, was Dr. D. de Sola Pool. He is the author of the following words:

> "In the ghetto the observance of Judaism was natural and almost inevitable. The regimen of Jewish life was the atmosphere that was breathed."

Another famous Jewish rabbi, Dr. M. H. Segal, expresses the view that Jewry in the more modern portions of Europe and America was really kept alive by the infusions of immigrants from Poland and Lithuania. Asserting, in agreement with other Jewish leaders, that the Jewish center of the world had been in Russia and Poland until just before the 1914 war, Dr. Segal says:

"The war (1914-1918) has destroyed the last traces of the declining Jewish society which had dragged out its feeble existence in the semi-medieval ghettos of Poland and Lithuania. With all their growing feebleness, these communities were yet the last refuge of Judaism in the Dispersion. In them there still survived something of the old Jewish life, some of the old Jewish institutions, practices and traditions. These communities also supplied such vitality as they could afford to the attenuated and atrophied Judaism in the communities of the more modern states of Europe and America."

The idea is not at all uncommon - that large infusions of "real Jews" from the Old World ghettos are desirable and necessary in order to keep Judaism alive in countries like the United States. Israel Friedlaender whose name is held in honor by the Jews, also recognized the service of the ghetto stream to Judaism. In his lecture, "The Problem of Judaism in America," he speaks about the de-Judaizing tendencies of absolute freedom, such as the Jew has always enjoyed in the United States. This tendency, he says, is corrected in two ways - by anti-Semitic influences and "by the large stream of Jewish emigration, on the other hand, which, proceeding from the lands of oppression to the lands of freedom, carries with it, on or under the surface, the preserving and reviving influences of the ghetto." This same authority, in an article entitled "The Americanization of the Jewish Immigrant," frankly prefers the Jew fresh from the ghetto to the Jew who has been influenced by American life.

To "Americanize" means, in our ordinary speech, to bring into sympathy with the traditions and institutions of the

United States, but the Jews do not mean only the United States when they say "America." They mean also South and Central America - where so many revolutions have occurred. There are large numbers of Jews in Argentina, and many are found in other countries. It would probably give a wrong slant to the fact to say that the Jewish leaders are wholly anti-America, but it is true to say that they are against the "Americanization" of the Jewish immigrant stream. That is, that the trend of "Americanism" is so different from the trend of "Judaism" that the two are in conflict. This does not indicate treason toward American nationalisms perhaps, so much as it indicates loyalty toward Jewish nationalism. But the reader must himself be the judge, on the facts given in this book, as to how far the difference really goes and the effect of the struggle between the two ideas. The fact of the antagonism which exists between the two is clear and complete. The Gentiles do not notice that antagonism, but the Jews are always and everywhere keenly aware of it. This throws a very strong light on all the revolutionary programs to break up the present control of society, by sowing dissensions between so-called capital and labor, by cheapening the dignity of government through corrupt politics, by trivializing the mind of the people through theaters and movies, but it is in the study of Jewish money-making out of war that the clues are found to most of the great abuses of which the Jews have been guilty. "Wars are the Jews' harvests," is an ancient saying. Their predilection for the quartermaster's department has been observed anciently and modernly. Their interest being mostly in profits and not in national issues; their traditional loyalty being to the Jewish nation, rather than to any other nation; it is natural that they should be found to be the merchants of goods and information in times of war - that is, the war profiteers and spies. As the unbroken program is traced through the Revolutionary War, through the Civil War, and through the Great War, the only change observable is the increasing power and profit of the Jews. Although the number of Jews resident in the American colonies was small, there were enough to make a mark on the Revolutionary War; and while there was no wholesale legislation against Jews as there was in the Civil War, there were the same actions against individuals for the same causes which in 1861-5 obtained more extensively.

Jews And The "Religious Persecution" Cry

No intelligent Jew in the United States ever was asinine enough to declare that the Jewish Question is a religious question and that investigation of that question in these articles constituted "religious persecution." But it is apparently all that remains for the "Gentile fronts" to shout about. From what can be learned of them they are for the most part men of no religion themselves and they use the term "religious persecution" as a red rag which they think will stir people into action. It is curious how the cry of "religious persecution" is used to evoke the spirit of persecution against the alleged persecutors.

Neither directly nor by implication is it held in these articles that the Jewish Question is a religious question. On the contrary, supported by the highest Jewish authorities, it is firmly stated that the Jewish Question is one of race and nationality.

There is no religious persecution of the Jews in the United States, unless the agitation of the various humane societies for the abolition of "kosher killing" may be considered as such - the method of slaughtering animals for food which is needlessly cruel. But even this objection can only with difficulty be stretched into interference with "the religion of the Jews." The Jewish method of slaughter as now practiced is not commanded in the Old Testament but in the Talmud, and is, therefore, not religious in the authoritative sense, but traditional. Moreover, there is positive evidence that modern methods achieve the Jewish purpose (the disposal of the blood of the carcass) much better than does the Jewish method. This is the only instance where even remotely the religion of the Jews has been touched.

The fact is that while there is no "religious persecution" of the Jews, there is very much real religious persecution by the Jews. That is one of the outstanding characteristics of organized Jewish life in the United States, its active, unceasing, powerful and virulent attacks upon any and all forms of Christianity which may chance to come to public notice. Now and again we hear of outbreaks of sectarian bigotry between Catholics and Protestants, but these are not to be compared with the steady, relentless, alert, anti-

Christian activity of the Jewish organizations. There are doctrinal disputes within the Christian Churches, but none that challenge the basis of Christianity itself; organized Judaism, however, is not content with doctrinal disputation, but enlists its vast commercial and political power against everything that it regards as, in its own words, "Christological manifestations."

No President of the United States has yet dared to take his inaugural oath on the open pages of the New Testament - the Jews would denounce him. Various governors of American states, having used the word "Christian" in their Thanksgiving proclamations, have been obliged to teach Americanism in our cities because it held that Christianity and good citizenship were synonymous!

No public man in America has ever given public evidence of his Christian faith without rebuke from the Jews. Not only do the Jews disagree with Christian teaching - which is their right and no one questions it - but they excise it on demand of the Jews. Everything that would remind the child in school that he is living in the midst of a Christian civilization, in a nation declared by its Supreme Court to be founded on the Christian principles, has been ordered out of the public schools on Jewish demand. In a nation and at a time when a minority of Jews can print every year a record of the apologies they have extorted from public officials for "having inadvertently used the term 'Christian'," it is desirable that this charge of "religious persecution" should be placed where it belongs.

The Jew glories in religious persecution as the American glories in patriotism. Religious prejudice is the Jews' chief expression of their own patriotism. It is the only well-organized, active and successful form of religious prejudice in the country because they have succeeded in pulling off the gigantic trick of making not their own attitude, but any opposition to it, bear the stigma of "prejudice" and "persecution." That is why the Jew uses these terms so frequently. He wants to label the other fellow first. That is why any investigation of the Jewish Question is so wickedly advertised as anti-Semitism - the Jew knows the advantage of labeling the other man.

This theme "religious persecution," will not be found anywhere within the whole range of the Jewish Question, except on the Jewish side. There is, in the United States, a religious prejudice, but it is strictly Yiddish. If the Christian population bothered one-hundredth-thousandth part as much about Jewish religion as the Jews bother about Christian observances, the whole fabric of Talmudic teaching would be consumed in the bright light to which general attention would bring it, the bright light from which it has always been concealed. Sheer analysis in the interest of mental health would compel the Jewish people to abandon the darkness which holds them now. Jewish Talmudism owes its existence today to the indifference with which it is regarded. This is the far opposite extreme of "religious persecution."

Religious prejudice is just as unpleasant to write about as it is to experience in any other way. It is totally contrary to the genius of the American and the Anglo-Saxon. We have always regarded religion as a matter of conscience. To believe as he will is part of every man's fundamental liberty. Holding these hereditary principles, one chooses to study that active stream of influence in America which is known as the Jewish stream, and immediately upon doing so, one finds himself classed with the bigots and torturers of other times.

It is time to show that the cry of “bigot” is raised mostly by bigots. There is a religious prejudice in this country, there is, indeed, a religious persecution, there is a forcible shoving aside of the religious liberties of a majority of the people, and this prejudice and persecution and use of force is Jewish and nothing but Jewish.

A study of history and of contemporary Jewish journalism shows that Jewish prejudice and persecution is a continuous phenomenon wherever the Jews have obtained power, and that in neither action nor word has any disability placed upon the Jew equaled the disabilities he has placed and still contemplates placing upon non-Jews. There is no Christian church that the Jews have not repeatedly attacked.

If there is in the world any extra-ecclesiastical undertaking by Catholics which has won the undivided approval of the entire Christian world it is the Passion Play of Oberammergau. Yet in a volume entitled “A Rabbi's Impressions of the Oberammergau Passion Play,” Rabbi Joseph Krauskopf, of Philadelphia, has stigmatized that noble production as reeking with falsehoods and vicious anti-Semitism. In the rabbi's eyes, of course, it is, for to him the entire Christian tradition is a poisonous lie. The whole fabric of Christian truth, especially as it concerns the person of Christ is "the hallucinations of emotional men and hysterical women." "Thus," says the rabbi, "was invented that cruel story, that has caused more misery, more innocent suffering, than any other work of fiction in the range of the whole world's literature."

And thus the simple peasants of Oberammergau, presenting the Catholic faith in reverent pageant, are labeled anti-Semites.

These are not isolated instances. When the Methodist Church put on the great pageant entitled "The Wayfarer," Rabbi Stephen S. Wise (American Zionist leader when this original was published, and one of the most active political leaders of Zionist Jewry in the United Nations; Ed.) played critic and made the solemn and silly statement that had he been a South Sea Islander (instead of the itinerant platform performer which he is) his first impulse, after seeing "the Wayfarer," would have been to rush out into the street and kill at least three Jews. It says a great deal, perhaps, for the channel in which Rabbi Wise's impulses run, but the tens of thousands of Methodists who saw "The Wayfarer" will not be inclined to attribute such a criticism to the spirit of tolerance which Rabbi Wise so zealously counsels the Christians to observe.

The Episcopal Church also has felt the attack of the Jews. Recently (June, 1921: Ed.) the Jewish Press raised a clamor that the Episcopal Church was not competent to seek to interfere with it. It is not religious tolerance in the midst of religious difference, but religious attack that they preach and practice. The whole record of the Jewish opposition to Christmas, Easter and other Christian festivals, and their opposition to certain patriotic songs, shows the venom and directness of that attack. One parallel between the Protocols and the real hopes of the Jews is written in the common Jewish prophecy that Christianity is doomed to perish. It will perish, to all intents and purposes, by becoming Judaism.

Jewish intolerance today, yesterday and in every age of history where Jews were able to exert influence or power, is indisputable except among people who do not know the record. Jewish intolerance in the past is a matter of history; for the future it is a matter of Jewish prophecy. One of the strongest causes militating against the full Americanization of several millions of Jews in this country is their belief - instilled in them by their religious authorities - that they are "chosen," that this land is theirs, that the inhabitants are idolators, that the day is coming when the Jews will be supreme.

How can they otherwise act than in agreement with such declarations? The supercilious attitude adopted by the Jews toward the stock that made America is merely a foreshadowing of what would be the complete attitude if power and influence made it possible. Bolshevism, which began with the destruction of the class that contained all the promise of a better Russia, is an exact parallel for the attitude that is adopted in this courts regarding the original stock.

Chapter 4: Are The Jews A Nation?

No Gentile knows how many Jews there are in the United States. The figures are the exclusive property of the Jewish authorities. The government of the United States can provide statistics on almost every matter pertaining to the population of the country, but whenever it has attempted in a systematic way to get information about the Jews who are constantly entering the country, and the number now resident here, the Jewish lobby at Washington steps in and stops it. The Jews conceal their strength because Jewish influence at the Capitol has been strong enough to win on all matters affecting Jewish interests, at all times.

Immigration into the United States became a business 40 years ago - a strictly Jewish business. There is a perfect organization which overcomes the numerous objections which arise against the admission of known revolutionary Jews, European Jews are potential revolutionaries. America has not been called "The Jews' Country" in the smaller nations of Europe for nothing, and the alarming increase in Jewish immigration brings the question to public attention again. A national conviction is forming upon the subject, for it is apparent that the strictly Jewish business of getting Jews into the United States moves like an army which, having done duty in Europe for the subjugation of that continent, has transferred itself to America. Jewish secret societies in America are the principal aides in this long stampede to America. They are able to "arrange" the passport work, they "arrange" avoidance of the health regulations. The laws of the country are set aside in open contempt. The Jewish immigrants can come from anywhere and are coming from anywhere; their first glimpse of life here shows a Jewish control as potent and complete as it is in Russia. They see officials of Jewish secret societies override officials of the United States Immigration Bureau; why should they not behave as if they own the United States? No wonder that they literally beat down the walls and gates with all the éclat of a victorious invasion. It is an invasion, nothing less, and it is inspired and helped by influences within the United States. When it is not secret it is thinly cloaked with sentiment "these people are fleeing from persecution."

After the tide of Jewish invasion into the United States; in the 1880's became too wide for anyone to ignore the dangers, the census authorities asked Congress for permission to classify people by "race" a well as by "country of birth." The strongest opposition was led in Congress by the Jews, principally by Simon Guggenheim and Julian WV. Mack. Hearings had to be ordered to know what elements were comprising the population; whether the United States was an Anglo-Saxon, Semitic, Latin nation, or what. The Jewish opposition to the hearings disclosed four matters very clearly: (1) the Jew is opposed to any restrictive legislation against his entrance into a country; (2) the Jew is opposed to any racial classification of himself after he has entered a country; (3) the Jewish argument to the Gentile authorities is that the Jew represents religion and not race; (4) the Jew has one view to present to the Gentiles, and another which he cherishes among his own people, on this question of Race. When Americans disregarded as untenable the argument of "religion, not race," the Jewish spokesmen were able to fall back on the fact that their powerful organizations did not want certain things and would not have certain things - argument or no argument, commission or no commission. The Jewish lobbyists had their way. There is no enumeration of Jews in the United States. There are classifications for all other races and nations, but none for the Jew. None of the other races made objection, but the Jew is not distinguished at all. What is the result today? If you ask the government of the United States how many Frenchmen there are in the country, it can give you the figures. If you ask for the number of Poles, it is there. If you ask for the number of Africans, it is known. Down a long list you may make your inquiries, you will find that the government knows. But ask the government of the United States how many Jews are in the country - and it cannot tell; there are no records.

Race Or Religion?

What have the Jews themselves to say about "race or religion?" The following quotations put the reader in possession of information regarding the Jew's own thought of himself as a member of a separate people, quite aside from the consideration of his religion.

Leo N. Levi, President of B'nai B'rith, 1900-1904:

> "The distinctive character of the Jew does not arise solely from his religion. It is true that his race and religion are indissolubly connected, but whatever be the cause of this junction of the race idea with the religion, it is very certain that the religion alone does not constitute the people. A believer in the Jewish faith does not by reason of that fact become a Jew. On the other hand, however, a Jew by birth remains a Jew, even though he abjures his religion."

Graetz, the historian of the Jews, whose monumental work is one of the standard authorities, says that the history of the Jews, even since they lost the Jewish State, "still possesses a national character; it is by no means merely a creed or church history."

Moses Hess, one of the historic figures through whom the whole Jewish Program has flowed down from its ancient sources to its modern agents, wrote a book entitled "Rome and Jerusalem" in which he stated the whole matter with clearness and force:

> "The Jews are something more than mere 'followers of a religion,' namely, they are a race, a brotherhood, a nation." (p. 71).
> "A Jew belongs to his race and consequently also to Judaism, in spite of the fact that he or his ancestors have become apostates." (pp. 97-98).
> "Every Jew is, whether he likes it or not, solidly united with the entire nation." (p. 163).
> "Jewish religion is, above all, Jewish patriotism." (p. 61).

Louis D. Brandeis, Justice of the Supreme Court of the United States and world leader of the Zionist movement, wrote in his book "Zionism and the American Jews," -

> "Despite the meditations of pundits or the decrees of councils, our own instinct and acts, and those of others, have defined for us the term 'Jew'."

Rabbi Morris Joseph, sometime of the West London Synagogue of British Jews, writes in his book "Israel a Nation," -

> "Israel is assuredly a great nation . . . Israel is recognized as a nation by those who see it; no one could possibly mistake it for a sect. To deny Jewish nationality you must deny the existence of the Jew."

The Jewish barrister, Bertram B. Benas, writes in "Zionism - the National Jewish Movement," --

> "The Jewish entity is essentially the entity of a People."

Leon Simon, a brilliant and impressive Jewish scholar and writer, makes an important study of the question of "religion and nationality," in his volume, "Studies in Jewish Nationalism." He makes out a case for the proposition that the religion of the Jews is Nationalism, and that Nationalism is an integral part of their religion: "The Messianic Age means for the Jew not merely the establishment of peace on earth and good will to men, but the universal recognition of the Jew and his God (p. 14). "Judaism has no message of salvation for the individual soul, as Christianity has; all its ideas are bound up with the existence of the Jewish nation." (p. 20).

> "The idea that Jews are a religious sect, precisely parallel to Catholics and Protestants, is nonsense."

Arthur D. Lewis, a Jewish writer, in his "The Jews a Nation," also bases nationality on the racial element:

> "The Jews were originally a nation, and have retained more than most nations one of the elements of nationality - namely, the race element; this may be proved, of course, by the common-sense test of their distinguishability. You can more easily see that a Jew is a Jew than that an Englishman is an Englishman."

The idea that the Jews comprise a nation is the most common idea of all - among Jews. Not only a nation with a past, but a nation with a future. More than that - not only a nation, but a Super-Nation. We can go still further on the authority of Jewish statements: we can say that the future form of the Jewish Nation will be a kingdom.
Elkan N. Adler says:

> "No serious politician today doubts that our people have a political future."

This future political definiteness and power was in the mind of Moses Hess when he wrote in 1862 - mark the date! - in the preface of his "Rome and Jerusalem," these words:

> "No nation can be indifferent to the fact that in the coming European struggle for liberty, if may have another people as its friend or foe."

Hess, complaining of the inequalities visited upon the Jews, was saying that what the individual Jew could not get because he was a Jew, the Jewish Nation would be able to get because it would be a nation. He warns the Gentile nations to be careful, because in that "coming struggle" there would be another nation in the list, the Jewish Nation, which could be the friend or foe of any it chose.
Dr. Israel Friedlaender says:

> "It is enough for us to know that the Jews have always felt themselves as a separate race, sharply marked off from the rest of mankind."

As to the problems of the Jewish Nation, there is plenty of Jewish testimony to the fact that the influence of Americanism is harmful to Jewish life; that is, they are in antagonism, like two opposite ideas. And that Zionism is the modern rallying point for Jewish nationalism. The actual beliefs of the most active and influential part of Jewry in America are demonstrated in a work published by the Zionist Organization of America, "Guide to Zionism,"

> "The name of their national religion, Judaism, is derived from their national designation. An unreligious Jew is still a Jew, and he can with difficulty escape his allegiance only by repudiating the name of Jew." (p. 5).

Jewry nowhere subscribes in the persons of its greatest teachers and its most authoritative representatives to the theory that the Jew is only "a brother of the faith." Often he is not of the faith at all, but he is still a Jew. The "religion, not race" argument exposes the double minds of those political leaders who, instead of straightforwardly meeting the Jewish Question, endeavor to turn all inquiry aside by an impressive confusion of the Gentile mind.

There are two Jewish Programs in the world - one which it is intended the Gentiles should see, and one which is exclusively for the Jews. In determining which is the real program, it is a safe course to adopt the one that is made to succeed. It is the program sponsored by the so called Zionists which is succeeding. That is the program whose sponsors stand for the racial and national separateness of the Jews.

Regardless of what may be said to the Gentiles for the purpose of hindering or modifying their action, there is no question of what the Jew thinks of himself: he thinks of himself as belonging to a People, united to that people by ties of blood which no amount of creedal change can weaken, heir of that People's past and agent of that People's political future. He belongs to a race; he belongs to a nation. He seeks a kingdom to come on this earth, a kingdom which shall be over all kingdoms, with Jerusalem the ruling city of the world. That desire of the Jewish nation may be fulfilled; and the relationships between Jewish nationalism and the nationalism of the peoples among whom the Jews dwell are pointers to the potential victory.

The Policy Of "Misrepresentation"

To these exposures of the "religion, not race," arguments, the Jews have complained that they are being misrepresented. It is their usual complaint. They are always being "misrepresented" and "persecuted" except when they are being praised for what they are not. If the Jews were fully understood by the Gentiles, if the Christian churches, for example, were freed from their delusion that the Jews are Old Testament people, and if the churches really knew what Talmudic religion is, the "misrepresentation" would be still stronger.

The downfall of Russia was prepared by a long and deliberate program of misrepresentation of the Russian people, through the Jewish world press and Jewish diplomatic service. The name of Poland has been drawn (December, 1920: Ed.) in filth through the press of the United States under Jewish instigation; a vilification of Poland whose sole crime was that she wished to save herself from the Jews. But whenever a hand has been raised to prevent the Jews overrunning the people and secretly securing the control of the major instruments of life, the Jews have raised the cry of "misrepresentation." They never meet the question outright. False denials, pleas for sympathy, and a base campaign for smearing others with their own crimes, and an unworthy attempt to link others with them in their fall, constitute their whole method of defense. And a concentration of all the political, economic, legal weapons at their command are flung at the head of the outspoken critic of the Jew who persists in defending his right to national existence free from Jewish infiltration, influence and control.

The policy of "misrepresentation" succeeds because there is a feeling strongly entrenched in Gentiles that somehow the Jews are the "chosen people," and that it is dangerous to oppose them in anything; whoever opposes the Jew is damned. "The fear of the Jews" is a very real element in life. It is just as real among the Jews as among non-Jews. The Jew himself is bound in fear to his people, and he exercises the fear of the curse throughout the sphere of religion - "I will curse them that curse thee." It remains to be proved, however, that opposition to the destructive tendencies of Jewish influences all along the principal avenues of life is a "cursing" of the Jews.

If the Jews were really Old Testament people (which they are not), if they were really conscious of a "mission" for the blessing of all the nations, the very things in which they offend would automatically disappear. If the Jew is being "attacked" it is not because he is a Jew but because he is the source and life of certain tendencies and influences which, if they are not checked, mean the destruction of moral society. The only real misrepresentation in society is regarded as the Jews' privilege.

Disraeli Portrays The Jews

Benjamin Disraeli, Earl of Beaconsfield and Prime Minister of Great Britain, was a Jew and gloried in it. He wrote many books, in a number of which he discussed his people in an effort to set them in a proper light. The British Government was not then so Jewish as it has since become, and Disraeli was easily one of the greatest figures in it. In his book, "Coningsby," there appears a Jewish character named Sidonia, in whose personality and through whose utterances, Disraeli sought to present the Jew as he would like the world to see him.

Yet here is the International Jew, full dress; he is the Protocolist, too, wrapped in mystery, a man whose fingers sweep all the strings of human motive, and who controls the chief of the brutal forces - money.

If a non-Jew had written a Sidonia, so truthfully showing the racial history and characteristics of the Jews, he would have been subjected to that terrific pressure which the Jews apply to every truth teller about themselves.
Disraeli caused his Jewish hero, Sidonia, to remark:

> "The world is governed by very different personages from what is imagined by those who are not behind the scenes," and even more illuminating lines by Disraeli which half compel the thought that, after all, he was writing to warn the world of Jewish ambition for power: "You never observe a great intellectual movement in Europe in which the Jews do not greatly participate. The first Jesuits were Jews. That mysterious Russian Diplomacy which so alarms western Europe is organized and principally carried on by Jews. That mighty revolution which is at this moment preparing in Germany, and which will be, in fact, a second and greater Reformation, and of which so little is yet known in England, is entirely developing under the auspices of Jews."

Just how the Jews work to break down the established order of things, by means of ideas, as the Protocols claim, is shown in a conversation of Sidonia:

> "The Tories lose an important election at a critical moment; 'tis the Jews come forward to vote against them. The Church is alarmed at the scheme of a latitudinarian university, and learns with relief that funds are not forthcoming for its

> establishment; a Jew immediately advances and endows it."

If these words had been written by a non-Jew, the cry of "anti-Semitism" would ring through the land. Yet Sidonia adds: "And every generation they (the Jews) must become more powerful and dangerous to the society that is hostile to them."

"Latitudinarianism" is the doctrine of the Protocols in a word. It is the break-up by means of a welter of so-called "liberal" ideas which construct nothing themselves, but have the power to destroy the established order.

Several generations have passed since Disraeli's words were written. The Jew still regards every form of non-Jewish society as hostile to him. They have become more powerful and more dangerous. Those who would measure the danger - look around !

The Jew says that the Protocols are inventions. Is Benjamin Disraeli an invention? Was this Jewish Prime Minister of Great Britain misrepresenting his people? He showed that in Russia, the very country where the Jews of his time complained they were least free, the Jews were in control. He showed that the Jews knew the technique of revolution, foretelling in his book the revolution that shortly broke out in Germany. How did he foreknow it? Because that revolution was developing under the auspices of Jews, and, though it was then true that "so little is yet known in England," Disraeli the Jew knew it, and knew it to be Jewish in origin and development and purpose. One point is clear; Disraeli told the truth. He presented his people before the world with correctness. He described Jewish power, Jewish purpose and Jewish method with a certainty of touch that betokens more than knowledge - he shows racial sympathy and understanding. Why did he do it? Disraeli the flamboyant, most oriental of courtiers and suave of politicians, with a keen financial ability. Was it that typically racial boastfulness, that dangerous, aggressive conceit in which the Jew gives up most of his secrets? No matter; he is the one man who told the truth about the Jews without being accused of "misrepresenting" the Jews.

Chapter 5:
The Jewish Political Program

Theodor Herzl, one of the greatest of the Jews and founder of modern Zionism, was perhaps the farthest-seeing public exponent of the philosophy of Jewish existence that modern generations have known. He was never in doubt of the existence of the Jewish nation. He proclaimed its existence on every occasion. He said,

> "We are a people - One people."

He clearly saw that what he called the Jewish Question was political. In his introduction to "The Jewish State" he says:

> "I believe that I understand anti-Semitism,

> which is really a highly complex movement. I consider it from a Jewish standpoint, yet without fear or hatred. I believe that I can see what elements there are in it of vulgar sport, of common trade jealousy, of inherited prejudice, of religious intolerance and also of pretended defense. I think the Jewish Question is no more a social than a religious one, notwithstanding that it sometimes takes these and other forms. It is a national question, which can only be solved by making it a political world-question to be discussed and controlled by the civilized nations of the world in council."

Not only did Herzl declare that the Jews formed a nation, but in relating the action of this Jewish nation to the world Herzl wrote:

> "When we sink, we become a revolutionary proletariat, the subordinate officers of the revolutionary party; when we rise, there rises also our terrible power of the purse."

This view, which appears to be the true view in that it is the view which has been longest sustained in Jewish thought, is brought out also by Lord Eustace Percy, and re-published, apparently with approval, by the Canadian "Jewish Chronicle." It will repay careful reading.

"Liberalism and Nationalism, with a flourish of trumpets, threw open the doors of the ghetto and offered equal citizenship to the Jew. The Jew passed out into the Western World, saw the power and the glory of it, used it and enjoyed it, laid his hand indeed upon the nerve centers of its civilization, guided, directed and exploited it, and then - refused the offer . . . Moreover - and this is a remarkable thing - the Europe of nationalism and liberalism, of scientific government and democratic equality is more intolerable to him than the old oppressions and persecutions of despotism . . . "In a world of completely organized territorial sovereignties he (the Jew) has only two possible cities of refuge: he must either pull down the pillars of the whole national state system or he must create a territorial sovereignty of his own. In this perhaps lies the explanation both of Jewish Bolshevism and of Zionism, for at this moment Eastern Jewry seems to hover uncertainly between the two. In Eastern Europe Bolshevism and Zionism often seem to grow side by side, just as Jewish influence molded Republican and Socialist thought throughout the nineteenth century, down to the Young Turk revolution in Constantinople hardly more than a decade ago - not because the Jew cares for the positive side of radical philosophy, not because he desires to be a partaker in Gentile nationalism or Gentile democracy, but because no existing Gentile system of government is ever anything but distasteful to him."

All that is true, and Jewish thinkers of the more fearless type always recognize it as true. The Jew is against the Gentile scheme of things. He is, when he gives his tendencies full sway, a Republican as against the monarchy, a Socialist as against the republic, and a Bolshevist as against socialism.

What are the causes of this disruptive activity? First, his essential lack of democracy. Jewish nature is autocratic. Democracy is all right for the rest of the world, but the Jew wherever he is found forms an aristocracy of one sort or another. Democracy is merely a tool of a word which Jewish agitators use to raise themselves to the ordinary level in places where they are oppressed below it; but having reached the common level they immediately make efforts for special privileges, as being entitled to them - a process which the late Peace Conference (Versailles: Ed.) will remain the most startling example. The Jews today are the only people whose special and extraordinary privileges are written into the world's Treaty of Peace. (Original published in July, 1920: refer also to the present United Nations: Editor).

In all the explanations of anti-Jewish feeling which modern Jewish spokesmen make, these three alleged causes are commonly given - these three and no more: religious prejudice, economic jealousy, social antipathy. Whether the Jew knows it or not, every Gentile knows that on his side of the Jewish Question no religious prejudice exists. Economic jealousy may exist, at least to this extent, that his uniform success has exposed the Jew to much scrutiny. The finances of the world are in control of Jews; their decisions and their devices are themselves our economic law.

Economic jealousy may explain some of the anti-Jewish feeling; it cannot account for the presence of the Jewish Question except as the hidden causes of Jewish financial success may become a minor element of the larger problem. And as for social antipathy - there are many more undesirable Gentiles in the world than there are undesirable Jews, for the simple reason that there are many more Gentiles.

None of the Jewish spokesmen mention the political cause, or if they come within suggestive distance of it, they limit it and localize it. The political element inheres in the fact that the Jews form a nation in the midst of the nations. It is not the fact that the Jews remain a nation in the midst of the nations; it is the USE made of that inescapable status, which the world has found to be reprehensible. The nations have tried to reduce the Jews to unity with themselves, but destiny seems to have marked them out to continuous nationhood. Both the Jews and the World will have to accept that fact. The Jewish world program, and the political basis of anti-Jewish feeling which that program creates, is exposed by Jewish cosmopolitanism with regard to the world, and by Jewish nationalistic integrity with regard to themselves.

Jewish Nationalism And The Protocols

No one now pretends to deny, except a few spokesmen who really do not rule the thought of the Jews but are set forth for the sole benefit of influencing Gentile thought, that the socially and economically disruptive elements abroad in the world today are not only manned but also moneyed by Jewish interests.

For a long time this fact was held in suspense owing to the vigorous denial of the Jews and the lack of information on the part of those agencies of publicity to which the public looked for its information. But now the facts are coming forth. Herzl's words are being proved to be true - "when we sink, we become a revolutionary proletariat, the subordinate officers of the revolutionary party." These words were first published in English in 1896!

Just now these tendencies are working in two directions, one for the tearing down of the Gentile states all over the world, the other for the establishment of a Jewish state in Palestine. The latter project engaged the attention of the whole world. The Zionists make a great deal of noise about Palestine, but it can scarcely be designated as more than an unusually ambitious colonization scheme. The Jewish "home" idea so sedulously cultivated is a very useful smokescreen for the confiscation of the immeasurable sources of mineral and oil wealth. It is also serving as a very useful public screen for the carrying on of secret activities.

International Jews, the controllers of the world's governmental and financial power, may meet anywhere, at any time, in war or peace time, and by giving out that they are only considering the ways and means of opening up Palestine to the Jews, they easily escape the suspicion of being together on any other business.

Though Jewish nationalism exists, its enshrinement in a state to be set up in Palestine is not the project that is engaging the whole Jewish nation. The Jews will not move into Palestine just yet; they will not move in at all merely because of the Zionist movement. Quite another motive will be the cause of the exodus out of the Gentile nations, when the time for that exodus fully comes.

The world has long suspected - at first only a few, then the secret departments of the governments, next the intellectuals among the people, now more and more the common people themselves - that not only are the Jews a nation distinct from all other nations and mysteriously unable to sink their nationality by any means they or the world may adopt to this end, but that they also constitute a state; that they are nationally conscious, not only, but consciously united for a common defense for a common purpose. Revert to Herzl's definition of the Jewish nation as held together by a common enemy, and then reflect that this common enemy is the Gentile world! Does this people which knows itself to be a nation remain loosely unorganized in the face of that fact? It would hardly be like Jewish astuteness in other fields! The interest of the Protocols is their bearing on the questions: Have the Jews an organized world system? What is its policy? How is it being worked?

These questions all receive full attention in the Protocols. Whosoever was the mind that conceived them possessed a knowledge of human nature, of history and of statecraft which is dazzling in its brilliant completeness, and terrible in the objects to which it turns its powers. If, indeed, one mind alone conceived them. It is too terribly real for fiction, too well-sustained for speculation, too deep in its knowledge of the secret springs of life for forgery. Jewish attacks upon it thus far make much of the fact that it came out of Russia. That is hardly true. It came by way of Russia.

The internal evidence makes it clear that the Protocols were not written by a Russian, nor originally in the Russian language, nor under the influence of Russian conditions, but they found their way to Russia and were first published there about 1905 by a Professor Nilus, who attempted to interpret the Protocols by events then going forward in Russia.

They have been found by diplomatic officers in manuscript in all parts of the world. Wherever Jewish power is able to do so, it has suppressed them, sometimes under the extreme penalty.

Their persistence is a fact which challenges the mind. Sheer lies do not live long, their powcr soon dics. Thc Protocols are more alive than ever. They have penetrated higher places than ever before. They have compelled a more Serious attitude to them than ever before. The Protocols are a World Program - there is no doubt anywhere of that - whose program is stated within the articles themselves. But as for outer confirmation, which would be the more valuable - a signature, or six signatures, or twenty signatures, or a 50-year unbroken line of effort fulfilling that program?

The point of interest for this and other countries is not that a "criminal or a madman" conceived such a program but that, when conceived, this program found means of getting itself fulfilled in its most important particulars. The document is comparatively unimportant; the conditions to which it calls attention are of a very high degree of importance.

The Fourteenth Protocol --

> "When we become rulers we shall regard as undesirable the existence of any religion except our own, proclaiming One God with Whom our fate is tied as The Chosen People, and by Whom our fate has been made one with the fate of the world. For this reason we must destroy all other religions. If thereby should emerge contemporary atheists, then, as a transition step, this will not interfere with our aims.

The Fifth Protocol --

> "A world coalition of Gentiles could cope with us temporarily, but we are assured against this by roots of dissension among them so deep that they cannot be torn out. We have created antagonism between the personal and national interests of the Gentiles by arousing religious and race hatreds which we have nourished in their hearts for twenty centuries. "

Chapter 6: An Introduction to the "Jewish Protocols"

The documents most frequently mentioned by those who are interested in the theory of Jewish World Power rather than in the actual operation of that power in the world today, are those 24 documents known as "The Protocols of the Learned Elders of Zion." The Protocols have attracted much attention in Europe, having been the center of an important storm of opinion in England, but discussion of them in the United States has been limited. Who it was that first entitled these documents with the name of the "Elders of Zion" is not known. It would be possible without serious mutilation of the documents to remove all hint of Jewish authorship, and yet retain all the main points of the most comprehensive program for world subjugation that has ever come to public knowledge.

Yet to eliminate all hint of Jewish authorship would be to bring out a number of contradictions which do not exist in the Protocols in their present form. The purpose of the plan revealed in the Protocols is to undermine all authority in order that a new authority in the form of an autocracy may be set up. Such a plan would not emanate from a ruling class which already possessed authority, although it might emanate from anarchists. But anarchists do not avow autocracy as the ultimate condition they seek. The authors might be conceived as a company of French Subversives such as existed at the time of the French Revolution and had the infamous Duc d'Orleans as their leader, but this would involve a contradiction between the fact that those Subversives have passed away, and the fact that the program announced in these Protocols is being steadily carried out, not only in France, but throughout Europe, and very noticeably in the United States.

In their present form which bears evidence of being their original form, there is no contradiction. The allegation of Jewish authorship seems essential to the consistency of the plan. If these documents were the forgeries which Jewish apologists claim them to be, the forgers would probably have taken pains to make Jewish authorship so clear that their anti-Semitic purpose could easily have been detected. But only twice is the term "Jew" used in them. After one has read further than the average reader usually cares to go into such matters, one comes upon the plans for the establishment of the World Autocrat, and only then is it made clear of what lineage he is to be.

But all through the documents there is left no doubt as to the people against whom the plan is aimed. It is not aimed against aristocracy as such. It is not aimed against capital as such. Very definite provisions are made for the enlistment of aristocracy, capital and government for the execution of the plan. It is aimed against the people of the world who are called "Gentiles." It is the frequent mention of "Gentiles" that really decides the purpose of the documents. Most of the destructive type of "liberal" plans aim at the enlistment of the people as helpers; this plan aims at the degeneration of the people in order that they may be reduced to confusion of mind and thus manipulated. Popular movements of a "liberal" kind are to be encouraged, all the disruptive philosophies in religion, economics, politics and domestic life are to be sown and watered, for the purpose of so disintegrating social solidarity and a definite plan, herein set forth, may be put through without notice, and the people then molded to it when the fallacy of these philosophies is shown.

The formula of speech is not, "We Jews will do this," but "The Gentiles will be made to think and do these things." With the exception of a few instances in the closing Protocols, the only distinctive racial term used is "Gentiles."

Racial Divergencces

To illustrate: the first indication of this kind comes in the First Protocol in this way:

> "The great qualities of the people - honesty and frankness - are essentially vices in politics, because they dethrone more surely and more certainly than does the strongest enemy. These qualities are attributes of Gentile rule; we certainly must not be guided by them."

> "On the ruins of the hereditary aristocracy of the Gentiles we have set up the aristocracy of our educated class, and over all the aristocracy

> of money. We have established the basis of this new aristocracy on the basis of riches, which we control, and on the science guided by our wise men."

> "We will force up wages, which, however, will be of no benefit to workers, for we at the same time will cause a rise in prices of prime necessities, pretending that this is due to the decline of agriculture and of cattle raising. We will also artfully and deeply undermine the sources of production by instilling in the workmen ideas of anarchy, and encourage them in the use of alcohol, at the same time taking measures to drive all the intellectual forces of the Gentiles from the land."

The above point continues:

> "That the true situation shall not be noticed by the Gentiles prematurely, we will mask it by a pretended effort to serve the working classes and promote great economic principles, for which an active propaganda will be carried on through our economic theories"

These quotations will illustrate the style of the Protocols in making references to the parties involved. It is "we" for the writers, and "Gentiles" for those who are being written about. This is brought out very clearly in the Fourteenth Protocol:

> "In this divergence between the Gentiles and ourselves in ability to think and reason is to be seen clearly the seal of our election as the chosen people, as higher human beings, in contrast with the Gentiles who have merely instinctive and animal minds. They observe, but they do not foresee, and they invent nothing (except perhaps material things). It is clear from this that nature herself predestined us to rule and guide the world."

This, of course, has been the Jewish method of dividing humanity from the earliest times. The world was only Jew and Gentile; all that was not Jew was Gentile. The use of the word Jew may be illustrated by this passage from the Eighth section:

> "For the time being, until it will be safe to give responsible government positions to our brother Jews, we shall entrust them to people whose past and whose characters are such that there is an abyss between them and the people."

This is the practice known as using "Gentile fronts" which is extensively practiced in the financial world today in order to cover up the evidences of Jewish control. How much progress has been made since these words were written down, is indicated by the party convention at San Francisco, when the name of Judge Brandeis was proposed for President. It is reasonably to be expected that the public mind will be made more and more familiar with the idea of Jewish occupancy - which will be really a short step from the present degree of influence which the Jews exercise - of the highest office in the government. There is no function of the American Presidency in which the Jews have not already secretly assisted in a very important degree. Actual occupancy of the office is not necessary to enhance their power, but to promote certain things which parallel very closely the plans outlined in the Protocols.

Another point which the reader of the Protocols will notice is that the tone of exhortation is entirely absent from these documents. They are not propaganda. They are not efforts to stimulate the ambitions or activity of those to whom they are addressed. They are as cool as a legal paper and as matter-of-fact as a table of statistics. There is none of the "Let us rise, my brothers" stuff about them. There is no "Down with the Gentiles" hysteria. These Protocols, if indeed they were made by Jews and confined to Jews, or if they do contain principles of a Jewish World Program, were certainly not intended for the firebrands but for the carefully prepared and tested initiates of the higher groups.

Problem Of Origin

Jewish apologists have asked, "Is it conceivable that if there were such a world program on the part of the Jews, they would reduce it to writing and publish it?" But there is no evidence that these Protocols were ever uttered otherwise than in spoken words by those who put them forth. The Protocols as we have them are apparently the notes of lectures which were made by someone who heard them. Some of them are lengthy; some of them are brief. The assertion which has always been made in connection with the Protocols since they have become known is that they are the notes of lectures delivered to Jewish students somewhere in France or Switzerland. The attempt to make them appear to be of Russian origin is absolutely forestalled by the point of view, the references to the times and certain grammatical indications. The tone certainly fits the supposition that they were originally lectures given to students, for their purpose is clearly not to get a program accepted but to give information concerning a program which is represented as being already in process of fulfillment. There is no invitation to join forces or to offer opinions. Indeed it is specifically announced that neither discussion nor opinions are desired. ("While preaching liberalism to the Gentiles, we shall hold our own people and our own agents in unquestioning obedience." "The scheme of administration must emanate from a single brain . . . Therefore, we may know the plan of action, but we must not discuss it, lest we destroy its unique character . . . The inspired work of our leader therefore must not be thrown before a crowd to be torn to pieces, or even before a limited group.")

Moreover, taking the Protocols at their face value, it is evident that the program outlined in these lectures was not a new one at the time the lectures were given. There is no evidence of its being of recent arrangement. There is almost the tone of a tradition, or a religion, in it all, as if it had been handed down from generation to generation through the medium of specially trusted and initiated men. There is no note of new discovery or fresh enthusiasm in it, but the certitude and calmness of facts long known and policies long confirmed by experiment.

The point of age of the program is touched upon at least twice in the Protocols themselves. In the First Protocol this paragraph appears:

"Already in ancient times we were the first to shout the words, 'Liberty, Equality, Fraternity,' among the people. These words have been repeated many times since by unconscious poll-parrots, flocking from all sides to this bait, with which they have ruined the - prosperity of the world and true personal freedom . . . The presumably clever and intelligent Gentiles did not understand the symbolism of the uttered words; did not observe their contradiction in meaning; did not notice that in nature there is no equality . . ."

The other reference to the program finality is found in the Thirteenth Protocol:

"Questions of policy, however, are permitted to no one except those who have originated the policy and have directed it for many centuries."

Can this be a reference to a secret Jewish Sanhedrin, self-perpetuating within a certain Jewish caste from generation to generation? Again, it must be said that the originators and directors here referred to cannot be at present any ruling caste, for all that the program contemplates is directly opposed to the interests of such a caste. It cannot refer to any national aristocratic group, like the Junkers of Germany, for the methods which are proposed are the very ones which would render powerless such a group. It cannot refer to any but a people who have no open government, who have everything to gain and nothing to lose, and who can keep themselves intact amid a crumbling world. There is only one group that answers that description.

Gentile Ingenuousness

The criticisms which these Protocols pass upon the Gentiles for their ingenuousness are just. It is impossible to disagree with a single item in the Protocol's description of Gentile mentality and venality. Even the most astute of the Gentile thinkers have been fooled into receiving as the motions of progress what has only been insinuated into the common human mind by the most insidious systems of propaganda. It is true that here and there a thinker has arisen to say that science so-called was not science at all. It is true that here and there a thinker has arisen to say that the so-called economic laws both of conservatives and radicals were not laws at all, but artificial inventions. It is true that occasionally a keen observer has asserted that the recent debauch of luxury and extravagance was not due to the natural impulses of the people at all, but was systematically stimulated, foisted upon them by design. It is true that a few have discerned that more than half of what passes for "public opinion" is merely hired applause and booing and has never impressed the public mind.

But even with these clues here and there, for the most part disregarded, there has never been enough continuity and collaboration between those who were awake, to follow all the clues to their source. The chief explanation of the hold which the Protocols have had on many of the leading statesmen of the world for several decades is that they explain whence all the false influences come and what their purpose is. It is now time for the people to know.

Whether the Protocols are judged as proving anything concerning the Jews or not, they constitute an education in the way the masses are turned about like sheep by influences which they do not understand. It is certain that once the principles of the Protocols are known widely and understood by the people, the criticism which they now rightly make of the Gentile mind will no longer hold good.

Divide And Rule

Is there likelihood of the program of the Protocols being carried through to success? The program is successful already. In many of its most important phases it is already a reality. But this need not cause alarm, for the chief weapon to be used against such a program, both in its completed and uncompleted parts, is clear publicity. Let the people know. Arousing the people, alarming the people, appealing to the passions of the people is the method of the plan outlined in the Protocols. The antidote is merely enlightening the people.

The Protocols are found upon analysis to contain four main divisions. These are not marked in the structure of the documents but in the thought. There is a fifth, if the object of it all is included, but this object is assumed throughout the Protocols, being only here and there defined in terms. And the four main divisions are great trunks from which there are numerous branches.

There is first what is alleged to be the Jewish conception of human nature, by which is meant Gentile nature. Secondly, there is the account of what has already been accomplished in the realization of the program - things already done. Thirdly, there is a complete instruction in the methods to be used to get the program still further fulfilled. Fourth, the Protocols contain in detail some of the achievements which, at the time these words were uttered, were yet to be made. Some of these desired things have been achieved in the meantime, for it should be borne in mind that between 1905 and the present time there have been set in motion many powerful influences to attain certain ends. The achievement to be made was the break up of Gentile solidarity and strength, expedited, of course, by the great wars in Europe. The method expounded is one of disintegration. Break up the people into parties and sects. Sow abroad the most promising and utopian of ideas and you will do two things: you will always find a group to cling to each idea you throw out; and you will find this partisanship dividing and estranging the various groups. The authors of the Protocols show in detail how this is to be done. Not one idea, but a mass of ideas are to be thrown out, and there is to be no unity among them. The purpose is not to get the people thinking one thing, but to think so diversely about so many different things that there will be no unity among them. The result of this will be vast disunity, vast unrest - and that is the result aimed at. When once the solidarity of Gentile society is broken up - and the name "Gentile society" is perfectly correct, for human society is overwhelmingly Gentile - then this solid wedge of another idea which is not at all affected by the prevailing confusion can make its way unsuspected to the place of control. It is well enough known that a body of 20 trained police or soldiers can accomplish more than a disordered mob of a thousand persons. So the minority initiated into the plan can do more with a nation or a world broken into a thousand antagonistic parties, than any of the parties could do. "Divide and rule" is the motto of the Protocols. Take for illustration these passages:

This from the First Protocol:

> "Political freedom is an idea, not a fact. It is necessary to know how to apply this idea when there is need of a clever bait to gain the support of the people for one's party, if such a party has undertaken to defeat another party already in power. This task is made easier if the opponent has himself been infected by principles of freedom or so-called liberalism, and for the sake of the idea will yield some of his power."

Consider this from the Fifth Protocol:

> "To obtain control over public opinion, it is first necessary to confuse it by the expression from various sides of so many conflicting opinions . . . this is the first secret. The second secret consists in so increasing and intensifying the shortcomings of the people in their habits, passions and mode of living that no one will be able to collect himself in the chaos, and, consequently, people will lose all their mutual understanding. This measure will serve us also in

> breeding disagreement in all parties, in disintegrating all those collective forces which are still unwilling to submit to us and in discouraging all personal initiative which can in any way interfere with our undertaking."

And this from the Thirteenth Protocol:

> ". . . and you may also notice that we seek approval, not for our acts, but for our words uttered in regard to one or another question. We always announce publicly that we are guided in all our measures by the hope and the conviction that we are serving the general good."

Protocols Claim Partial Fulfillment

Besides the things they look forward to doing, the Protocols announce the things they are doing and have done. Looking about the world today it is possible to see both the established conditions and the strong tendencies to which the Protocols allude - the terrible completeness of the World Plan which they disclose. A few general quotations will serve to illustrate the element of present achievement in the assertions of these documents, and in order that the point may be made clear to the reader the key words will be emphasized.

Take this from Protocol Nine:

> "In reality there are no obstacles before us. Our super-government has such an extra-legal status that it may be called by the energetic and strong

> word - dictatorship. I can conscientiously say that, at the present time, we are the lawmakers. We create courts and jurisprudence. We rule with a strong will because we hold in our hands the remains of a once strong party, now subjugated by us."

And this - from the Eighth Protocol:

> "We will surround our government with a whole world of economists. It is for this reason that the science of economics is the chief subject of instruction taught by the Jews. We shall be surrounded by a whole galaxy of bankers, industrialists, capitalists, and especially by millionaires because, actually, everything will be decided by an appeal to figures."

These are strong claims, but not too strong for the facts that can be marshalled to illustrate them. They are, however, but an introduction to further claims that are made and equally paralleled by the facts. All through the Protocols, as in this quotation from the Eighth, the pre-eminence of the Jews in teaching political economy is insisted upon, and the facts bear that out. They are the chief authors of those vagaries which lead the mob after economic impossibilities, and they are also the chief teachers of political economy in our universities, the chief authors of those popular textbooks in the subject, which hold the conservative classes to the fiction that economic theories are economic laws. The idea, the theory, as instruments of social disintegration are common to both the university Jew and the Bolshevik Jew. When all this is shown in detail, public opinion upon the importance of academic and radical economics may undergo a change. And, as claimed in the quotation just given from the Ninth Protocol, the Jewish world power does today constitute a super-government. It is the Protocol's own word, and none is more fitting. No nation can get all that it wants, but the Jewish World Power can get all that it wants, even though its demands exceed Gentile equality. "We are the lawmakers," say the Protocols, and Jewish influences have been lawmakers in a greater degree than any but the specialists realize. In the past decades Jewish international rule has quite dominated the world. Wherever Jewish tendencies are permitted to work unhindered, the result is not "Americanization," nor "Anglicization" nor any other distinctive nationalism, but a strong and ruling reversion back to essential "Judaization."

Conquest Of Religion And Press

This from the Seventeenth Protocol will be of considerable interest, perhaps, to those clergymen who are laboring with Jewish rabbis to bring about some kind of religious union:

> "We have taken good care long ago to discredit the Gentile clergy and thereby to destroy their mission, which at present might hamper us considerably. Their influence over the people

> diminishes daily. Freedom of conscience has been proclaimed everywhere. Consequently it is only a question of time when the complete crash of the Christian religion will occur."

A curious paragraph in this Protocol claims for the Jewish race a particular skill in the art of insult:
"Our contemporary Press will expose governmental and religious affairs and the incapacity of the Gentiles, always using expressions so derogatory as to approach insult, the faculty of employment which is so well known to our race."
And this from the Fifteenth Protocol:

> "Under our influence the execution of the laws of the Gentiles is reduced to a minimum. Respect for the law is undermined by the liberal interpretation we have introduced in this sphere. The courts decide as we dictate, even in the most important cases in which are involved fundamental principles or political issues, viewing them in the light in which we present them to the Gentile administration through agents with whom we have apparently nothing in common, through newspaper opinion and other avenues."

Claims of control of the Press are numerous, here are emphatic statements from the Fourteenth Protocol:

> "In countries called advanced, we have created a senseless, filthy and disgusting literature. For a short time after our entrance into power we shall

> encourage its existence so that it may show in greater relief the contrast between it and the written and spoken announcements which will emanate from us."

And in the Twelfth Protocol:

> "We have attained this (Press control) at the present time to the extent that all news is received through several agencies in which it is centralized from all parts of the world. These agencies will then be to all intents and purposes our own institutions and will publish only that which we permit."

This from the Seventh Protocol bears on the same subject:

> "We must force the Gentile governments to adopt measures which will promote our broadly conceived plan, already approaching its triumphant goal, by bringing to bear the pressure of stimulated public opinion, which has been organized by us with the help of the so-called 'great power' of the Press. With a few exceptions not worth considering, it is already in our hands."

To resume the Twelfth Protocol:

> "If we have already managed to dominate the mind of Gentile society to such a point that almost all see world affairs through the colored lenses of the spectacles which we place before their eyes, and if now there is not one government with barriers erected against our

> access to that which by Gentile ingenuousness is called state secrets, what then will it be when we are the recognized masters of the world in the person of our universal ruler?"

The Jewish nation is the only nation that possess the secrets of all the rest. The fact that they can get whatever they want when they want it is the important point - as many a secret paper could testify if it could talk, and as many a custodian of secret papers could tell if he would. The real secret diplomacy of the world is that which hands over the world's so-called secrets to a few men who are members of one race; there is no government in the world so completely at their service as our own at present.

Note on the Dispersal

The Protocols do not regard the dispersal of the Jews abroad upon the face of the earth as a calamity, but as a providential arrangement by which the World Plan can be the more easily executed, as see these words of the Eleventh Protocol.

> "God gave us, His Chosen People, as a blessing, the dispersal, and this which has appeared to all to be our weakness has been our whole strength. It has now brought us to the threshold of universal rule."

The claims to accomplishment which are put forth in the Ninth Protocol would be too massive for words were they

not too massive for concrete realization, but there is a point where the word and the actuality meet and tally:
"In order not to destroy prematurely the Gentile institutions, we have laid our efficient hands on them, and rasped the springs of their mechanism. They were formerly in strict and just order, but we have replaced them with a liberal disorganized and arbitrary administration. We have tampered with jurisprudence, the franchise, the press, freedom of the person, and, most important of all, education and culture, the comer stone of free existence.

> "We have misled, stupefied and demoralized the youth of the Gentiles by means of education in principles and theories patently false to us, but which we have inspired. Above existing laws, without actual change but by distorting them through contradictory interpretations, we have created something stupendous in the way of results."

Everyone knows that, in spite of the fact that the air was never as full of theories of liberty and wild declarations of "rights," there has been a steady curtailment of "personal freedom." Instead of being socialized, the people, under a cover of socialistic phrases, are being brought under an unaccustomed bondage to the state; laws of every kind are hedging upon the harmless liberties of the people. A steady tendency toward systematization, every phase of the tendency based upon some very learnedly stated "principle," has set in, and curiously enough, when the investigator pursues his way to the authoritative center of these movements for the regulation of the people's life, he finds Jews in power!

Splitting Society By "Ideas"

The method by which the Protocols work for the breakdown of society is evident. An understanding of the method is necessary if one is to find the meaning of the currents and cross-currents which make so hopeless a hodge-podge of the present times. People who are confused and discouraged by the various voices and discordant theories of today, each seeming to be plausible and promising, may find a clear clue to the value of the voices and the meaning of the theories if they understand that their confusion and discouragement comprise the very objective which is sought. The uncertainty, hesitation, hopelessness, fear; the eagerness with which every promising plan and offered solution is grasped - these are the very reactions which the program outlined in the Protocols aims to produce. The condition is proof of the efficacy of the program.

It is a method that takes time, and the Protocols declare that it has taken time, indeed centuries. Students of the matter find the identical program of the Protocols, announced and operated by the Jewish race, from the first century onward.

It has taken 1900 years to bring Europe to its present degree of subjugation - violent subjugation in some countries, political subjugation in some, economic subjugation in all - but in America the same program, with almost the same degree of success, has only required about 50 years! The center of Jewish power, the principal sponsors of the Jewish program, are resident in America, and the leverage which was used at the Peace Conference to fasten Jewish power more securely upon Europe, was American leverage exercised at the behest of the strong Jewish pressure which was brought from the United States for that purpose. And these activities did not end with the Peace Conference.

The whole method of the Protocols may be described in one word, Disintegration. The undoing of what has been done, the creation of a long and hopeless interim in which attempts at reconstruction shall be baffled, and the gradual wearing down of public opinion and public confidence, until those who stand outside the created chaos shall insert their strong, calm hand to seize control - that is the whole method of procedure.

The Protocols distinctly declare that it is by means of the set of ideas which cluster around "democracy," that their first victory over public opinion was obtained. The idea is the weapon. And to be a weapon it must be an idea at variance with the natural trend of life. It must be a theory opposed to the facts of life. And no theory so opposed can be expected to take root and become the ruling factor, unless it appeals to the mind as reasonable, inspiring and good. The Truth frequently seems unreasonable; the Truth frequently is depressing; the Truth sometimes seems to be evil; but it has this eternal advantage, it is the

Truth, and what is built thereon neither brings nor yields to confusion. This first step does not give the control of public opinion, but leads up to it. It is worthy to note that it is this sowing of "the poison of liberalism," as the Protocols name it, which comes first in order in those documents. Then, following upon that, the Protocols say:

> "To obtain control over public opinion it is first necessary to confuse it."

Truth is one and cannot be confused, but this false, appealing liberalism which has been sown broadcast, and which is ripening faster under Jewish nurture in America than ever it did in Europe, is easily confused because it is not truth. It is error, and error has a thousand forms. Take a nation, a party, a city, an association in which "the poison of liberalism" has been sown, and you can split that up into as many factions as there are individuals simply by throwing among them certain modifications of the original idea. That is a piece of strategy well known to the forces that invisibly control mass-thought. Theodor Herzl, the arch-Jew, a man whose vision was wider than any contemporary statesman's and whose program paralleled the Protocols, knew this many years ago when he said that the Zionist (cryptic for "Jewish") state would come before the Socialist state could come; he knew with what endless divisions the "liberalism" which he and his predecessors had planted would be shackled and crippled. The process of which all Gentiles have been the victims, but never the Jews - never the Jews! - is just this: First, to create an ideal of "broad-mindedness." That is the phrase which appears in every Jewish remonstrance against public mention of the Jew and his alleged World Program: "We thought you were too broad-minded a man to express such thoughts." It is a sort of key word, indicative of the state of mind in which it is desired that the Gentiles be kept. It is a state of flabby tolerance. A state of mind which mouths meaningless phrases about Liberty, phrases which act as an opiate on the mind and conscience and which allow all sorts of things to be done under cover.

The phrase, the slogan, is a very dependable Jewish weapon. ("In all times people have accepted words for acts." - Protocol 5.) The reality behind the phrase the Protocols frankly admit to be non-existent.

Men are born believers. For a time they may believe in "broad-mindedness" and under the terrific social pressure that has been set up in its favor they will openly espouse it. But it is too shallow to satisfy any growing roots of life. They must believe, deeply, something. For proof of this, notice the undeniable strength of the negative beliefs which are held by men who fancy that they believe nothing. Therefore, some who are highly endowed with independence of spirit, root down into those prohibited matters which at some point touch Jewish concerns - these are the "narrow" men. But others find it more convenient to cultivate those departments which promise a highway whereon there shall be no clashes of vital opinion, no chance of the charge of "intolerance"; in short they transfer all their contemplative powers to the active life; even as it is written in the Protocols - "To divert Gentile thought and observation, interest must be deflected to industry and commerce." It is just this Deflection to the materialistic base that offer the Protocolists, and similarly Jewish propagandists, their best hold. "Broad-mindedness" - in leaving vital matters severely alone-descends quickly into material-mindedness. Within this lower sphere all the discord which distresses the world today is to be found.

It means, as everything about us shouts, the prostitution of service to profits and the eventual disappearance of the profits: It means that the high art of management degenerates into exploitation. It means reckless confusion among the managers and dangerous unrest among the working men. But it means something worse: it means the splitting up of Gentile society. Not a division between "Capital" and "Labor," but thc division between the Gentile at both ends of the working scheme, as the Protocols confirm: "To make it possible for liberty definitely to disintegrate and ruin Gentile society, industry must be placed on a speculative basis."

With Jewish capital at one end of the Gentile working scheme putting the screws on the manufacturers, and with Jewish agitators and disruptionists and subversives at the ether end of the Gentile working scheme putting the screws on the workmen, we have a condition at which the world-managers of the Protocol program must be immensely satisfied. See Protocol Nine:

"We might fear the combined strength of the

> Gentiles of vision with the blind strength of the masses, but we have taken all measures against such a possible contingency by raising a wall of mutual antagonism between these two forces. Thus, the blind force of the masses remains our support. We, and we alone, shall serve as their leaders. Naturally, we will direct their energy to achieve our end."

The indication that they are highly satisfied is that they are not only not doing anything to relieve the world situation, but are apparently willing to have it made worse. The privations which are scheduled for it (unless Gentile flabbiness before the Jewish power, high and low, receives a new backbone), will bring the United States to the verge, if not across the very line, of Bolshevism. The Jews know the whole method of artificial scarcity and high prices. It was practiced in the French Revolution and in Russia. All the signs of it are in this country too.

It is not difficult to see the genealogy of the Jewish ideas of liberalism from their origin to their latest effects upon Gentile life. The confusion aimed at is here! Bewilderment characterizes the whole mental climate of the people today. They do not know what to believe. First one set of facts is given to them, then another. First one explanation of conditions is given to them, and then another. The fact-shortage is acute. There is a whole market-full of explanations that explain nothing, but only deepen the confusion. The government itself seems to be hampered, and whenever it starts on a line of investigation finds itself mysteriously tangled up so that procedure is difficult. This governmental aspect is also clearly set forth in the Protocols. Add to this the onslaught on the human tendency toward religion, which is usually the last barrier to fall before violence and robbery unashamed stalk forth To conclude this general view of the method, rather this part of the method, the confusion itself, which all Jewish influences converge to produce, it is expected to produce another more deeply helpless state. And that state is Exhaustion. It needs no imagination to see what this means. Exhaustion is today one of the conditions that menace the people. The war and its strain began the exhaustion; the "peace" and its confusions have about completed it. The people believe in little and expect less. Confidence is gone. Initiative is nearly gone. The failure of movements falsely heralded as "people's movements" has gone far to make the people think that no people's movement is possible. So say the Protocols:

> "To wear everyone out by dissensions, animosities, feuds, famine, inoculation of diseases, want, until the Gentiles see no other way of escape except by an appeal to our money power." -- Protocol 10.

> "We will so wear out anal exhaust the Gentiles by all this that they will be compelled to offer us an international authority, which by its position will enable us to absorb without disturbance all the governmental forces of the world and thus form

> a super-government. We must so direct the education of the Gentile Society that its hands will drop in the weakness of discouragement in the face of any undertaking where initiative is needed." - Protocol 5.

The Jews have never been worn out or exhausted. They have never been nonplussed. This is the true psychic characteristic of those who have a clue to the maze. It is the unknown that exhausts the mind, the constant wandering around among tendencies and influences whose source is not known and whose purpose is not understood. Walking in the dark is wearing work. The Gentiles have been doing it for centuries. The others, having a pretty accurate idea what it was all about, have not succumbed. Even persecution is endurable if it is understandable, and the Jews of the world have always known just where it fitted in the scheme of things. Gentiles have suffered more from Jewish persecutions than have the Jews for after the persecutions were over, the Gentile was as much in the dark as ever; whereas Judaism simply took up again its century-long march toward a goal in which it implicitly believes, and which, some say who have a deep knowledge of Jewish roots in the world and who, too, may be touched with exhaustion, they will achieve. However, this may be the revolution which would be necessary to unfasten the International Jewish system from its grip on the world, would probably have to be just as radical as any attempts the Jews have made to attain that grip. There are those who express serious doubts that the Gentiles are competent to do it at all. Maybe not. Let them at least know who their conquerors are.

Chapter 7: How The Jews Use Power

Two organizations, both of which are as notable for their concealment as for their power, are the New York Kehillah and the American Jewish Committee. The Kehillah is the most potent factor in the political life of New York; it is the organization which today wields so large an influence on the rest of the world, which consciously issues a program which on one side is pro-Jewish and on the other anti-Gentile. It is the central group, the inner government, whose ruling is law and whose act is the official expression of Jewish purpose. It offers a real and complete instance of a government within a government in the midst of America's largest and politically most powerful city, and it also constitutes the machine through which pro-Jewish and anti-Gentile propaganda is operated and Jewish pressure brought to bear against certain American ideas. That is to say, the Jewish government of New York constitutes the essential part of the Jewish Government of the United States.

The word "Kehillah" has the same meaning as "Kahal," which signifies "community," "assembly" or government. It represents the Jewish form of Government in dispersion. In the Babylonian captivity, in Eastern Europe today, the Kahal is the power and protectorate to which the faithful Jew looks for government and justice. The New York Kehillah is the largest and most powerful union of Jews in the world, the center of Jewish world power has been transferred to that city. That is the meaning of the heavy migration of Jews all over the world toward New York in recent decades. It is to them what Rome is to the Catholic and what Mecca is to the Moslem.

The Kehillah is a perfect answer to the deceptive statement that the Jews are so divided among themselves as to render a concert of action impossible. That is one of the statements made for Gentile consumption. All experience shows, even to the most casual observer of Jewish activities, that the capitalist and the bolshevik, the rabbi and the union leader are all united under the flag of Judah. Touch the conservative capitalist who is a Jew, and the red communist who is also a Jew will spring to his defense. It may be that sometimes they love each other less, but altogether they hate the non-Jew more, and that is their common bond. The Kehillah is an alliance, more offensive than defensive, against the “Gentiles."

It is a strange and impressive spectacle which the Kehillah presents, of a people of one racial origin, with a vivid belief in itself and its future, disregarding internal differences, to combine privately in a powerful organization for the racial, material and religious advancement of its own race, to the exclusion of all others.

The American Jewish Committee came into being in 1906. There had been a government investigation into the "White Slave Traffic," the result of which was a direct set of public opinion into channels uncomplimentary to the Jews, and a defensive movement was begun. The Kehillah organized protests against the statement by General Bingham, then police commissioner of the City of New York, that 50 per cent of the crime in the metropolis was committed by Jews. Very soon afterward, General Bingham disappeared from public life, and a national magazine of power and influence which had embarked on a series of articles setting forth the government's finding in the White Slave investigation was forced to discontinue after printing the first article.

The Kehillah has mapped out New York just as the American Jewish Committee has mapped the United States, and practically every Jew belongs to one or more lodges, secret societies, unions, orders, committees and federations. The list is a prodigious one. The purposes interlace and the methods dovetail in such a manner as to bring every phase of American life not only under the watchful eye, but under the swift and powerful action of experienced compulsion upon public affairs.

At the meeting which organized the Kehillah a number of sentiments were expressed which are worthy of consideration today, Judah L. Magnes, then rabbi of Temple Emanu-el, chairman of the meeting, set forth the plan:

"A central organization like that of the Jewish

> community of New York City is necessary to create a Jewish public opinion," he said.

Rabbi Asher was loudly applauded when he said:

> "American interests are one, Jewish interests are another thing."

The delegates at the first open meeting in 1906 represented 222 Jewish societies - religious, political, industrial and communal. Just over a year later the number of Jewish organizations under the jurisdiction of the Kehillah aggregated 688, and in 1921 well over 1,000. When the aggressive program of the Kehillah to make New York a Jewish city, and through New York to make the United States a Jewish country, was announced some of the more conservative Jews of New York were timorous. They did not expect that the American people would stand for it. They thought the American people would immediately understand what was afoot and oppose it. There were others who doubted whether the same Kehillah authority could here be wielded over the Jews as was wielded in the old country ghettos. An official of the Kehillah wrote:

> "There were those who doubted the ultimate success of this new venture in Jewish organization. They based their lack of belief on the fact that no governmental authority could possibly be secured; in other words, that the Kehillah of New York could not hope to wield the same power, based on governmental coercion, as

the Kehillahs of the Old World."

There is much in this paragraph to indicate the status of the Kehillah in Jewish life. Add to this fact that all the Jews who entered America lived under the Kehillahs of the old world, whose power was based on coercion, and the situation is simple. Regimentation, the destruction of individual liberty which has risen to curse the world, is the basic principle of Jewish government of the Jews, by the Jews.

What else can happen when world government of the Gentiles by the Jews for the bankers becomes established?

However, the misgivings of some Jews were not justified. The Americans made no protest. The Kehillah went ahead with its campaign and America submitted. New York became Jewish. American life, American thought, and American politics, became Jewish-dominated in the decades that followed. But with it all, the Jews exhibit a sense of the insecurity of this usurpation of power. It does not belong to those who have seized it; it does not belong either by right of numbers, or by right of superior ability, or yet by right of a better use made of that power. They have taken power in America by audacity; they have taken it in such a way as to make resentment of it seem like an anti-racial movement - and that is why they have held it as long as they have. That is the only way to explain the meekness of the Americans in this matter, and it also accounts for the sense of insecurity which even the Jews feel in the position they hold. The American is the slowest person in the world to act on any line that savors of racial or religious prejudice. This makes for a seeming aloofness from matters like the Jewish Question. This also leads uninformed public men to sign protests against. "anti-Semitism" which are really designed to be protests against the publication of Jewish facts. The foundation, organization and rapid success of the Kehillah in New York is an object lesson set in the sight of the world, as to what the Jew can do and will do when he exalts himself to the seat of rule.

As to the Kehillah being officially representative, it may be added that the Kehillah has in it representatives of the Central Conference of American Rabbis, Eastern Council of Reform Rabbis, Independent Order of B'nai B'rith, Independent Order of B'rith Shalom, Independent Order of Free Sons of Israel, Independent Order of B'rith Abraham, Federation of American Zionists - orthodox Jews, reform Jews, "apostate Jews," rich Jews, poor Jews, law-abiding Jews and red revolutionary Jews. At the 1918 Convention there were present: Jacob H. Schiff, banker; Louis Marshall, lawyer, president of the American Jewish Committee; Adolf S. Ochs, proprietor of the "New York Times"; Otto A. Rosalsky, judge of the General Sessions Court; Otto H. Kahn, of the banking house of Kuhn, Loeb and Company - AND -- Benjamin Schlesinger, who had lately returned from Moscow where he had a conference with Lenin; Joseph Schlossberg, general secretary of the Amalgamated Clothing Workers of America; Marc Pine, also a recent consultant with the Bolshevik rulers of

Russia; David Pinski; Joseph Barondess, labor leader. The high and the low were there; the first world war was closing, the Russian revolution had been won. Judge Mack, who headed the War Risk Insurance Bureau of the United States Government, and the little leader of the reddest group in the East End - they all met in the Kehillah, as Jews. Adolph Ochs of the great "New York Times" together with the most feverish scribbler on a Yiddish weekly that calls for blood and violence, all of them of all classes, bound together in a solidarity which has been achieved by no other people so perfectly as by Judah. Banded together for the purpose of "protecting Jewish rights."

The Jewish Demand For "Rights" In America

What rights have Americans that Jews in America do not possess? Against whom are the Jews organized and against what? What basis is there for the cry of "persecution"? None whatever, except the Jews' own consciousness that the course they are pursuing is due for a check. The Jews always know that. They are not in the stream of the world, and every little while the world finds out what Judah always knows. The program of the Kehillah was ostensibly to "assert Jewish rights." No Jewish rights have ever been interfered with in America. The expression was a euphemism for a campaign to interfere with non-Jewish rights.

The New York Kehillah is the pattern and parent Jewish community in the United States, the visible entourage of the Jewish government, the dynamo which motivates those "protests" and "mass meetings" which are frequently heralded throughout the country, and the arsenal of that kind of dark power which the Jewish leaders know so well how to use. It is the "whispering gallery," where the famous whispering drives are originated and set in motion and made to break in lying publicity over the country. The liaison between this center of Jewish power and the affairs of the people of the United States is made by the American Jewish Committee. The Committee and the Kehillah are practically identical as far as the national Jewish program is concerned. Through their foreign associations they are also identical as far as the world program is concerned.

The United States is divided into 12 parts by the American Jewish Committee and every State belongs to a district headed by the most powerful and representative Jews. The Committee represents the focusing point of the religious, racial, financial and political will of Jewry. It is also the executive committee of the New York Kehillah. New York Jewry is the dynamo of the national Jewish machinery. Its national instrument is the American Jewish Committee. Among its direct leaders and supporters today are the owners of powerful newspapers, officials in Federal, State and City administration, influential office holders on public boards and corporations, members of the judiciary and police departments, financiers and heads of banking houses, mercantile and manufacturing establishments, labor leaders and political party organizers of all colors.

There are certain announced purposes of these associations, and there are certain purposes which are not announced. The announced purposes may be read in printed pages; the purposes not announced may be read in the records of attempted acts and achieved results. To keep the record straight let us look first at the announced purposes of the American Jewish Committee, then of the Kehillah; next at the line which binds the two together; and then at the real purposes as they are to be construed from a long list of attempts and achievements. The American Jewish Committee, officially organized in 1906, announced itself as incorporated for the following purposes:

1. To prevent the infraction of the civil and religious rights of the Jews in any part of the world.
2. To render all lawful assistance and to take appropriate remedial action in the event of threatened or actual invasion or restriction of such rights, or of unfavorable discrimination with respect thereto.
3. To secure for Jews equality of economic, social and educational opportunities.
4. To alleviate the consequences of persecution wherever they may occur, and to afford relief from calamities affecting the Jews.

It is an exclusively Jewish program. The Charter of the Kehillah empowered it, among other things, to establish an educational bureau, to adjust differences between Jewish residents or organizations by arbitration or by means of boards of mediation or conciliation; while the Constitution announces the purpose to be:

"To further the cause of Judaism in New York City and to represent the Jews in this city with respect to all local matters of Jewish interest."

Where the American Jewish Committee and the Kehillah join forces is shown as follows:

Committee was a national organization, the Jewish Community (Kehillah), of New York City, if combined with it, would have a voice in shaping the policy of Jewry throughout the land. It is expressly understood that the American Jewish Committee shall have exclusive jurisdiction over all questions of a national or International character affecting the Jews generally."

It will be seen, therefore, that the Kehillah and the American Jewish Committee are one. The capital of the United States, in Jewish affairs, is New York. Perhaps that may throw a sidelight on the efforts which are constantly made to exalt New York as the spring and source of all the thoughts of the day. (Editor's Note: and now the seat of the United Nations system of world government)! New York, the Jewish capital of the United States, has been made the financial center, the art center, the political center of the country. But its art is oriental sensuousness, its politics those of a Judaized Tammany. It is the home of anti-American propaganda, of pro-Jewish hysteria, a mad confusion of mind that now passes all over the world as the true picture of America.

The doctrine with which so large a mass as the citizens of America have been inoculated is making havoc with the whole American program today. It is "broadening" America out of all semblance to its distinctive self and blurring out of recognition those determining ideals and ideas on which American institutions were based.

"Jewish Rights" Clash with American Rights

This study of the Jewish Question in the United States is not based upon religious differences. The religious element does not enter except when it is injected by the Jews themselves; they persistently inject it in three ways: First, in their allegation that any study of the Jews is "religious persecution"; second, by their own records of what their activities in the United States consist of; third, by the impression which is very misleading if not corrected, that the Jews are the Old Testament people. The Jews are not the Old Testament people and the Old Testament can be found among them only with difficulty. They are a Talmudical people who have preferred the volumes of rabbinical speculation to the words of the ancient prophets.

In this series of articles, we have set aside every non-Jewish statement on this religious question, and have accepted only that which proceeds from recognized Jewish sources. It has been most illuminating, in studying the proceedings of the New York Kehillah and the

American Jewish Committee, and their affiliated organizations, as represented by their activities throughout the country, to find how large a part of these activities have a religious bearing, as being directly and combatively anti-Christian.

That is to say, when the Jews set forth in the public charters and constitutions of their organizations that their only purpose is to "protect Jewish rights," and when the public asks what are these "Jewish rights" which need protection in this free country, the answer can be found only in the actions which the Jews take to secure that "protection."

Thus interpreted, "Jewish rights" seem to be summed up in the "right" to banish everything from their sight and hearing that suggests Christianity or its Founder. It is just there, from the Jewish side, that religious intolerance makes its appearance.

Attacks On Christianity

Previous to the formation of the Kehillah and the Jewish Committee, this sort of attack on the rights of Americans was sporadic, but since 1906 it has increased in number and insistence. Under cover of the ideal of Liberty we have given the Jews liberty to attack Liberty. What America has been tolerating is intolerance itself. Let us look rapidly down the years and see one phase of that attack. It is the attack upon Christianity. Here are a few items from the record. They are recorded over a period of years following the rise of Jewish power in America:

- 1899-1900. The Jews attempt to have the word "Christian" removed from the Bill of Rights of the State of Virginia.
- 1906-1907. The Jews of Oklahoma petition the Constitutional Convention protesting that the acknowledgment of Christ in the new State constitution then being formulated would be repugnant to the Constitution of the United States.
- The Jews force "The Merchant of Venice" to be dropped from public schools in Texas, Ohio.
- 1907-1908. Widespread demand by the Jews for the complete secularization of the public institutions of this country, as a part of the demand of the Jews for their constitutional rights.
- Supreme Court Justice Brewer's statement that this is a Christian country widely controverted by Jewish rabbis and publications.
- Jews agitate in many cities against Bible reading. Christmas celebrations or carols in Philadelphia, Cincinnati, St. Paul and New York met with strong Jewish opposition.
- 1908-1909. Protests made to Governor of Arkansas against "Christological expressions" employed by him in his Thanksgiving Day proclamation.
- Professor Gotthard Deutsch protests against "Christological prayers" at the high school graduating exercises at Cincinnati.
- Jewish community in Tamaqua, Pennsylvania defeats resolutions providing daily Bible reading in schools.

- Local Council of Jewish Women of Baltimore petitions school board to prohibit Christmas exercises.
- Boycotts were instituted in New York against merchants who opened on Saturday.
- Special efforts at this period to introduce the idea of the Jewish Sabbath into public business. Jews refused to sit as jurors in court, thus postponing cases.
- 1909-1910. On demand of the Jews, the school board of Bridgeport, Pennsylvania, votes to discontinue the recitation of the Lord's Prayer in the school.
- In Newark, New Jersey, the rabbis ask the night schools to discontinue Friday evening sessions, because the Jewish Sabbath begins at sundown on Friday.
- The work of introducing the idea of Jewish national holidays into public life especially active.
- 1910-1911. An attempt to have Hebrew officially recognized was frustrated by Supreme Court Judge Goff.
- Chicago Jews have election date changed because the official date fell on the last day of the Passover. Jews oppose Bible reading and singing of hymns in Detroit schools. Rabbis force Hartford, Connecticut, school board to drop "The Merchant of Venice" from reading list. New York Kehillah does two contradictory things; favors bill to permit Jews to do all kinds of business on Sunday, and pledges itself to co-operate in the strict enforcement of the Sunday laws.

- 1911-1912. Jews in Passaic, New Jersey, petition school board to eliminate Bible reading and all Christian songs from the schools. At request of a rabbi, three principals of Roxbury, Mass., public schools agree to banish Christmas tree and omit all references to the season from their schools. A Jewish delegate to the Ohio Constitutional Convention suggests that the Constitution be made to forbid Christian religious references in schools. The Council of the University Settlement, at the request of the New York Kehillah, adopts this resolution: "That in the holiday celebrations held annually by the Kindergarten Association at the University Settlement every feature of any sectarian character, including Christmas trees, Christmas programs and Christmas songs, shall be eliminated."
- 1912-1913. Jews at Jackson, Tennessee, seek an injunction to prevent the reading of the Bible in City schools. Annual Convention Independent Order B'nai B'rith at Nashville, Tennessee, adopts resolution against reading of the Bible and singing Christian songs in public schools. Chicago Board of Education, scene of much Jewish agitation, approves recommendation of sub-committee to remove Christmas from the list of official public holidays in schools.
- 1913-1914. The energies of the Jewish powers were concentrated on the task of preventing the United States from changing the immigration laws in a

manner to protect the country from undesirable aliens.

- 1914-1915. More Kehillah attempts to secure modification of the Sunday laws.
- 1915-1916. Jewish opposition to various movements towards making the schools free to use the Bible.
- 1916-1917. Jews busy carrying out an immense campaign against the "literacy clause" of the Immigration Bill. On demand of the Jews the New Haven Connecticut, Board of Education prevents the reading of "The Merchant of Venice," and extends the prohibition to "Lamb's Tales from Shakespeare."
- 1918-1919. Provost Marshal Crowder, in charge of the Selective Draft U.S. Forces, had issued an order to all medical examiners, under direction of the Surgeon General, stating "The foreign-born, especially Jews, are more apt to malinger than the native-born." Louis Marshall, head of the American Jewish Committee, telegraphed demanding that the "further use of this form shall be at once discontinued." President Wilson ordered the excision of the paragraph.
- The United States Shipping Board sent an advertisement to the "New York Times," calling for a file clerk and stating that a "Christian" was preferred - by which is meant always a non-Jew - the paper rejected it. Louis Marshall again went into action and protested to Bainbridge Colby, Woodrow Wilson's Secretary of State, demanding "Not because of any desire for inflicting punishment, but for the sake of

example and the establishment of a necessary precedent this offense should be followed by a dismissal from the public office of the offender, and the public should be informed the reason." Attention is called to the tone which the American Jewish Committee adopts when addressing high American officials in the name of Jewry. It is not to be duplicated in the addresses of any other representative of any other race or faith.

- The Plattsburg Manual, published for officers in the United States officers' training camps, contained the statement that "the ideal officer is a Christian gentleman." The A J.C. at once protested against "Christological manifestations," and the Manual was changed to read "the ideal officer is a courteous gentleman." The Anti-Defamation Committee claimed that 160 American cities had excluded "The Merchant of Venice" from the public schools.
- 1919-1920. The Kehillah was so successful in its campaign that it was possible for a Jewish advertiser in New York to say that he wanted only Jewish help, but it was not possible for a non-Jewish advertiser to state his non-Jewish preference. And so it goes on, year after year, right up to the present day. The incidents quoted are typical not occasional. They represent what is transpiring all the time in the United States as the Jews pursue their "rights." There is no interference with Jewish ways and manners. The Jew may use his own calendar, keep his own days, observe

his own form of worship, live in his own ghetto, exist on a dietary principle all his own, slaughter his cattle in a manner which no one who knows about it can approve - he can do all these things without molestation, without the slightest question of his right in them. But, the non-Jew is the "persecuted one." He must do everything the way the Jew wants it done; if not he is infringing on Jewish "rights."

The Cry Of "Anti-Semitism"

What people are now coming to see is that it is American rights that have been interfered with, and the interference has been made with the assistance of their own "broad-minded" tolerance. The Jews' interference with the religion of others, and the Jews' determination to wipe out of public life every sign of the predominant Christian character of the United States, is the only active form of religious intolerance in the country today. Not content with the fullest liberty to follow their own faith in peace and quietness, in a country where none dare make them afraid, the Jews declare - we read it in their activities - that every sight and sound of anything Christian is an invasion of their peace and quietness, and so they stamp it out wherever they can reach it through political means. To what lengths this spirit may run is shown in the prophecies of the Talmud, and in the "reforms" undertaken by the Communists of Russia and Eastern Europe.

That is not all; not content with their own liberty, not content with the "secularization," which means the de-Christianization of all public institutions, the third step observable in Jewish activities is the actual exaltation of Judaism as a recognized and specially privileged system. The program is the now familiar one wherever the Jewish program is found: first, establishment; second, the destruction of all that is non-Jewish or anti-Jewish; third, exaltation of Judaism in all its phases.

Put the Lord's Prayer and certain Shakespeare plays out of the public schools, but put Jewish courts in the public buildings - that is the way it works. Secularization is preparatory to Judaization. The New York Kehillah is an illustration of how it is done, and the American Jewish Committee is an illustration of the type of men who do it.

The work of the Kehillah is claimed to be "educational" by its defenders, on the few occasions when it is attacked. It is certainly that. The best educated members are those who come from the Eastern European ghettos where the Kehillah idea was fully understood and practiced and where Jewish - community - government exercised unrestricted sway. Whatever other phase of education the Kehillah may be interested in, it certainly stresses most the education to separateness. Dr. S. Benderley, director of the Bureau of Education, gave away the objects of the Kehillah "education" thus:

"The problem before us was to form a body of young Jews who should be on the one hand true Americans, a part of this Republic, with an intense interest in building up

American ideals; and yet, on the other hand, be also Jews in love with the best of their own ideals, and not anxious merely to merge with the rest and disappear among them. That problem confronts Orthodox and Reform Jews alike. It is not merely a religious but a civic problem."

That is separatism and exclusiveness as an educational program, and its result cannot help being training in ideas of racial superiority and exclusivism.

It is the Jews' unceasing consciousness of the "Goy" that constitutes the disease of Judaism, this centuries-long tradition of separateness. There is no such thing as "anti-Semitism." There is, however, much anti-Goyism. In all the countries of the world there is no anti-Arab sentiment of which anyone knows. None of the Semite people have been distinguished by the special dislike of any other people. There is no reason why anyone should dislike the Semites.

It is very strange, however, that the Semite people should be a unit in disliking the Jews. Palestine, which still only has a handful of Jews, is peopled by Semites who so thoroughly dislike the Jews that serious complications are threatening the Zionist advances being made there. This surely is not anti-Semitism. Semites are not against Semites. They are at odds with Jews.

When Aryan and Semite are kept conscious through many centuries that the Jew is another and superior race, and when it is known that neither Aryan nor Semite are touchy on the race question, what is the answer? Only this, that the whole substance of such a situation must be supplied by the Jews. There is no such thing as anti-Semitism. There is only a very little and a very mild anti-Jewism. But a study of Jewish publications, books, pamphlets, declarations, constitutions and charters, as well as a study of organized Jewish action in this and other countries, indicates that there is a tremendous amount of anti-Goyism, or anti-Gentilism.

Chapter 8: Jewish Influences in American Politics

Within the memory of even young men, Tammany Hall has been the synonym of all political trickery in the vocabulary of popular criticism. Tammany Hall was held up as the worst example of boss rule, political corruption, brute force, that it was possible to find in the world. Its very name became a stigma in the decades before the first world war. But even the most unobservant newspaper reader must have observed the gradual fading out of Tammany Hall from public comment, the cessation of the bitter criticism, the entire absence of headlines bristling with ugly charges, and the calling of the hosts of good citizenship to do battle against the grim bossism that maintained its headquarters in New York.

Why the change in recent years? Is it due to the dying out of Tammany Hall as a political force? No, Tammany Hall is still there, as any New York politician will tell you. The Tammany tiger has not changed its stripes.

There was a time when fearless publications told the truth about Tammany, but they have either gone out of existence or have fallen under control of the Jews. There was a time when public bodies like the Citizens' Union organized to oppose Tammany and to keep a volunteer vigil on its activities; these groups have succumbed to Jewish contributions and officership and no longer stand guard.

The outcry against Tammany seemed to be hushed the moment that Tammany patronage fell into the hands of the New York Jews, where it now remains, the Kehillah being the real political center, and Tammany but a distributing station - a sort of "Gentile front" for the more powerful Kehillah. The Judaization of Tammany is now complete, for the Irish element has been overcome by Jewish money.

Tammany was one of the strongest political organizations ever seen in the United States. Potent not only in municipal and state politics, but often exercising a decisive influence on national affairs. It was, without exaggeration, unequalled in any country in the world.

If there is one quality that attracts Jews, it is power. Wherever the seat of power may be, thither they swarm obsequiously. As Tammany was power and the gate of power, it was natural that the Jews of the biggest Jewish city in the world should court it. Doubtless, they were also affected by the incongruity of the fact that in the biggest

Jewish city, the most solid political power was non-Jewish.

When the German Jewish banker, Schoenberg, went to America under the name of August Belmont to represent the interests of the Rothschilds, his keen eye at once took in the situation. He became a member and supporter of Tammany. It was good business for this Jewish banker, because the funds of the Rothschilds were heavily invested in New York transport. The properties of city tractions are, as in all American cities, at the mercy of the local Tammany power, by whatever name it may be known. Belmont eventually attained the coveted eminence of Grand Sachem of the Tammany Society. Belmont-Schoenberg opened the way for the rest of the Jews; the Freedman's, Untermeyer's, Straus's; financiers, lawyers, politicians, business men and union sharks. There soon followed the wholesale appointment of Jews to the judiciary of New York until New York became a political and legal Jewish preserve; and onwards to the Supreme Court where Jewish influence never looked back since the now distant day of the Jewish capture of Tammany Hall.

It was necessary for a Jewry that planned to control the judiciary, as well as to provide special protection for certain Jewish enterprises that are near enough to the borderline of the law to merit question, it was necessary to obtain control of the supreme political engine through which favors are disbursed in local politics. The peculiar system of local, state and national government in the

United States made it easy for the control of such organizations to be gained by money.

The Jew's natural political home seems to be in the Republican Party, for thither he returns after venture elsewhere; but his predilection for the Republican Party does not move the Jew to make the mistake of being exclusively the partisan of one group. It is better, he knows, to control all groups. Strong as Jewry became in Tammany, it was even stronger in the ranks of the Republican Party, while New York socialism was, and is, completely headed and manned by Jews. This renders it extremely easy for the Jews to swing support in whichever direction they choose, and for Kehillah to fulfill any threat it may make. It also insures that any Jewish candidate on any ticket will be elected.

Because of the powerful Irish control of Tammany at the beginning, the Jews worked cautiously. The Kehillah adopted the ancient policy, not of putting forward their own people, but non-Jews who could be useful to Judah. The difference between pro-Jewish politicians who are not themselves Jews, and politicians of the Jewish race, is that the former can sometimes go further than the Jew in office can, without detection. Thus, in the early days of Tammany, indeed until just before World War I there was always a "Gentile front" in Tammany offices basking in the glory of Tammany publicity, but always in the background there was his "Jewish control." This is the formula for citizens who wish to know the meaning of things otherwise unexplained - "look for the 'Jewish control'." To this end, therefore, the Jews have been strong in all parties, so that whichever way the election went, the Jews would win. In New York it is always the Jewish party that wins. Whoever wins New York rules the Government.

As always election campaigns are staged as an entertainment, a diversion for the people; they are permitted to think and act as if they are really making their own government, but it is always the Jews that win. And if after having elected their man or group, obedience is not rendered to the Jewish control, then you speedily hear of "scandals" and "investigations" and "impeachments" for the removal of the disobedient.

Usually a man with a "past" proves the most obedient instrument, but even a good man can often be tangled up in campaign practices that compromise him. It has been commonly known that Jewish manipulation of American election campaigns have been so skillfully handled, that no matter which candidate was elected, there was ready made a sufficient amount of evidence to discredit him in case his Jewish masters needed to discredit him. To arrange this is part of the thoroughness of Jewish control. And, of course, the American people have been sufficiently trained to roar against the public official immediately the first Jewish hound emits its warning bay. Amazing as is the technique of the Jewish political process, the readiness with which the American people can be counted on to do their part in forwarding the game is still more amazing.

Aliens and Tammany Leadership

The strength of Tammany had exactly the same source as the strength of the Kehillah, namely, in the foreign population; the difference being that the Kehillah had a more compact foreign mass to draw upon. But both the Kehillah leaders and the Tammany leaders have always been alertly aware of the fact that their power depended upon an uninterrupted flow of immigration. It is always the foreigner that makes the best material for the Kehillah's purpose, until America became so thoroughly un-Americanized as to make intensive immigration no longer essential. It was only then that immigration began to slow down. The third great influx of immigration into the United States occurred in 1884 and was really the cause of the beginning of the degeneration of New York, and then of American political life. The great wave was composed of Russian, Austrian and Hungarian Jews, whose arrival was followed by a memorable period of crime, the marks of which remain to this day.

At that time the police department and the police courts before which all criminal cases in the city were first brought, were in the hands of Tammany Hall under the notorious Boss Croker. The result of the Jewish control was a partnership between local government and crime which has not been duplicated outside of Semitic countries. Immigrant Jews of the shadier type organized an association called The Max Hochstim Association, which was known as the "Essex Market Court Gang." One of its chief leaders was Martin Engel, Tammany leader of the Eighth District. The "king" of this Jewish district was a man named Solomon who had changed his name to the less revealing one of "Smith," and who became known as "Silver Dollar Smith," because of the fact that he ruled his little empire from the Silver Dollar Saloon. This saloon was just opposite the Essex Market Court, which was thronged daily by hordes of Yiddish criminals, the bondsmen, the false witnesses and lawyers. The Max Hochstim Association became the first organized White Slavery Group in America, and the revelations made by the United States Government Investigation Committee are shuddering exposures of that lowest form of depravity - a coolly conducted, commercialized, consolidated traffic in women. The traffic was made to yield dividends to politicians, to Tammany Jews in particular; it was during the official investigation that the Max Hochstim Association became known as the "Essex Market Court Gang." Out of the old police court in the "red light" Essex Market district, New York, comes a word which has fixed itself in common English speech. A lawyer named Scheuster, whose practices were quite characteristic, made himself very obnoxious to Justice Osborne. Whenever another Yiddish lawyer attempted a shady trick the judge would openly denounce it as "Scheuster practice," and so it came that the first men in the profession to bear the name of "shyster" were the Yiddish lawyers of Essex Market Court, New York.

Jews and The Write Slave Scandal

It is a surprising fact that, although these matters are written in official documents, and although the same matters have been written into the record of every similar investigation which has been made, Jewish leaders persist in denying that the leaders in this particular form of depravity are Jews. When the United States Government made a nation-wide investigation, it found and recorded the same facts. The New York Kehillah came into existence as a defense organization at a time when the exposure of the Jewish White Slave Traffic threatened to overwhelm the New York ghetto.

The exposure which resulted when the white people of New York finally succeeded in getting the forces of the law to function impartially for a little while, caused many of the implicated Jews to change their names. These names are now representative of some of the best Jewish families, whose concealed bar sinister is the fact that the foundation of the family fortune was laid in the red light districts. The Max Hochstim Association was not the only organization of its kind to be unearthed. Another was the New York Independent Benevolent Association, which was organized in 1896 by a party of Jewish white slave dealers. Gangs like these formed the backbone of Tammany power in the slum districts; their principal field of operations was the cheap dance halls, their cover the "benevolent associations" in the East Side, all run by Jewish leaders, chiefly Russian and Galician Jews, as the official report exposes. They were slavers as their forbears were in the days of Rome's decline; they were bootleggers before the days of prohibition; and they constituted a strong support of the international narcotic ring which to this day has defied the law by corrupting the officers of the law.

In the decade before the first world war, in seizing control and exploiting New York, the Jews made one of their cyclically recurring mistakes; they carried things too far with too high a hand. They survived the exposure, however, and retained their power. It is this Jewish tendency to boast and overdo that has always given the game away.

Superficial observers and writers have noted the recurrent protests against Jewish presumption and bumptiousness and have explained them as being recurrent spasms of a vile poison which is supposed to reside in the blood of the Gentile - the vile poison of anti-Semitism. That is, of course, the conventional Jewish propaganda explanation, and many Gentile clergy, writers and politicians innocently retail it; many other Gentile worshippers of Jewish money cynically connive at the treachery. It always breaks out after wars, say some of these writers. Why after wars? Because in wars the world sees more clearly than at other times the real purpose and personality of the Jew. Thus, it is not anti-Semitism that breaks out - it is Judaism, gross and exaggerated Semitism; and the serum that forms in the social body to encyst and control the germ of Judaism comes in the form of public exposure and protest. That serum is working now - the serum of publicity; and the Jewish program cannot endure it.

Study the history of all things whatsoever into which the Jews inject themselves, from summer resorts to empires, and you see the same cycle appearing.

The Jewish conquest of Tammany, however, is only one phase of the conquest of New York. The Jewish objective is more than political. Merely to insure that the lucrative and powerful officers of the city shall be their own people, is not the end in view. New York has been turned into the Red Center of America. There most of the alien treason carried on against the government of the United States has its source. Tammany is a convenient cover for ostensible political activity as the Kehillah is for the more radical racial and anti-American racial activity.

Chapter 9: Bolshevism and Zionism

Communism works in the United States through precisely the same channels as it used in Russia and through the same agents - Revolutionary and Predatory Unionism, as distinct from Business and Uplift Unionism, and Jewish agitators. When Martens, the so-called Soviet Ambassador, "left" the United States after being deported, he appointed as the representative of Communism in the United States one Charles Recht, a Jew, a lawyer by profession, who maintained an office in New York. This office was the rendezvous of all the Jewish labor union leaders in the city, many of the labor leaders throughout the country, and frequently of American government officials and other political leaders known to be the henchmen of Jewish aspirations in the United States and sympathizers with predatory radicalism. The organization has since spread from coast to coast, from north to south. The situation of Communist headquarters in New York was, and is, important because from that center lines of authority and action radiate to all the other cities of the Union. New York is the laboratory in which the emissaries of revolution learn their lesson, and their knowledge is daily increased by the counsel and experience of travelling delegates straight out of Russia.

American citizens do not realize that all the public disturbances, the labor differences, strikes and political confusions of which they read are not mere sudden outbreaks, but the deliberately planned movements of leaders who know exactly what they are doing.

Mobs are methodical; there is always an intelligent core which gets done under the appearance of excitement what has been planned beforehand. Up through the French Revolution, up through the German Revolution, up through the Russian Revolution, and the world disorders since, came the previously chosen men, and to this day the groups thus raised to power have not lessened their power - and they are Jewish groups. Russia is not more Jewish controlled than France; Germany tried in vain to loosen the grip of Judah from her throat. So it is in America.

The first step of the Jewish organizations supporting Communism in the United States was the control and expansion of the Hebrew labor movement among the millions of immigrants during 50 years; with the view to eventual Jewish control of all labor unions. The Jews have captured American trade union movements as completely as if they had stormed them with the bayonet.

There is a mass of moving literature (mostly written by Jews) pretending to describe the glowing hearts with which these alien throngs of liberty-loving-democrats, workers' comrades, look upon America, their intense longing for the "American way of life," their love of the people and American institutions. The actions of these people and the utterances of their leaders all too clearly give the lie to this fair picture which gullible American Gentiles would fain believe.

The resistance offered to the "American way of life," consisting in the limitations put on the Americanization program, has been sufficient to convince alert observers that, so far as the Jewish invasion is concerned, it is not their desire to go the way America is going, but to influence America to go the way they are going. They talk a great deal of what they bring to America but nothing at all of what they found there. America is presented to them as a big piece of putty to be molded as they desire. "The Melting Pot," a term which the Jewish writer Zangwill gave currency, is not a dignified name for the Republic, and it is more and more challenged as descriptive of the process that goes on. There are some substances in the pot that will not melt; but more significant still, there are rapidly increasing influences who want to melt the pot!

The two divisions of Jewish wealth and political power are - first, German Jewish, represented by the Schiffs, the Speyers, the Warburgs, the Kahns, the Lewisohns and the Guggenheims. These play the game with the aid of the financial resources of the non-Jews. The other division is composed of the Russian and Polish Jews who monopolize the lower ranks of trade and industry. Between them their grip and influence is absolute. They may sometimes have internecine quarrels regarding the division of the spoils, and eager publicists may zealously call attention to these quarrels as evidence of the utter lack of unity among the Jews, but in the Kehillah and elsewhere they understand each other quite well, and on the question of Jew vs. "goy" they are indivisibly one.

There is a distinction between what this Jewish coalition would do and what it could do, but its will and power never so closely correspond as when the non-Jewish element in the nation is asleep. Never are Jewish will and power so widely divorced as when the non-Jewish mind is alert. The only thing to fear is not the alert Jew, but the consequences of sleepiness among the Gentiles. The Jewish program is checked the moment it is perceived and identified.

Jewish-Red-Links

There are more Communists in the United States than there are in Soviet Russia. Their aim is the same and their racial character is the same. If they have not yet been able to do in America what they have done in Eastern Europe, it is because of the greater dissemination of information, the higher degree of intelligence, and particularly the wider diffusion of the agencies of government, than ever obtained in Russia and Eastern Europe. The power house of Communist influence and propaganda in the United States is in the Jewish trade unions which, almost without exception, adhere to a Bolshevik program for the respective industries and for the country as a whole. The fact proves most embarrassing to the Jewish leaders in the recognized political parties very frequently. It is bad enough that Russian Bolshevism, Communism, should be so predominantly Jewish, but to confront the same situation in the United States is a problem which Jewish leaders have to use much ingenuity and deception to explain away or avoid. Yet the International Jew of America cannot be absolved from bearing sole responsibility for it. Russian Bolshevism came out of the East Side of New York where it was fostered by the encouragement - the religious, moral and financial encouragement - of Jewish leaders.

Leon Trotsky (Braunstein) was an East Sider. The forces which fostered what he stood for centered in the Kehillah and the American Jewish Committee. Both were interested in the work he set out to do - the overthrow of an established government, one of the allies of the United States in World War One. Russian Bolshevism was helped to its objective by Jewish gold from the United States -

and by the ignorance and indolence of the Gentile citizens of the United States whose crimes of omission are almost as grave as those of bolshevik commission.

Now that the influence of Communism is found to be numerically stronger here than in Russia, the fact causes no little embarrassment to "patriotic" Jews. The big Jewish labor organizations are the direct offspring of the Jewish Socialist Bund of Russia. Bundists swarmed to the United States after the abortive revolution of 1905 at which time they failed to put Bolshevism over in Russia, and these Bundists gave their time to the Bolshevising of the Hebrew Trade Unions in America. An Agitation Bureau was formed which propagated radical Socialism through the medium of the Yiddish language. The Bundists incorporated in 1905 in New York an organization known as "The Workmen's Circle" and "swelled the ranks of the Jewish trade unions," to quote the Kehillah's Register. After a brief attempt to propagate Socialism without reference to the Jewish Question, it was given up, and in 1913 a resolution was adopted declaring that the whole purpose of the work was Jewish. This is attributed, in the Kehillah record, to the spread of "the idea of Jewish nationalism."

What amazes the student of the Jewish Question in the United States is the ingenuousness which permitted Jewish Bolshevism to flaunt itself so openly. The only explanation that seems at all adequate is that the Jews never dreamed that the American people would become sufficiently awake to challenge them. The occasional exposure of Jewish tactics in America comes as a surprise to the Jewish leaders, and is accounted for because they are confident they have gained too strong a grip on the American mind to make such challenges possible.

But, the Jewish leaders must admit that the Jewish Question does not consist in American citizens uncovering the facts and helping other citizens to become aware of them; the Jewish Question inheres in the facts themselves and in Jewish responsibility for the facts.

If it is "anti-Semitism" to say that Communism in the United States is Jewish, so be it; but to the unprejudiced mind it will look very like Americanism.

Will Jewish Zionism Bring Armageddon?

When the British Army passed into Jerusalem in the memorable capture of the city in 1917, the Protocols went in with it. A symbolic circle was thus closed, though not in the way the Protocolists had hoped. The man who carried the Protocols knew what they signified, and they were carried not in triumph but as the plans of the enemies of world liberty.

Zionism is the best advertised of all present Jewish activities and has exerted a greater influence upon world events than the average man realizes. In its more romantic aspects it makes an appeal to Christians as well as to Jews, because there are certain prophecies which are held to concern the return of the Jews to Jerusalem. When this return takes place, certain great events are scheduled to ensue.

Because of this admixture of the "religious" sentiment, it is sometimes difficult for a certain class of people to scrutinize modern Political Zionism. They have been too well propagandized into believing that political Zionism and the "return" promised by the prophets are the same thing. Having succumbed to the initial confusion of mistaking Judah for Israel they have entirely mistaken the ancient writings that relate to these two and have made the tribe of Judah (whence comes the name of Jew) the hub around which all history and humanity swing. Judah was the single tribe with which Israel could not live in peace over 2,000 years ago, and which has the baleful gift of stirring up the same kind of dissension today. Yet no one ever thought of charging the Ten Tribes of Israel with "anti-Semitism."

Zionism is challenging the attention of the world today because it is creating a situation out of which many believe the next war will come.

To adopt a phraseology familiar to students of prophecy, it is believed by many students of world affairs that Armageddon will be the direct result of what is now beginning to be manifested in Palestine.

With Zionism as a dream of pious Jews this investigation has nothing to do. With Zionism as a political fact, every government is now compelled to have something to do. It is a bigger question than any other world question, it lies back of all world problems, large or small, national or international, and is rapidly proceeding under cover of many other interests.

It is worthy of note that Zionism in the active modern political sense took its rise racially and geographically where Bolshevism arose, namely, in Russia, and that there was always a close relationship between the Zionists of Russia and the New York Kehillah, as was evidenced by public utterances made in Russia after the revolution in which the Kehillah was extolled.

At the time war was declared in 1914, the Zionist Inner Actions Committee was spread about in various countries. For example: Dr. Schmarya Levin, of Berlin, was in the United States and remained there. He was a Russian rabbi, German scholar, and cosmopolitan. Although, in 1914, the Zionist center and seat of Inner Actions Committee was at Berlin, he remained in the United States and became recognized as the leader of the leaders of Zionism, until the great Jewish shift to Versailles. Another member of the Inner Actions Committee was Jacobson, who was in Constantinople.

> "When he saw that Constantinople could no longer be a center of Zionist politics, he left and went to Copenhagen, Denmark, where in a neutral country he could be of practical usefulness to the Zionists by transmitting information and funds." ("Guide to Zionism," page 80).

In fact, the entire Inner Actions Committee, with headquarters in Berlin, moved freely through a war-locked world, the only two exceptions being Warburg and Hantke and there was no need for the Berlin Warburg to move about, for there were others who represented him.

Dr. Levin gave his sanction for the shifting of the center of Jewish gravity from Berlin to America, and "As early as August 80, 1914, a month after the outbreak of war, an extraordinary conference of American Zionists was called in New York."

What this change of seat meant, has formed the subject of much discussion. In 1914 the Jews apparently knew more about the probable duration of the Great War than did the principals. It was not to be a mere excursion through Belgium, as some fancied. There was time to dicker, time to show the value of certain Jewish support to the governments. Germany gladly pledged the land of Palestine to the Jews, but the Jews had already seen what Wilhelm II had done in that ancient country when he enthroned himself on the Mount of Olives. Evidently the Allies won in the contest of making promises and submissions to Jewry, for on November 2, 1917, when General Allenby was pushing up through Palestine with his British Army, Arthur James Balfour, the British Foreign Secretary, issued the famous declaration approving Palestine as a national home for the Jewish people.

> "The wording of it came from the British Foreign Office, but the text had been revised in the Zionist offices in America as well as in England. The British Declaration was made in the form in which the Zionists desired it, and the last clauses were added in order to appease a certain section of timid anti-Zionist opinion." ("Guide to Zionism,"

pp. 85-86.)

Now read the Declaration and note the italicized clauses just referred to:

> "His Majesty's Government view with favor the establishment in Palestine of a national home for the Jewish people and will use their best endeavors to facilitate the achievement of this object, it being clearly understood that nothing will be done which may prejudice the civil and religious rights of non-Jewish communities in Palestine, or the rights and political status enjoyed by Jews in any other country."

Zionism is of particular interest, not merely because of the quarrels which have arisen among the leaders over money - it is the war of "interest" against "capital" - but also because of the light it throws on the two great armies of Jews in the world, the way in which they use their power where they can, and the trouble that always embroils the nations which become Jewish tools.

People sometimes ask why Jewry. which is capitalistic, should favor Bolshevism, which is the announced enemy of capital.

It is an interesting question. Why should a New York Jewish financier, an officer of the government of the United States, help finance a "Red" publication which even our tolerant government cannot stomach? In addition to the fact that it is only "Gentile capital" that is attacked, the answer is that the Jew who has fallen for the worship of the Golden Calf is anxious to keep in the good graces of the Jew of the East - the Mongolian Jews - who are rampaging against orderly systems of society. It quite useful when there is a revolution in Paris to have 600 houses which you may own spared by the incendiary mobs - as were Rothschild's houses. Zionism has been one of the subjects upon which Western and Eastern Jews can unite.

Indeed, it was the Eastern Jew that compelled the Western Jew to take a favorable stand on the matter. The Jews who are receiving the freedom of our cities today in their various aspects as "German" and "British" scientists are Eastern Jews. They have come to a contest with the Jews of America on the question of Money. The Jews of America have smothered some very ugly charges. The Jews of the East, more recently of Germany or England, are not likely to be browbeaten by the money-bags of Jewish New York, for the Eastern type of Jew knows of a situation in which money is the most useless thing in the world - and that is why he is feared and favored by Western Jewry of the Golden Calf.

Cunning Jewish defenders occasionally capitalize the "split" in Jewry. There is no such thing. The real split in Jewry will come if and when Jews of vision begin to support the attempts which have been made to liberate the Jews from their leaders. This internal squabble means nothing but the squabble of leaders; but when the Jews themselves divide, one side for twentieth century light and the destruction of the power of selfish leaders, then we may begin to hope. When the Jew recognizes the honesty of his critics and the righteousness of what they charge, when the Jew advances in civilization then there may be a "split," but not before. The division in Jewry as evidenced by the contempt of the revolutionary party for the financial party, and as even more strongly evidenced by the fear of the revolutionary party by the financial party, was brought about by the earlier insincerity of the Western Jew's Zionism. The Western Jew said that the United States is the Promised Land, profits and interest are the "milk and honey" and New York is Jerusalem; the Eastern Jew had another view.

A knowledge of Political Zionism is essential also as an authoritative illustration of what the Jew does when he is in power. Heretofore there has been Russia to illustrate this, but now there is Palestine. With every fact against them, with every traveler and observer giving them the lie direct, there are still Jewish spokesmen and poor befuddled "Gentile fronts," as well as corrupt Gentile politicians and writers, who insist that Communism is not Jewish and that Russia is not governed by Jews. It is just this constant denial of facts, this failure to use their opportunity to be honest, that is going to be the judgment of Jewish leaders. Communism all over the world, not in Russia only, is Jewish.

More to the present point is Palestine, where the unity of revolutionary and financial Jewry is never more clearly established. It is impossible for the most irresponsible Jewish spokesman to deny that Palestine is Jewish. The government is Jewish, the plan of procedure is Jewish, the methods are Jewish. Palestine will do to illustrate the genius of the Jew when he comes to power.

Professor Albert T. Clay, in the "Atlantic Monthly" (will anyone declare that this long-established and thoroughly respectable Boston publication is "anti-Semitic"?) warns us that the information about Palestine which we receive in America comes to us through the Jewish Telegraph Service (which is the Associated Press of worldwide Jewry) and the Zionist propaganda.

> "The latter," he says, "with its harrowing stories of pogroms in Europe, and its misrepresentations of the situation in the Near East, has been able to awaken not a little sympathy for the Zionist propaganda."

This propaganda of pogroms - "thousands upon thousands of Jews killed" - amounts to nothing except as it illustrates the gullibility of the Press. No one believes this propaganda and governments regularly disprove it. But the fact that it continues indicates that something besides the facts is necessary to keep the scheme going. In Jerusalem as this is being written (1921: Ed.) martial law is proclaimed. There has been a struggle between the native inhabitants, whom the Balfour Declaration sought to protect, and the new-come Jews. The Jews were well armed and the natives fought with whatever weapons they could find on the spot; the conclusion of all impartial observers being that the Jews prepared for and sought the fight with unprepared Arabs.

The mark of disorder perpetrated by the Jews is all over the place, the "persecuted" turned persecutor, and lest this should be charged to the general wildness of the people in Palestine let it be said that the Jewish rioters (most of whom are thugs from Eastern Europe) are only expressing in deeds what the "cultivated" American and English Jews have expressed in words - namely, that the lawful inhabitants of the land ought to be driven out, in spite of governmental promises to the contrary. One of the first rioters during that bloody Easter after World War I, Jabotinsky, whom the British authorities sentenced to 15 years in prison, was released immediately on the arrival of the Jew Sir Herbert Samuel. Jabotinsky was one of the original Russian Bolsheviks come down to practice the gentle arts of that tribe in Palestine. The Government of Palestine since the British occupation was, and is, Jewish. Sir Herbert Samuel was the British High Commissioner, representing the power of the British Government which took up the Mandate for Palestine. This founded the Jewish power which has been maintained and increased to its present virulent state. The head of the judicial department was also a Jew. Christian or Moslem judges who did not give the Jew a shade the better of the proceedings were ousted - a condition familiar in New York. Chaim Weizmann became head of the Department of Works, and later emerged as the successor to Levin as the leader of Zionism. The Jewish government of the "new Palestine" was very much like that of Bolshevik Russia - mostly foreign. Practically every big American city was represented in the first Bolshevik government of Russia. There is another full-fledged government waiting in America for service whenever necessary.

Land-Grabbing

The methods adopted to get the land of Palestine away from the Arabs in the early days of the Zionist invasion were such as will fill the world with indignation once the world is permitted to know what was done. That it was done with the knowledge and approval of Zionist Commissioner Samuel is indicated by the fact that he suspended the activities of a British officer who endeavored to stop the abuse. It was the old game of lending money at exorbitant rate of interest to Arabs hard pressed by the ravages of war and crop failure, and then seizing their land when they could not pay. The bank that did this was the Anglo-Palestine Bank, a Zionist concern. This British officer, to save the people and the land, made arrangements with a British bank to lend them money at 6.5% with five years to pay. If payment failed, the land was to go to the government for redistribution, not to the Zionist bank. This was the humane plan which the Zionist High Commissioner forbade, whereupon the British officer resigned. The well-considered action of Jewry in power.

Then follows what is described by every impartial observer as an arrogant attempt to expropriate everything in sight. The only schools that had been established in Jerusalem had been built and manned by the Gentiles, although the tiny group of Jews permanently resident in Jerusalem have been the pensioners of world-wide Jewry for centuries. As long ago as 1842 Dr. Murray M'Cheyne noted that the Jerusalem Jews cared nothing for the schools, but Christians with a warm regard for the Holy City set about to improve the miserable condition of the Jewish inhabitants. Thus it came that at the time of the Zionist invasion a considerable number of Jewish children were in attendance at the schools. The new-come Zionist leaders demanded that the best of the schools be given up to them. Of course, this was refused. "The Council of Jerusalem Jews" then caused it to be published in the Hebrew daily that parents who did not withdraw their children from the schools would be punished. Now look at the typical punishments threatened:

(i) If any parent refused whose name was on the list of the American Relief Fund, the relief would be withdrawn.

(ii) Doctors would be forbidden to visit families that had children attending the enlightened schools.

(iii) Their names would be sent to the black-list at the places where circumcision was performed, so that new-born descendants of the recalcitrants might be refused the rites of Moses.

(iv) They would be denied all share in Zionist benefits or funds.

(v) If they were in business they would be boycotted.

(vi) If they were workmen, they could get no work.

> "Anyone who refused, let him know that it was forbidden for him to be called by the name of Jew. They will be fought by all lawful means. Their names will be put upon a monument of shame and their deeds made to reproach them to the last generation. If they are supported, their support will cease. If they are rabbis, they will be removed from office. They shall be put under the ban and persecuted, and all the world will know that in this justice there has been no mercy."

It is the spirit of Jewish Bolshevism all over again. It is tyranny, not the tyranny of strength, but of meanness and darkness. It is the spirit which produced the Irgun terrorism, the Jewish hatred, malice and vengeance which lurks for all critics of Jewry and opponents of Zionist ambitions.

This spirit which obtained at the beginning of a movement, which the innocent Christian world has been taught by propaganda to regard as a profoundly religious and respectable exodus, explains all that has happened in the years since the Zionists took over Palestine. It staggers the imagination to forecast what will be done in a period of full and unquestioned rule.

It is very clear that Jewish nationalism will develop along the line of enmity to the rest of the world.

There are three elements of danger in the situation: the overwhelming predominant Bolshevist element that is being poured into Palestine; the intense, egotistic and challenging nationalism that Zionists exhibit even before they get a potato patch - the taste for world politics and world power; and the racial confusion which now exists in Palestine.

These combined are dynamite. The first is more vital than many realize. The few Jews who have gone to Palestine at great sacrifice and for pious reasons are complaining that instead of the Psalms of David the people are singing songs of the Red Revolution, and instead of meeting for instruction and prayer there are riotous gatherings extolling Russian leaders as Messiahs and the Soviet as the Kingdom of Heaven.

Palestine has been called the center of the earth. The power that controls Palestine controls the world. Although exercising no sovereignty over the land itself, Great Britain's control of adjacent waters and of Egypt and Persia and India forms the key of her power.

The white race has thus far been the Chosen People to whom dominion of the earth has been given. Palestine is the key to world military strategy and trade. In question 12 of the Questions and Answers published by the department Education, Zionist Organization of America, this occurs:

12. What are the commercial possibilities of Palestine? The location of Palestine between three continents favors foreign trade.

All this lends itself to dreams of future glory, as do the unlimited mineral and oil resources of Palestine estimated by scientists in astronomical figures.

Many Christian friends of the Jew have pleased themselves by conceiving a universal Hague at Jerusalem and a new social order going out to bless the nations from Zion. It is the idea conveyed by men like A. A. Berle in books like "The World Significance of a Jewish State."

Americans do not understand the delicate racial situation in Palestine. Zionist propaganda has always been accepted on the assumption that Palestine is the Jews' land and that they only need help to go back. It is an historical and political fact that Palestine has not been the Jew's land for more than 2,000 years - and then for only a brief while. At the close of the 1914-1918 war there were in Palestine over 600,000 Arabs and only 50,000 Jews. Neither numerically nor industrially have the Jews held the land. Yet as the result of a "war bargain" it is handed over to them as regardless of the native inhabitants as if Belgium had been handed over to Mexico. Many of thc natives are Semites, like the Jews, but they do not want the Jews among them. The Balfour Declaration, as well as the terms of the Mandate, recognized the rights of the native races. Everyone who knows about the people who have been native to Palestine for thousands of years recognizes their right, everybody except the Jews.

It is now that the last clauses, added as the Zionist historian declares, "in order to appease a certain section of timid anti-Zionist opinion?' begin to get a meaning for the reader.

Was the purpose only to quiet disturbing questions until all the arrangements were made? Evidently. It was then a dishonest appeasement! Such may have been the Zionists' intention, but no one expects perjury on the part of the responsible nations.

General Allenby promised the native Arabs of Palestine that their rights would be respected. So did the Balfour Declaration. So did the San Remo Conference. So also did President Wilson in the twelfth of his Fourteen Points. But Judah says, "Let them get out!" "The last clauses were added in order to appease a certain section of timid anti-Zionist opinion." "Let them give up their land to us, we want it!" The delightful Jewishness of it! The watchmen on the towers of the world are alarmed at what is brewing in Judah's cauldron.

Chapter 10: Jewish Supremacy in Theatre and Cinema

The Theater has long been a part of the Jewish program for the guidance of public taste and the influencing of the public mind. Not only is the theater given a special place in the program of the Protocols, but it is the instant ally night by night and week by week of any idea which the "power behind the scenes" wishes to put forth. It is not by accident that in Russia, where they now have scarcely anything else, they still have the Theater, specially revived, stimulated and supported by Jewish-Bolshevists because they believe in the Theater just as they believe in the Press; it is one of the two great means of molding popular opinion.

Not only the "legitimate" stage, so-called, but the motion picture industry - the fifth greatest of all industries - is also entirely Jew-controlled; with the natural sequence that the civilized world is increasingly antagonistic to the trivializing and demoralizing influence of that form of entertainment as at present managed.

As soon as the Jew gained control of American liquor, we had a liquor problem with drastic consequences. As soon as the Jew gained control of the "movies" we had a movie problem, the consequences of which are visible.

It is the peculiar genius of that race to create problems of a moral character in whatever business they achieve a majority.

Every night hundreds of thousands of people give from two to three hours to the Theater, every day literally millions of people give up from 30 minutes to 8 hours to the "Movies"; and this simply means that millions of Americans every day place themselves voluntarily within range of Jewish ideas of life, love and labor; within close range of Jewish propaganda, sometimes cleverly, sometimes clumsily concealed. This gives the Jewish masseur of the public mind all the opportunity he desires; and his only protest now is that exposure may make his game a trifle difficult.

The Theater is not only Jewish on its managerial side, but also on its literary and professional side. More and more plays are appearing whose author, producer, star and cast are entirely Jewish (vaudeville-music hall-performers are predominantly Jewish). They are not great plays, they do not last long. This is natural enough, since the Jewish theatrical interests are not seeking artistic triumphs, they are not seeking the glory of the American stage, nor are they striving to develop great actors. Their interest is solely financial and racial. There is a tremendous Judaizing movement on. The work is almost complete. The American feel has gone out of the Theater; a dark, Oriental atmosphere has come instead.

Down to 1885 the American Theater was still in the hands of the Gentiles; from that year dates the first invasion of Jewish influence. This date almost coincides with the beginning of the organization and co-ordination of the Jewish world scheme for domination called Zionism, and this year marks not only the beginning of the Jewish wedge of control, but something far more important.

It is not important that theater and music hall managers are now Jews whereas they were formerly Gentiles. The importance begins with the fact that with the change of managers there came also a decline in the art and morals of the stage, and that this decline became accelerated as the Jewish control became widespread. Jewish control means that everything has been deliberately and systematically squeezed out of the American Theater except its most undesirable elements, and these undesirable elements have been exalted to the highest place of all. The Great Age of the American Theater is past, the Great Actors have passed, and they have left no successors. A Hebrew hand fell on the stage, and the natural genius of the stage was not welcome. A new form of worship was to be established.

"Shakespeare spells ruin," was the utterance of a Jewish manager. "High-brow stuff" (meaning anything not salacious) is also a Jewish expression. These two sayings, one appealing to the managerial end, the other to the public end of the Theater, have formed the epitaph of the classic era.

The present-day average intelligence appealed to in the Theater does not rise above 13 to 18 years. "The tired business man" stuff (another Jewish expression) has treated the theater-going public as if it were composed of morons. The appeal is frankly to a juvenile type of mind which can easily be molded to the ideas of the Hebraic theatrical monopoly.

Clean, wholesome, constructive plays - the few that remain - are supported mainly by the rapidly vanishing race of theatergoers who survive from an earlier day, and by those younger people whose minds have been shielded by these survivors from the contamination of the Jewish theater.

The great majority of the present generation has been educated to support plays of an entirely different type. Tragedy is taboo; the play of character, with a deeper significance than would delight the mind of a child, is out of favor; the comic opera has degenerated into a flash of color and movement - a combination of salacious farce and jazz music, supplied by a Jewish songwriter (the great purveyors of jazz) and the rage is for extravaganza and burlesque. The bedroom farce has been exalted into the first place, the historical drama has given way to fleshly spectacles set off with overpowering scenic effects, the principal component of which is an army of girls whose drapery does not exceed five ounces in weight.

Frivolity, sensuality, indecency, appalling illiteracy and endless platitude are the marks of the degenerate American Theater under Jewish control.

That, of course, is the real meaning of all the "Little Theater" movements which have begun in so many cities and towns in the United States. The art of the drama, having been driven out of the theater by the Jews, is finding a home in thousands of study circles throughout the country. The people cannot see real plays; therefore, they read them. The plays that are acted could not be read at all, for the most part, any more than the words of the jazz songs can be read; they don't glean anything. The people who want to see real plays and cannot, because Jewish managers won't produce them, are forming little dramatic clubs of their own, in barns and churches and schools. The drama fled from exploiters and has found a home with its friends.

Mechanics and Fake "Stars"

The major changes which the Jews have made in the theater are four in number. First, they have elaborated the mechanical side, making human talent and genius less necessary. They have made the stage "realistic" instead of interpretative. Great actors needed very little machinery; the men and women on the pay rolls of the Jewish managers are helpless without machinery. The outstanding fact about the vast majority of present day performances of any pretension is that the mechanical part dwarfs and obscures the acting: and this is the reason - knowing that the Jewish policy is death to talent, the Jewish producer prefers to put his faith and his money in wood, canvas, paint, cloth and tinsel. Wood and paint never show contempt for his sordid ideals and his betrayal of his trust. Thus we have in the theater today dazzling effects of light and motion - but no ideas. A great many stage employees, but no actors, drills and dances without end, but no drama. The Jew has put in the glitter but he has taken out the profounder ideas. Second, the Jews have introduced Oriental sensuality to the stage. The mark of the filthy tide has risen until it has engulfed the whole theater. In New York, where Jewish managers are thicker than they ever will be in Jerusalem, the limit of theatrical adventures into the realm of the forbidden is being pushed further and further. The sale of narcotics is illegal, but the instilling of moral poison is not. The whole atmosphere of "cabaret" and "midnight frolic" entertainment is of Jewish origin and importation. Montmarte has nothing at all in the nature of lascivious entertainment that New York cannot duplicate. But, neither New York nor any other American city has that Comédie Française which strives to counterbalance the evil of cosmopolitan Paris. Where have the writers for the

Stage a single chance in this welter of sensuousness? Where have the actors of tragic or comic talent a chance in such productions? It is the age of the chorus girl, a voluptuous creature whose mental caliber has nothing to do with the concern of drama, and whose stage life cannot in the very nature of things be a career.

A third consequence of Jewish domination of the American stage has been the appearance of the "Star" system, with its advertising appliances. The Theater is swamped in numerous "stars" that never really rose and certainly never shone, but which were hoisted high on the advertising walls of the Jewish theatrical syndicates in order to give the public the impression that these feeble lantern lights were in the highest heaven of dramatic achievement. The trick is a department store trick. It is sheer advertising strategy. Whereas in normal times a discriminating public made the "star" by their acclaim, nowadays the Jewish managers determine by their advertisements who the star shall be.

The Jew seeks immediate success in all but racial affairs. In the breakdown of the Gentile theater, success cannot be too swift for him. The training of artists takes time. It is far simpler to have the advertisement bills, the venal critics of the Press, serve as a substitute. The Jewish manager of the day diverts attention from the dramatic poverty of the theater by throwing confetti, limbs, lingerie and spangles dazzlingly into the eyes of his audience.

Rise of The Jewish Theatrical Trust

These three disastrous results of Jewish control of the Theater are all explained by a fourth; the secret of the change is found in the Jewish passion to commercialize everything it touches. The focus of attention has been shifted from the Stage to the box office. The banal policy of "give the public what they want" is the policy of the panderer and not that of creative genius. It entered the theater with the first Jewish invasion in 1885, when two alert Jews established in New York a so-called booking-agency and offered to take over the somewhat cumbersome system by which managers of theaters in the big but distant towns in the country arranged engagements for the ensuing season. The old process involved extensive correspondence with producing managers in the East and many local managers were obliged to spend several months in New York to make up a season's bookings. The advantage of a central booking concern relieved local managers of much time, labor and thought, all details were handled for him and his next season's bookings were arranged for him. In this manner was laid the foundation of the later day Theatrical Trust. The booking firm which gave birth to the iron control of the theater was that of Klaw & Erlanger. This is the key to the whole problem of the decline of the American stage. The rise of the Theatrical Trust completed the destruction of the personal touch in their relationship between manager and company. The old "personal" system made possible the development of genius in accordance with the organic laws which determine its nurture, growth and fruition.

The fact of Jewish control of the theater is not itself a ground for complaint. If certain Jews, working separately or in groups, have succeeded in wrenching this rich business from its former Gentile control, that is purely a matter of commercial interest. It is precisely on the same footing as if one group of Gentiles had won the control from another group of Gentiles. In this, as in other business matters, however, there is the ethical test of how the control was gained and how it is used. Society is usually willing to receive the fact of control with equanimity, providing the control is not used for anti-social purposes.

The fact that the old-time Gentile producing managers usually died poor while Jewish producing managers wax immensely rich would indicate that the Gentile managers were better artists and poorer business men than the Jewish managers. At least poorer business men, perhaps; and in any case working on a system whose chief object was to produce plays not merely profits.

The advent of Jewish control put the theater on a more commercialized basis than it had previously known. It really represented applying the Trust Idea of the theatre before it had been largely applied to industry.

The early control of theaters in strategic cities, the block booking agencies for artists and productions, and the running out of business of the independent theaters and stock companies by excessive charges for plays that had already been used in the regular theaters of the Trust, really served Jewish interests in another way. The motion picture industry was coming to the front. It was a Jewish enterprise from the first. There was never any need to drive the Gentiles out of that, because the Gentiles never had a chance to get in. Thus the driving out of the independent theater manager and the stock companies threw the empty theaters over to the "movies" and the benefit was again confined to a racial group.

The Theatrical Trust, which began as Jewish, was at the beginning of the twentieth century in full control of the field. It reduced what was essentially an art to a timeclock, cash-register system, working with the precision of a well-controlled factory. It suppressed individuality, initiative, killed off competition, drove out the independent manager and the natural genius, excluded all but foreign playwrights of established reputations, fostered the popularity of inferior talent which was predominantly Jewish, foisted countless "stars" of mushroom growth upon a helpless public while driving real artists into obscurity; it handled plays, theaters and actors, like factory products and began a process of vulgarizing and commercializing everything connected with the theater.

Critics "Controlled"

It is quite possible that many who read this are not interested in the theater, and are, in fact, convinced that the theater and cinema are a menace. But, what principally makes these things a menace? This - that the stage and cinema today represent the principal cultural element of 90 per cent of the people. What the average young person absorbs as to good form, proper deportment, refinement as contrasted with coarseness, correctness of speech or choice of words, customs and feelings of other nations, fashion of clothes, ideas of religion and law, are derived from what is seen at the cinema and theater. The masses' sole idea of home and life of the rich is derived from the stage and the movies.

More wrong notions are given, more prejudices created by the Jewish controlled theater-cinema in one week than can be charged against a serious study of the Jewish Question in a century. People sometimes wonder where the ideas of the younger generation come from - this is the answer.

The Jewish control of the public mind was not gained without opposition, but one by one the defenders of the American tradition were beaten or surrendered to overwhelming influences. The Jewish Theatrical Trust was attacked by the Editor of the New York "Dramatic Mirror" as far back as December 25, 1897. He was the famous dramatic critic Harrison Grey Fiske. He wrote:

"What then should be expected of a band of adventurers of infamous origin, of no breeding and utterly without artistic taste? Let it be kept in mind that the ruling number of these men who compose the Theatrical Trust are absolutely unfit to serve in any but the most subordinate places in the economy of the stage, and that they ought not to be tolerated even in these places except under a discipline, active, vigorous and uncompromising. Their records are disreputable and in some cases criminal, and their methods are in keeping with their records."

Fiske's article was reprinted in March, 1898. The Jews, of course, acted as one man as is always the case when one Jew is censured for wrong doing or when one group of Jews are exposed for malpractices. All the Jews in the United States came to the rescue of the Theatrical Trust. Pressure was brought to bear on news companies which handled the circulation of magazines in the United States. Leading hotels were induced to withdraw the "Dramatic Mirror" from their newsstands. "Mirror" correspondents were refused admittance to theaters controlled by the Trust. Any number of underground influences were set in operation to "get" Fiske and his business.

Libel suits were brought against Fiske for gigantic damages for the strictures he had printed upon the personal characters of members of the Trust. For once the Trust members came off badly. They were revealed to be a much lower type of men than the American public had supposed was in charge of the American theater.

The fight of the dramatic critics, first against the bribery and then against the bludgeoning of the Theatrical Trust makes a story of which echoes have frequently come to the public through the Press. Conciliatory at first, with managers, actors, playwrights and critics, the Trust, as soon as it gained power, showed its claws beneath the velvet. It had millions of dollars of the public coming its way, why should it care? Whenever a critic opposed its methods or pointed out the inferior, coarse and degrading character of the Trust productions, he was barred from the Trust's theaters, and local managers were instructed to demand his discharge from his newspaper. In almost every case the demand was complied with, the papers being threatened with the loss of advertising. In all the years since, the Trust has hounded and black-listed critics who tell the truth and have prevented their employment by newspaper.

The rage of the day is not plays but playhouses. The theatrical business entered upon its real estate phase with the coming of the Trust. There is money in renting chairs at the rate of 1 to 3 dollars an hour. The renting of chairs is a reality. The Stage has become an illusion, since it came under the influence and control of a group of former bootblacks, newsboys, ticket speculators, prize ring habitués, and Bowery characters.

The public does not see and does not know these gods before whom they pour their millions yearly, nor does the public know from what Source theatrical vileness comes. It is painful to listen to fledgling philosophers discuss the "tendencies of the stage," or expiate learnedly on the "divine right of Art," to be as flippant and filthy as it pleases, when all the time the "tendency" and "art" is determined by men whose antecedents would make Art scream.

The Theatrical Trust does not exist in the form it did ten years ago; it grew arrogant and bred secret enemies among its own people. A new force arose, but it was also Jewish. Instead of one, the American people now have a dual dictatorship of the stage.

It is perfectly natural that the complete Judaization of the theater should result in its being transformed into the "show business," a mere matter of trade and barter. The producers are often not equipped culturally for anything more than the baldest business. They can hire what they want, mechanics, costumers, painters, writers, musicians. With their gauge of public taste and their models of action formed upon the race track and the prize ring; with their whole ideal modeled upon the ambition to pander to depravity, instead of serving legitimate needs, it is not surprising that the standards of the Theater should now be at their lowest mark.

The Jewish manager whenever possible employs Jewish actors and actresses. Gentile playwrights and actors are steadily diminishing in number for want of a market. The "cover name" conceals from the public that the actors and actresses who purvey "entertainment" are, in large and growing proportion, Jewish.

The All-Jewish "Movies"

Jews did not invent the art of motion picture photography; they have contributed next to nothing to its mechanical or technical improvement; they have not produced any of the great artists, either writers or actors, which have furnished the screen with its genuine material. Motion photography, like most other useful things in the world, is of non-Jewish origin. But by the singular destiny which has made the Jews the greatest cream-skimmers of the world, the benefit of it has not gone to the originators, but to the usurpers, the exploiters. When millions of people crowd through the doors of the movie houses at all hours of the day and night, literally an unending line of human beings in every habitable comer of the land, it is worth knowing who draws them there, who acts on their minds while they quiescently wait in the darkened theater, and who really controls the massive bulk of human force and ideas generated and directed by the suggestions of the screen.

Who stands at the apex of this mountain of control? It is stated in the sentence: The motion picture influence of the United States, of the whole world, is exclusively under the control, moral and financial, of the Jewish manipulators of the public mind.

The moral side of the movies' influence is now a world problem. Everybody who has an active moral sense is convinced as to what is being done and as to what ought to be done. It is a business that frankly brutalizes taste and demoralizes morals and should not be permitted to be a law unto itself. But the propaganda side of the movies does not so directly declare itself to the public. That the movies are recognized as a tremendous propagandist institution is proved by the eagerness of all sorts of causes to enlist them. There is ample evidence that the Jewish promoters have not overlooked that end of it. This propaganda as at present observed may be described under the following heads: It consists in silence about the Jew as an ordinary being. Jews are not shown upon the stage and screen except in unusually favorable situations. This ill-concealed propaganda of the Jewish movie picture control is also directed against non-Jewish religions. A Jewish rabbi is never depicted on the screen in any but the most honorable attitude. He is clothed with all the dignity of his office and he is made as impressive as can be. Christian clergymen, as any movie "fan" will readily recall, are often subjected to all sorts of misrepresentation, from the comic to the criminal. This attitude is distinctly Jewish. Like many unlabeled influences in our life, whose sources lead back to Jewish groups, the object is to break down as far as possible all respectful or considerate thought about the clergy.

The Catholic clergy very soon made themselves felt in opposition to this abuse of their priestly dignity, and as a result of their vigorous resentment the Jew climbed down. You now never see a priest made light of on the screen. But the Protestant clergyman is still the elongated, sniveling, bilious hypocrite of anti-Christian caricatures. He is made to justify his deeds by appeals to "broad" principles - which really kills two birds with one stone; it degrades the representative of religion in the eyes of the audience, and at the same time it insidiously inoculates the audience with the same dangerous ideas. A Hebrew may not be depicted on the screen as the owner of a sweat shop - though all sweat shop owners are Jews; but you may make a Christian clergyman anything from a seducer to a safe-cracker - and get away with it. Remembering what is written in the Protocols, a question arises. It is written:

> "We have misled, stupefied and demoralized the youth of the Gentiles by means of education in principles and theories, patently false to us, but which we have inspired."
> -- Protocol 9: "We have taken good care long ago to discredit the Gentile clergy."
> - Protocol 17: "It is for this reason that we must undermine faith, eradicate from the minds of the Gentiles the very principles of God and Soul, and replace these conceptions by mathematical calculations and material desires."
> -- Protocol 4: "Two possible views are open to choice: one, that this caricature of representatives of religion is simply that natural expression of a worldly state of mind; the other, that it is part of a traditional campaign of subversion. The former is the natural view among uninformed people. It would be the preferable view, if peace of mind were the object sought. But there are far too many indications that the second view is justified, to permit of its being cast aside."

The screen, whether consciously or just carelessly, is serving as a rehearsal stage for scenes of anti-social menace. There are no uprisings of revolutions except those that are planned and rehearsed. Revolutions are not spontaneous uprisings, but carefully planned minority actions. There have been few popular revolutions. Civilization and liberty have always been set back by those revolutions which subversive elements have succeeded in starting. Successful revolution must have a rehearsal. It can be done better in the motion pictures than anywhere else: this is the "visual education" such as even the lowest brow can understand. Indeed, there is a distinct disadvantage in being "high-brow" in such matters. Normal people shake their heads and pucker their brows and wring their hands, saying, "We cannot understand it." Of course, they cannot. But if they understood the low-brow, they would understand it, and very clearly. There are two families in this world, and on one the darkness dwells.

Reformers, of course, heartily agree with this as far as criminal portrayals are concerned. Police protest against the technique of killing a policeman being shown with careful detail on the screen. Business men object to daily lessons in safe-cracking being given in the pictures. Moralists object to the art of seduction being made the stock motif no matter what the subject. They object because they recognize it as evil schooling which bears bitter fruits in society. This kind of "visual education" is going on; there is now nothing connected with violent outbreaks which has not been put into the minds of millions by the agency of the motion pictures. It may be, of course, a mere coincidence. But coincidences are also realities.

There are other developments in "screendom" which are worthy of mention. One is the increasing use of non-Jewish authors to produce Jewish propaganda. Popular non-Jewish authors' books have been screened by Jewish producers and they are more effective as such propaganda because they are backed by non-Jewish names famous in the literary world. How much of it is due to the authors' desire to enter the field of pro-Semitic propaganda, and how much of it is due to their reluctance to refuse amiable suggestions from movie magnates who have already paid them liberal sums and are likely to pay them more, is another question.

With the "movie bug" so rampant in the country, it is next to impossible to supply enough good pictures for the stimulated and artificial demand. Some people's appetite calls for two or more pictures a day. Shallow pated women see them in the afternoon and several more at night. With all the brains and skill of the country engaged on the task it would be impossible to supply a fresh drama or comedy of quality, hot out of the studios every hour, like bread. Where the Jewish controllers have overstepped themselves is here: they have over-stimulated a demand which they are not able to supply, except with such material as is bound to destroy the demand. Nothing is more dangerous to the social value of the motion picture business than an exaggerated appetite for them, and this appetite is whetted and encouraged until it becomes a mania.

Chapter 11: Jewish Jazz Becomes Our National Music

Many people have wondered whence come the waves upon waves of musical slush that invade decent homes and set the young people of this generation imitating the drivel of morons. Popular music is a Jewish monopoly. Jazz is a Jewish creation. The mush, slush, the sly suggestion, the abandoned sensuousness of sliding notes, are of Jewish origin.

Monkey talk, jungle squeals, grunts and squeaks and gasps suggestive of calf love are camouflaged by a few feverish notes and admitted in homes where the thing itself, unaided by scanned music," would be stamped out in horror. The fluttering music sheets disclose expressions taken directly from the cesspools of modern capitals, to be made the daily slang, the thoughtlessly hummed remarks of school boys and girls.

Is it surprising that whichever way you turn to trace the harmful streams of influence that flow through society, you come upon a group of Jews? In baseball corruption - a group of Jews. In exploitative finance - a group of Jews. In theatrical degeneracy - a group of Jews. In liquor propaganda - a group of Jews. In control of national war policies - a group of Jews. In control of the Press through business and financial pressure - a group of Jews. War profiteers, 80 per cent of them - Jews. Organizers of active opposition to Christian laws and customs - Jews.

In this miasma of so-called popular music, which combines weak-mindedness with every suggestion of lewdness - again Jews.
The Jewish influence on American music is without doubt regarded as serious by those who know anything about it. Not only is there a growing protest against the Judaization of our few great orchestras, but there is a strong reaction from the racial collusion which fills the concert stage and popular platform with Jewish artists to the exclusion of all others. If they were superior artists, nothing against it could be said; they are only better known and racially favored in Jewish musical circles.
"Let me make a nation's songs and I care not who makes the laws," said one; in this country the Jews have had a very large hand in making both. It is the purpose of this article to put people in possession of the truth concerning the moron music which they habitually hum and sing and shout day and night, and if possible to help them to see the invisible Jewish baton which is waved above them for financial and propaganda purposes. Just as the American stage and motion picture have fallen under the control of Jews and their art-destroying commercialism, so the business of handling "popular songs" has become a Yiddish industry. The Jews who captured it in the early days of exploitation were for the most part Russian-born Jews, some of whom had personal pasts which were as unsavory as the past of many Jewish theatrical and movie leaders have been exposed to be.

In the early 1920's, Irving Berlin, Leo Feist and other officers of seven music publishing corporations in New York, were charged with violating the Sherman anti-Trust law in a suit brought by the United States Government. The defendants, it was alleged, controlled 80% of the available copyrighted songs used by manufacturers of phonographs, player piano rolls and other musical reproducing instruments, and fixed prices at which the records or rolls were to be sold to the public. The corporations involved in the action were the Consolidated Music Corporation; Irving Berlin, Inc.; Francis, Day and Hunter, Inc.; Shapiro, Bernstein & Co.; Watterson, Berlin & Snyder, Inc.; and M. Witmark & Sons, Inc. - all of New York. The agreement which the United States Government sought to dissolve was alleged to provide that the defendants would make contracts only through the Consolidated Music Corporation which they had organized. The other 20% of the song business was controlled by other Jewish music houses not included in that special group.

How The Jewish Song Trust Makes You Sing

Jews did not create the popular song; they debased it. The time of the entry of Jews into control of the popular song is the exact time when the morality of popular songs began to decline. The "popular" song, before it became a Jewish industry, was really popular. The people sang it and had no reason to conceal it. The popular song today is often so questionable a composition that performers with a vestige of decency must appraise their audience before they sing. Citizens of adult age will remember the stages through which the popular song has passed during recent decades. War songs persisted after the Civil War and were gradually intermingled with songs of a later time, picturesque, romantic, clean. The same and similar songs and ballads had a brief revival during World War I. These were not the product of song-factories, but the creation of individuals whose gifts were given natural expression. These individuals did not work for combines of publishers but for the satisfaction of their work, for individual artists of the music-hall stage. There were no great fortunes made out of songs, but there were many satisfactions in having pleased the public taste. The public taste, like every other taste, craves what it is given most to feed upon. Public taste is public habit. The public is blind to the source of that upon which it lives, and it adjusts itself to the supply. Public taste is raised or lowered as the quality of its pabulum improves or degenerates.

In a quarter of a century, given all the avenues of publicity like theater, movie, popular song, newspapers and radio - in the meantime having thrown the mantle of contempt over all counter-active moral agencies - you can turn out nearly the kind of public you want. It takes just about a quarter of a century to do the job.

In other days the people sang as they do now, but not in such doped fashion nor with such bewildered continuity. They sang because they wished to, not as an uncontrolled habit. They sang songs nonsensical, sentimental, heroic, but the "shady" songs were outlawed. The old songs come readily back to memory. Though years have intervened since they were the fashion, yet their quality was such that they do not die. The popular song of last month - who knows its name? But there are songs of long ago whose titles are familiar even to those who have not sung them. What margin did these songs leave for the suggestive and for the unwholesomely emotional? Sentiment was not lacking, but it was unobjectionable sentiment. Then came the Jews; the popular song underwent a change. An entirely new crop of titles appeared dealing with an entirely different series of subjects than the songs they displaced. Talented singers, tuneful singing vanished. The Jew and the African period, being the entrance of the jungle motif, the so-called "Congo" stuff, and other compositions which swiftly degenerated into a rather more bestial type than the beasts themselves arrive at. Running alongside this swamp strain was the "ragtime" style of music which was a development of the legitimate Negro minstrelsy. Lyrics disappeared before the numerous "cake-walk" songs that deluged the public ear. Seductive syncopation swamped the harmony of the real song. Minstrelsy took on a new life; glamorous youths mutter dirges in low monotones, voluptuous females with grossly seductive gestures moan nasal notes no real musician can recognize. "Piano acts" were made the rage; "jazz bands" made their appearance. By insensible gradations now easily traceable through the litter of songs with which recent decades are strewn, we have been able to see the decline in the popular song supply. Sentiment has been turned into sensuous suggestion. Romance has been turned into eroticism. The popular musical lilt slid into ragtime and ragtime has been superseded by jazz and crooning. Song topics became lower and lower until at last they are the dredges of the slimy bottom of the underworld.

The first self-styled "King of Jazz" was a Jew named "Frisco." The general directors of the whole downward trend have been Jews. It needed just their touch of cleverness to camouflage the moral filth and raise it half a degree above that natural stage where it begets nothing but disgust.

Plagiarism

In this business of making the people's songs the Jews have shown as usual, no originality but much adaptability - which is a charitable term used to cover plagiarism, which in its turn politely covers the crime of mental pocket-picking. The Jews do not create; they take what others have done, give it a clever twist, and exploit it. Plagiarism is the result of mediocre artists being spurred on by non-artistic promoters to produce something that can be dressed up with sufficient attractiveness to draw the public's money. The Jews bought up all the old song books, opera scores, collections of folk songs, and, if you stop to analyze some of the biggest "hits" of the early days of the Yiddish song manufacturing Trust, you will find they are woven on the motif and melody of the clean songs of the pre-swamp era. The music jazzed and swung out of recognition, the sentiment sensualized very much, and pushed upon their smutty road across the world. Because of absolute Jewish control of the song market, both in publishing and in theatrical performance, it is next to impossible for anything but a Jewish song to be published in the United States, or if published, to get a hearing. The proof of this is in the fact that the Yiddish trust owns all the business and the so-called "song-hits" all bear Jewish names.

The insidiousness of the Jewish menace to our artistic integrity is due partly to the speciousness, the superficial charm and oriental persuasiveness of Hebrew art, its glitter, its violently juxtaposed extremes of passion, its poignant eroticism and pessimism, and partly to the fact that the strain in us which might make head against it, the deepest, most fundamental strain in our nature is diluted and confused by a hundred other tendencies of the Jewish age. The Anglo-Saxon group of qualities and the AngloSaxon point of view, are the vital nucleus of the American temper. The Jewish domination of our music threatens to submerge and stultify them at every point.

Tin-Pan-Alley

America does not sing what it likes, but what the vaudeville "song-pluggers" popularize by repeated renditions, until the flabby minds of the audiences begin to repeat it on the streets.

The "song-pluggers" of theater, vaudeville and radio, are the paid agents of the Yiddish song agencies. Money, and not merit, dominates the spread of the moron music which is styled Jewish jazz and swing. Non-Jewish music is stigmatized as "high-brow." The people are fed from day to day on the moron suggestiveness that flows in a slimy flood out of "Tin-Pan-Alley," the head factory of filth in New York which is populated by the "Abies," the "Izzies," and the 'Moes" who make up the composing staffs of the various institutions. "Tin-Pan-Alley" is the name given to the region in Twenty-eighth street, between Broadway and Sixth Avenue, where the first Yiddish song manufacturers began business. Flocks of young girls who thought they could sing, and others who thought they could write song poems, came to the neighborhood allured by the dishonest advertisements that promised more than the budding Yiddish promoters could fulfill. Needless to say, scandal became rampant, as it always does when so-called "Gentile" girls are reduced to the necessity of seeking favors from the Jew. It was the constant shouting of voices, the hilarity of "parties," the banging of pianos and the blaring of trombones that gave the district the name of "Tin-Pan-Alley." All America is now one great Tin-Pan-Alley, its entertainment, its youth, its politics, a blare of moronic Judaism.

The diabolical cunning with which an unclean atmosphere is created and sustained through all classes of society and by the same influence, will not be overlooked by any observer. There is something Satanic about it, something calculated with demonic shrewdness.

And the stream flows on and on, growing worse and worse, to the degradation of the non-Jewish public and the increase of Jewish fortunes.

Ministers, educators, reformers, parents, citizens are amazed at the growth of looseness among the people, and rail at the evil results. They see the evil product and they attack the product. They rail at the young people who go in for this eroticism and suggestiveness. They deplore the sexual license, the delinquency and the infantilism of the younger people. But all this has a source! Why not attack the source? When a nation is bathed in sights, sounds and ideas of a certain character, drenched in them and drowned in them, by systematic, deliberate, organized intent, the point of attack should be the cause, not the effect.

Yet, that is precisely where the point of attack has not been made, presumably because of lack of knowledge, possibly because of fear.

It is little use blaming the people. The people are what they are made. Give the liquor business full sway and you have a population that drinks and carouses. The population could be turned into drug addicts if the same freedom was given to the illicit narcotic ring as is now given to the Yiddish popular song manufacturers. In such a condition it would be ingenuous to attack the addicts; common sense would urge the exposure of the panderers.

A dreadful narcotizing of moral modesty and the application of powerful aphrodisiacs have been involved in the present craze for crooning songs - a stimulated craze. The victims are everywhere. But too few of the opponents of this moral poison see the futility of scolding the young people thus diseased.

Common sense dictates a cleaning out, and a clearing out, of the sources of the disease. The source is in the Yiddish group of song manufacturers who control the whole output and who are responsible for the whole matter from poetry to profits.

Not So "Popular"

Next to the moral indictment against the so-called "popular" song is the indictment that it is not popular. There is no spontaneous popularity, public taste is not so discriminating. It is artificial popularity by constant plugging. It is a mere mechanical drumming on the minds of the public. It is flung at them at every movie and from every stage. It is advertised in flaring posters, gramophone records shriek forth day and night, dance bands plug it, radios plug it, and by sheer dint of repetition and suggestion the song catches on - until it is replaced by another. It is the old game of changing the styles to speed up business and make the people buy. Nothing lasts in the Yiddish game - styles of clothing, movies nor songs; it is always something "new" to stimulate the flow of money from the popular pocket into the moron music makers' coffers.

Two facts about the "popular" song are known to all: first, that for the most part it is indecent and the most active agent of moral miasma in the country, or if not the most active, then neck and neck with the "movies"; second, that the "popular" song industry is an exclusively Jewish industry.

There is work here for the Anti-Defamation League! That League knows how to put the screws on anyone who disparages the Jews! From important publishers down to inconsequential country newspapers, the Anti-Defamation League makes itself felt. There is work for it in the movies and the theater and popular song industries. Why does not the League put the screws on those Jews who have degenerated the movies and debauched the people in their "arts," sports, and entertainments? On those who have brought shame on the racial name? Why not? Is the answer that only non-Jews are to be controlled, and Jews let to run loose? Is the answer that the gentle Gentiles can be curbed as by bridle and bit and the Jews cannot? American Jewry is desperately afraid of opening a single seam in its armor by means of a single investigation or reform. They are afraid of how far the fire of correction may spread !

Chapter 12: Liquor, Gambling, Vice and Corruption

The Jew is the world's enigma. Poor in his masses, yet he controls the world's finances. Scattered abroad without country or official government, yet he presents a unity of race continuity which no other people has achieved. For some centuries living under legal disabilities in almost every land, he emerged to become the power behind many a throne.

The single description which will include a larger percentage of Jews than members of any other race is this: he is in business. From the sale of old clothes to the control of international trade and finance, the Jew is supremely gifted for business. More than any other race he exhibits a decided aversion to industrial employment which he balances by an equally decided adaptability to trade.

The Gentile boy is prepared to work his way up, taking employment in the productive or technical departments; but the Jewish boy prefers to begin as a salesman, clerk, anything so long as it is connected with the commercial side of the business.

In America alone most of the big business, the trusts, the banks, the natural resources and the chief agricultural products, especially tobacco, cotton and sugar, are in the control of Jewish financiers or their agents. Jewish journalists are a large and powerful group here. Large numbers of department stores are held by Jewish firms, and many of them, if not most, are run under Gentile names.

Jews are the largest and most numerous landlords of residential property in the whole country. They are supreme in the entertainment world. They absolutely control the circulation of publications throughout the country. More powerful than any race among us, they receive a daily amount of favorable publicity which would be impossible did they not have the facilities for creating and distributing it themselves.

Werner Sombart, a pro-Jewish writer, in his “Jews and Modern Capitalism,” says:

"If the conditions in America continue to develop along the same lines as in the last generation, if the immigration statistics and the same proportion of births among all the nationalities remain the same, our imagination may picture the United States of 50 or 100 years hence as a land inhabited only by Slavs, Negroes and Jews, wherein the Jew will naturally occupy the position of economic leadership."

The Jew is the only original internationalist capitalist, but as a rule he prefers not to emblazon that fact upon the skies; the arresting fact about the Jew is his worldwide unchallenged power coupled with comparative numerical inferiority.

Jews and The Bootlegging Evil

The claim made for the Jews that they are a sober race may be true, but that has not obscured two facts concerning them; namely, that they usually constitute the liquor dealers of countries where they live in numbers, and that in the United States they were the only race exempted from the operations of the Prohibition Law. In general, the Jews are on the side of liquor and always have been. They are the steadiest drinkers of all.

That is why they were able to secure exemption from the Prohibition Laws; their religious ceremonies require them to drink an amount which the law considered equal to 10 gallons a year. So the Prohibition Law of the United States - which was a part of the Constitution of the United States - was made legally ineffective to the extent of 10 gallons a year to a Jew. Racial privilege? No, the Jews did not raise that scare then, during the profitable Prohibition era. They knew it was easy to get 100 gallons through a 10 gallon loophole. In fact, millions of gallons of bootleg liquor came through that 10 gallon loophole.

It came as a surprise to the American people that the liquor business of the world had been in the hands of the Jews. In the United States the liquor business was almost exclusively in the hands of Jews for 25 years prior to Prohibition; during the period, in fact, when the liquor trade was giving point and confirmation to the more extreme Prohibition arguments!

In the volume, “The Conquering Jew,” published by Funk & Wagnalls Company in 1916, John Foster Fraser writes: "The Jews are masters of the whisky trade in the United States. Eighty per cent of the members of the National Liquor Dealers’ Association are Jews. It has been shown that sixty per cent of the business of distilling and wholesale trade in whisky is in the hands of Jews. As middle men they control the wine product of California. Jews visit the tobacco-growing States and buy up nearly all the leaf tobacco, so that the great tobacco companies have to buy the raw product from them. The Jews have a grip on the cigar trade."

It was also true of Europe, especially in Russia, Rumania and Poland. The Jewish Encyclopedia states that

"The establishment of the government liquor monopoly (in Russia in 1896) deprived thousands of Jewish families of a livelihood."

They controlled the liquor traffic, the vodka business which undermined Russia. In Rumania the whole "Jewish Question" was the liquor question. In Poland the same was true. In the United States whisky also became Jewish in the 19th century.

How the Jewish Liquor Trust Worked

An alcoholic spirit from grain may be made in any climate and by many methods. Neutral spirits, high wines and alcohol, are not indigenous anywhere. They can be made in any back room or cellar, in a very little time. Little care is required. A concoction of drugs and spirits, colored and flavored, fraudulently labeled "whisky" and passed over the bar, is a crime against distilling, against the human nervous system, and against society. As far back as 1904, Dr. Wiley, then chief of the United States Bureau of Chemistry, had a great deal to say about this. Few paid any attention to him because he did not point out that the evil he was attacking was fostered by a single class of men bent on gain at the cost of ruin to an American industry and to countless thousands of American citizens. The public supposed that Dr. Wiley was discussing a technical matter which interested American distillers only. It might have vastly interested the American citizens if anyone had but had the clear vision and the courage to expose the great Jewish whisky conspiracy.

Old Names Bought Up

The Jewish character of the whisky business since as far back as the Civil War may be visualized by the simple expedient of noting how many of the better known brands have at various dates come under Jewish control. It is an alarming list. Any citizen in any city of any size will have no trouble in confirming the statement that most of the rectifiers and wholesalers and brokers in the whisky trade of his city were, and still are, Jews. It is not only the fact that the liquor business is controlled by Jews that assumes importance, but it is in the additional fact that there was spread over America the machinery of a vicious system which while it was destined to ruin the liquor business, also ruined hundreds of thousands of citizens who trusted that "pure and unadulterated" meant what the words were intended to convey. Of course the stuff was "pure and unadulterated." So is carbolic acid - but it is not whisky.

Prohibition came sweeping the saloon away, but not depriving the Jewish compounder of his profits. Prohibition was swept away but the booze rackets remained.

"Nigger Gin"

In "Collier's Weekly," during the year 1908, solid truths appeared, which are in point today as proofs of what was transpiring. "Collier's Weekly" was the first journal in the land to print the names of Jews in connection with the liquor debauchery of the country. Even so, it had been going on a very long time. There was a specially scathing attack on what was called "Nigger gin," a peculiarly vile beverage which was compounded to act upon the Negro in a most vicious manner. The author, Will Irwin, spoke of this gin as

"The king iniquity in the degenerated liquor traffic of these United States."

This author and Collier's started a new fashion in giving publicity not only to the names of certain brands of liquors, but also the names of the men who made them - all were Jews! The maker of one brand of "nigger gin" which had spurred certain Negroes on to the nameless crime, was one Lee Levy. Mr. Irwin detailed some of his experiences investigating the gin sold by a number of companies, all bearing Jewish names. The gin was cheap, its labels bore lascivious suggestions and were decorated with highly indecent portraiture of white women. "I never saw it in any saloon which bars the Negro," he wrote.

Widely sold brands of cheap, noxious gins and other liquors, made by and brazenly sold under Jewish names, caused newspaper and police comments upon the peculiar lawlessness among negroes. With reference to the Negro Question, "nigger gin," the product of Jewish poisoned liquor factories, was its most provocative element.

The date of the appearance of this gin on the United States market is the period when Negro outbursts and subsequent lynching became serious. The localities where this gin was sold are those where the disorders prevailed.

The Reasoned Answer

The ancient Jewish policy of Divide-Conquer-Destroy tells the story of the liquor traffic. Jewish influence divided between distilling and compounding, drove out distilling, and in the end destroyed the traffic as a legalized entity - opening the way for the mass-organized bootlegger, gangster, and the lawlessness which created today's evil world.

It is extremely simple, so simple that it is overlooked. "Divide and Conquer," is the formula as the Jewish leaders conceive it, as, indeed, it is stated in the Protocols. The public is being constantly deceived by an appearance of complexity, where there is none. When you find the fever-bearing mosquito, yellow-fever is no longer a mystery. That which succumbs to complete Judaization, as Jewish leaders conceive it, may deserve to fall. The justification of its destruction may appear in the possibility of its Judaization.

The maintenance of the idea of drink in the minds of the people is due to Jewish propaganda. There is not a dialogue on the stage or screen that does not drip of drink patter. The idea of the abuse of drink will be maintained by means of the Jewish stage, Jewish jazz and Jewish comics, until somebody comes down hard upon it as being incentive of treason.

Jewish Gamblers Corrupt American Sports

There are men in the United States who say that baseball has received its death wound and is dying out of the lists of respectable sports. There are other men who say that American baseball can be saved if a clean sweep is made of the Jewish influence which has dragged it through a period of bitter shame and demoralization.

Whether baseball as a first-class sport is killed and will survive only as a cheap-jack entertainment; or whether baseball possesses sufficient intrinsic character to rise in righteous wrath and cast out the danger that menaces it, will remain a matter of various opinion. But there is one certainty, namely, that the last and most dangerous blow dealt baseball was curiously notable for its Jewish character.

Baseball is a trivial matter compared with some of the facts that are waiting publication, yet is it possible to see the operation of the Jewish Idea in baseball as clearly as in any other field. The process is the same, whether in war or politics, in finance or in sports.

To begin with, the Jews are not sportsmen. This is not set down in complaint against them, but merely as analysis. It may be a defect in their character, or it may not; it is nevertheless a fact which discriminating Jews unhesitatingly acknowledge. Whether this is due to their physical lethargy, their dislike of unnecessary physical action, or their cast of mind, others may decide; the Jew is not naturally an out-of-door sportsman; if he takes up golf it is because his station in society calls for it, not that he really likes it; and if he goes in for collegiate athletics, as some of the younger Jews are doing, it is because so much attention has been called to their neglect of sports that the younger generation thinks it necessary to remove that occasion of remark.

And yet, the bane of American sports is the presence of a certain type of Jew, not as a participant but as an exploiter and corrupter. There is a very full case made out in justification of the use of the terms “exploiter” and “corrupter” with regard to baseball. But it would be just as easy to make out the same sort of case with regard to wrestling and horse racing and professional pugilism. Wrestling is so completely ruled by Jews as to have become an outlawed sport. The story of wrestling is not only the story of demoralization of a sport but also the story of wholesale defrauding of the public. The same is true of horse-racing. The whole atmosphere of the sport is dishonest. The horses remain the only well-bred creatures connected with it.

Yet why should the art of breeding and training and testing fine horses be debasing? Only because a certain class saw in it a chance to play on the weakness of men for the sake of gain.

That explains the presence of the Jew in modern sports and it also explains why the Jewish Idea in sports, instead of being preservative, is corruptive. The Jew saw money where the sportsman saw fun and skill. The Jew set out to capitalize rivalry and to commercialize contestant zeal. It would seem to be high time that organized Jewry should undertake to control or repudiate those Jews who have been most instrumental in corrupting and nearly destroying our cleanest, most manly public sports.

It is worth noting that in Chicago, where the Jewish Anti-Defamation League has its headquarters, there was not a word of reproof sent out from Jews to the Jewish culprits chiding them for their activities. Not a word. But at the same time the pressure of the Anti-Defamation League was heavy on the whole American newspaper press to prevent the public statements that the whole baseball scandal was a Jewish performance from beginning to end. Heavy Jewish betting, the bribing of players, the buying of clubs, the cheating of the public, has been proved time and again in American courts. All along the line of investigation into sporting scandals the names of Jews are plentifully sprinkled.

If "fans" wish to know the trouble with American baseball, they have it in three words - too much Jew. "Gentile fronts" may rant out their parrot-like pro-Jewish propaganda, the fact is that a sport is clean and helpful until it begins to attract Jewish investors and exploiters and then it goes bad. The two facts have occurred in pairs too frequently in America and under too many dissimilar circumstances to have their relationship doubted. There are no variations on the Jewish corruption of American sports, principally baseball, racing, boxing and wrestling. In the fixing of results, the swindling of gamblers, the staging of frauds, the rottenness has been discovered between the Jewish investors and the venal contestants.

It should be emphasized that the principal Jewish abuses are nation-wide. This was shown in the United States Government's investigation of the White Slave Traffic; the bootlegging business, racetrack gambling, baseball pools - all a national network for the catching of "suckers." There is nothing unusual in this Jewish activity - from the clever "high-ups" to the degenerate "low-downs"; they are all part of a national group. They are part of the national machinery organized and operated for the purpose of separating "Gentile boobs" from their money.

If there were no "Gentile boobs," or if the "Gentile boob" would only take a straight look at the man behind the nationwide spiderweb, the gamblers and the Jewish sport-purveyors would be in another kind of business; with perhaps less money to flaunt in the faces of honest people.

Years before the public scandals broke, the Jew had crowded into all the lucrative sports; he remains in control of them, but only on the commercial side, seldom if ever in sympathy with sport as a real sportsman. The Jews are not even real gamblers, they are not sportsmen enough to gamble; they are the "sure-thing" men. The "Gentile boobs" who walk into their traps are the people who provide the money. Even in the field of money the Jew is not a sport - he is a gangster, ringing a gang of his ilk round him.

Wrestling

Wrestling is so tightly controlled by Jewish managers that a real wrestler is absolutely barred out, for fear he will be able to show that the handful of wrestlers hired by the Jewish Sports Trust are not wrestlers at all, but only impositions on the good nature of the public. The rottenness of the ancient sport of clean wrestling has surfaced in such disgusting orgies as "all in" and "mud" wrestling and, lately, wrestling contests between screaming viragos of the female sex. Wrestling is as much a Jewish business controlled in its every part as the manufacture of clothing.

Despite unending graft scandals baseball is still America's Number One sport. It cannot be killed as a business; it will always draw a gang on an afternoon, particularly a Sunday afternoon. It can be pepped up and "Jazzed" up to make it quite a show. But it can, it is being, killed as a sport, and those who value the game as a sport should wish its utter destruction rather than consent that it become the rendezvous for the gang that now fill the Jew-controlled burlesque houses. Baseball as a business has become a danger in American life, a mob center, a hang-out for the disorderly and criminal classes, as the racetrack and boxing ring have long since been.

The disease is caused by the Jewish characteristic which spoils everything by ruthless commercial exploitation. The disease may be too far gone for any cure.

Chapter 13: The World's Foremost Problem

Anyone who essays to discuss the Jewish Question in the United States or anywhere else must be fully prepared to be regarded as "anti-Semite," a "Jew-baiter." Nor need encouragement be looked for from politicians, people or Press. The people who are awake to the subject at all prefer to wait and see how it all turns out. There is a vague feeling that to use the word "Jew" openly, or to expose it nakedly in print, is somehow improper. Polite evasions like "Hebrew" and "Semite" (both of which are subject to the criticism of inaccuracy) are timidly assayed, and people pick their way gingerly as if the whole subject were forbidden, until some courageous thinker comes along with the word "Jew," and then the constraint is relieved and the air cleared.

The word "Jew" is not an epithet; it is a name, ancient and descriptive, with a significance for every period of human history, past, present and to come.

The chief difficulty in writing about the Jewish Question is the super-sensitiveness of Jews and non-Jews concerning the whole matter. There is probably not a newspaper in America, and certainly none of the advertising mediums which are called magazines, which would have the temerity even to breathe seriously the fact that such a Question exists. The Press in general is open to fulsome editorials in favor of everything Jewish, while the Jewish Press, which is numerous in the United States, takes care of the vituperative end.

The idea seems to be fixed in the Jew by inheritance that any public discussion of the Jewish Question is organized and inspired by a Jew-hater. That idea is sought to be fixed in the Gentile by propaganda; that any writing which does not simply cloy and drip sirrupy sweetness towards things Jewish is born of prejudice and hatred. It is, therefore, "full of lies, insult, insinuation, and constitutes an instigation to massacre." These terms can be found in current Jewish editorials.

What Is "Anti-Semitism"?

Anti-Semitism is a term which is bandied about too loosely. If it continues to be used indiscriminately and vituperatively about all who attempt to discuss Jewish characteristics and Jewish world-power, it will, in time, arrive at the estate of respectability and honor. It may be a useful clearing of the ground to define what anti-Semitism is not.

---

1. It is not a recognition of the Jewish Question. If it were, then it could be set down that the bulk of the American people are destined to become anti-Semites, for they are beginning to recognize the existence of a Jewish Question and will steadily do so in increasing numbers as the Question is forced on them from the various practical angles of their lives. The Question is here. We may be honestly blind to it. We may be timidly silent about it. We may even make dishonest denial of it. But it is here and in time all will have to recognize it. In time the polite "hush, hush," of over-sensitive or intimidated circles will not be powerful enough to suppress it.

But to recognize that Question will not mean that we have gone over to a national campaign of hatred and enmity against the Jews. It will only mean that a stream of tendency which has been flowing through our civilization has at last accumulated bulk and power enough to challenge attention, to call for some decision with regard to it, to call for the adoption of a policy which will not repeat the mistakes of the past and yet forestall any possible menace of the future.

2. The public discussion of the Jewish Question is not "anti-Semitism." Publicity is sanitary. But the kind of publicity given to certain aspects of the Jewish Question in this country has been very misleading. It

has been discussed more fully in the Jewish Press than elsewhere, but not with candor or breadth of vision. The two dominant notes - sounded over and over again with monotonous regularity - are Gentile unfairness and Christian prejudice. It is fortunate for the Jews generally that the Jewish Press does not circulate very widely among Gentiles, for it is probably the one established agency in the United States which, without altering its program in the least, could stir up anti-Jewish sentiment by the very simple expedient of a general reading among non-Jews. Jewish writers writing for Jewish readers, present unusual material for the study of race consciousness and its accompaniment of contempt for other races. On the side of the daily Press, there has been no serious discussion at all. When it mentions the Jews, it has stock complimentary phrases for the purpose. The publicity given to the Question in this country consists in misrepresentative criticism of the Gentiles by the Jewish Press, and misrepresentative praise of the Jews by the non-Jewish Press. An independent effort to give constructive publicity cannot, therefore, be laid to anti-Semitism, even when some of the statements which are made in the course of it arouse resentment of Jewish readers.

3. Nor is it anti-Semitism to say that the suspicion is abroad in every capital of civilization, and the certainty is firmly held by a number of important men, that there is active in the world a plan to control the

world, not by territorial acquisition, not by military aggression, not by governmental subjection, not even by economic control in the scientific sense, but by control of the machinery of commerce and exchange. It is not anti-Semitism to say that, nor to present the evidence which supports that, nor to bring the proof of that. Those who could best disprove it, if it were not true, are the International Jews themselves, but they have not disproved it.

Why Discuss the Jewish Question?

Because it is here, and because its emergence into public thought should contribute to its solution, and not to a continuance of those bad conditions which surround the Question in almost every country. The Jewish Question has existed in the United States for a very long time. Jews themselves have known it, even if Gentiles have not. There have been periods in our own country when it has broken forth with a sullen sort of strength which presaged dark things to come. Many signs portend that it is approaching an acute stage.

Not only does the Jewish Question touch those matters that are common knowledge, such as finance and commercial control, usurpation of political power, monopoly of necessities, and autocratic direction of the very news that the American people read; but it reaches into cultural regions and so touches the very heart of American life. The Question reaches down to South

America and threatens to become an important factor in Pan-American relations. It is interwoven with much of the menace of organized and calculated disorder which troubles the nations today. It is not of recent growth, but its roots go deep, and the long Past of the Problem is counterbalanced by prophetic hopes and programs which involve a very deliberate and creative view of the future.

The Answer - Too Much Power!!

Their heritage of tolerance has something to do with the extreme nervousness about public discussion of the Jewish Question on the part of many Gentiles, but perhaps their instinctive sense of the difficulty involved has more to do with it. The Gentile attitude is best expressed by the desire for silence - "Why discuss it at all?" Such an attitude is itself proof that here is a Problem we would evade if we could. Why discuss it at all? - the keen thinker clearly sees in the implications of such a question, the existence of a Problem whose discussion or suppression will not always be within the choice of easy-going minds.

Wherever you read of the Jewish Question being resolutely approached in the history of countries which have ever tackled it, wherever you go in the world today - in any country where the Jewish Question has come to the forefront as a vital issue, you will discover that the principal cause is the outworking of the Jewish genius to achieve the power of control. Here in the United States is the fact of this remarkable minority attaining in 50 years a degree of control that would be impossible to a ten times larger group of any other race. That creates the Jewish Question here.

No similar minority of any people would occasion comment, because we would not meet with a representative of them wherever we went in high places - in the innermost secrecy of the councils of the Big Four at Versailles; in the United States Supreme Court; in the councils of the White House; in the vast dispositions of world finance - wherever there is power to get or use. We meet the Jew everywhere in the upper circles, literally everywhere where there is power. And that is where the Jewish question begins - in very simple terms - How does the Jew so habitually and so "resistlessly" gravitate to the highest places? Who puts him there? Why is he put there? What does he do there? What does the fact of his being there mean to the world? That is the Jewish Question in its origin. From these points it goes on to others, and whether the trend becomes pro-Jewish or anti-Semitic depends on the amount of prejudice brought to the inquiry, and whether it becomes pro-Humanity depends on the amount of insight and intelligence.

The use of the word Humanity in connection with the word "Jew" usually throws a side meaning which may not be intended. In this connection it is usually understood that humanity ought to be shown toward the Jew. There is just as great an obligation upon the Jew to show his humanity toward the whole human race.

The Jew has been too long accustomed to think himself as exclusively the claimant on the humanitarianism of society; society has a large claim against him that he cease his exclusiveness, that he cease exploiting the world, that he cease making Jewish groups the end and all of his gains, and that he begins to fulfill, in a sense his exclusiveness has never yet enabled him to fulfill, the ancient prophecy he boasts that through him all the nations of the earth should be blessed.

The Jew cannot go on forever fulfilling the role of suppliant for the world's humanitarianism, he must himself show that quality to a society which seriously suspects his higher and more powerful groups of exploiting it with a pitiless rapacity, which in its wide-flung and long-drawn-out distress may be described as an economic pogrom against a rather helpless humanity.

Why The "International Jew"?

There has been used in this series the term "International Jew." It is susceptible of two interpretations; one, the Jew wherever he may be; the other, the Jew who exercises international control.

The real contention of the world is with the latter and his satellites, whether Jew or Gentile. This International type of Jew, this grasper after world-control, this actual possessor and wielder of world-control is a very unfortunate connection for his race to have. And the significance of this is that this type does not grow anywhere else than on a Jewish stem. There is no other racial or national type which puts forth this kind of person.

It is not merely that there are a few Jews among international financial controllers; it is that these world-controllers are exclusively Jews. Since world-control is an ambition which has only been achieved by Jews, and not by any of the methods usually adopted by would-be world-conquerors, it becomes inevitable that the question should center in that race.

It is not the point to insist that in any list of rich men there are often more Gentiles than Jews; we are not talking about merely rich men who have, many of them, gained their riches by serving a System, we are talking about those who control - and it is perfectly apparent that merely to be rich is not to control. The world-controlling Jew has riches, but he also has something much more powerful than that.

The International Jew rules not because he is rich, but because in a most marked degree he possesses the commercial and masterful genius of his race, and avails himself of a racial loyalty and solidarity the like of which exists in no other human group. He rules, at the top of affairs in every country worthwhile, by virtue of certain qualities which are inherent in the Jewish nature. Every Jew has these qualities even if not in the supreme sense, just as every Englishman has Shakespeare's tongue but not in Shakespeare's degree. And thus it is impracticable, if not impossible, to consider the International Jew without laying the foundations broadly upon Jewish character and psychology.

We may discount at once the too common accusation that this greater form of Jewish success is built upon dishonesty. It is impossible to indict the whole Jewish people or any other on a wholesale charge. No one knows better than the Jew how widespread is the belief that Jewish methods of business are all unscrupulous. There is no doubt a possibility of a great deal of unscrupulousness existing without actual legal dishonesty, but it is altogether possible that the reputation the Jewish people have long borne in this respect may have had other sources than actual and persistent dishonesty. To indicate one of these possible sources: The Jew at trade is naturally quicker than most other men. It is said that there are other races which are as nimble at a trade as is the Jew, but the Jew does not live much among them. Now, it is human nature for the man with slower, easy-going traditions to believe that the quicker man is too deft by far, and to become suspicious of his deftness. The slower mind is likely to conceive that the man who sees so many legitimate twists and turns to a trade, may also see and use a convenient number of illegitimate twists and turns. The Jews, as the records show for centuries, were a keen people in trade. The nimble eagerness of the Jew for trade bustled into the midst of trade traditions, he broke them all wherever he went. He went after trade, the old leisurely tradition was to make trade come to the trader. Everyone suspects the "sharp" fellow even though his sharpness may be entirely honest. A man who would break trade traditions would stop at nothing! The Jew was anxious to sell. If he could not sell one article to a customer, he had another on hand to offer him. The old tradition was that it was strictly unethical and non-business-like to handle more than one line of goods, or to deal in more than one "trade"; that it was contemptible and underhand to go out and get a brother tradesman's customers away from him. It is as easy as child's play to connect this energy with dishonesty. The Jew went after trade, pursued it, persuaded it. He was the originator of "quick turnover and quick profit." He originated the installment plan. The Jew's shops became bazaars, forerunners of our modern department stores, and the old custom of one shop for one line of goods was broken up . . . the Jew was not playing the game, the staid old-fashioned merchant thought. As a matter of fact he was playing the game, the game to get it all into his own hands - which he has practically done.

The Jew has shown that same ability ever since his entry into trade in the various countries he has established himself down the centuries. His power of analyzing the money currents amounts to an instinct. His establishment in one country represented another base from which the members of his race could operate. Whether by the natural outworking of innate gifts or the deliberate plan of race unity and loyalty, all the Jewish trading communities and relations, and as these trading communities increased in wealth, prestige and power, as they formed relations with governments and great interest in the countries where they operated, they simply put more power into the central community wherever it might be located, now in Spain, now in Holland, now in England.

Whether by intention or not, they became more closely allied than the branches of one business could be, because of the cement of racial unity; the bond of racial brotherhood cannot in the very nature of things exist among the Gentiles as it exists among the Jews.

Gentiles never think of themselves as Gentiles, and never feel that they owe anything to another Gentile as such; wherein lies their vulnerability. Thus they have been convenient agents of Jewish schemes at times and in places when it was not expedient that the Jewish controllers should be publicly known; but they have never been successful competitors of the Jew in the field of world-control.

From these separated Jewish communities went power to the central community where the master bankers and the master analysts of conditions lived. And back from the central community flowed information of an invaluable character and assistance wherever needed. It is not difficult to understand how, in such conditions, the nation that did not deal kindly with the Jews was made to suffer, and the nation that yielded to them their fullest desire was favored by them. They have made many nations feel the power of their displeasure and this system exists in greater power today. The co-ordination of Jewish activity has been a harmful thing for the world. This is the element which is bringing the Jewish Question to the bar of public opinion. May the International Jew go on as he has gone, or does his duty to the world require another use of his success?

Power Follows "The International Jew"

It is an important fact to be noted in connection with the "persecution" and consequent wanderings of the Jews about Europe that wherever they wandered the center of business seemed to go with them!

When the Jews were free in Spain, there was the world's gold center. When Spain drove out the Jews, Spain lost her financial leadership and has never regained it.

Students of the economic history of Europe have always been puzzled to discover why the center of trade should have shifted from Spain, Portugal and Italy, up to the northern countries of Holland, Germany and England. They have sought for the cause in many things, but none seemed to be completely explanatory. When it is shown that the change was coincident with the expulsion of the Jews from the South and their flight to the North, when it is known that upon the Jews' arrival the northern countries began a commercial life which has flourished to our day, the explanation does not seem difficult. Time and again it has been proved to be the fact that when the Jews were forced to move, the center of the world's precious metals moved with them.

It is also to be noted that the era of greatest national spiritual culture is shown during the period when the

Jews were expelled from England and Spain. These two great countries have given much to the world, the best of it they gave during their freedom from contact with Jewish ideas.

"When America Awakes!"

It is clearly proved that in the world today there is a central force which is playing a vast and closely organized game, with the world as its table and universal control for its stakes. Civilized people have long ago lost confidence in the argument that "economic conditions" are responsible for all the changes that occur. Under the camouflage of "economic law" a great many phenomena have been accounted for which were not due to any "law" whatever, except the law of the selfish human will as operated by the men who have the purpose and the power to use the nation as their vassals.

"Economic" reason no longer explains the condition in which the world finds itself today. Neither does the ordinary explanation of "the heartlessness of Capital." "Capital" has endeavored as never before to meet the demands of "Labor," and labor has gone to extremes in leading capital to new concessions - but what has it advantaged either of them? "Labor" has heretofore thought that "Capital" was the sky over it, and it made the sky yield. But behold, there was yet another higher sky which neither capital nor labor had seen in their struggles with one another. That sky is so far unyielding.

There is a super-capitalism which is supported wholly by the fiction that gold is wealth. There is a super-government which is allied to no government, which is free from them all, and yet which has its hands in them all. There is a race, a part of humanity, which has never yet been received as a welcome part, and which has succeeded in raising itself to a power that the proudest Gentile race has never claimed.

The "labor question," the wage question, the land question, cannot be settled, no question that confronts the peoples of the world can be settled, until first of all this matter of an international super-capitalistic government is settled.

"To the victor belongs the spoils" is an old saying. In a sense it is true that if all this power of control has been gained and held by a few men of a long-despised race, then either they are super-men whom it is powerless to resist or they are ordinary men whom the rest of the world has permitted to obtain an undue and unsafe degree of power. Unless the Jews are super-men, the Gentiles will have themselves to blame for what has transpired, and they can look for rectification in a new scrutiny of the situation and a candid examination of the experiences of other countries. When tracing all the anti-social and colossally harmful methods of world-control to their source, it is found that the responsible parties all have a common characteristic. Is it any wonder that the warning which comes across, the sea - "Wait until America becomes awake to the Jew!" has a new meaning?

Chapter 14: The High and Low Of Jewish Money-Power

Humanity has become wise enough to discuss those forms of physical sickness over which it formerly drew the veil of shame and secrecy, but political hygiene is not so far advanced. The main source of the sickness of our national body is charged to be the influence of the Jews, and although this was apparent to acute minds years ago, it is now said to have gone so far as to be apparent to the least observing. But while these influences were undermining the mass of the people, higher influences of Jewish origin were operating on the government.

The Jewish Problem in the United States is essentially a city problem; great cities are the areas in which most all national diseases have their origin. It is characteristic of the Jews to gather in numbers, not where land is open nor where raw materials are found, but where the greatest number of people abide. This is a noteworthy fact when considered alongside the claim that the Gentiles have ostracized them; the Jews congregate in their greatest numbers in those places and among those people where they complain they are least wanted!

The explanation most frequently given is this: the genius of the Jew is to live off people, not off land, nor off the production of commodities from raw materials, but off people. Let other people till the soil; the Jew, if he can, will live off the tiller. Let other people toil at trades and manufacture; the Jew will exploit the fruits of their work.

That is his particular genius. If this genius be described as parasitic, the term would seem to be justified by a certain fitness.

In no other city of the United States can the Jewish Problem be studied with greater profit than in the city of New York. There are more Jews in New York than anywhere else in the world; at least one Jew in every ten resides in New York. Jews exert more power in New York, and from New York, than they have ever exerted during the Christian era in any place, with the exception of present Russia. The Jewish Revolution of Russia was manned from New York. The Jewish government of Russia was transported almost as a unit from the lower East Side of New York. The general run of shop-keeping, from the great departmental stores to the smallest "junk" shop, is practically monopolized by Jews. The legal profession is predominantly Jewish. From news agencies that distribute news to the newspapers, to the newspaper that prints it, to the news-stand that distributes the national reading matter, the control and in most cases the ownership is entirely Jewish. In Wall Street the Jewish element is both numerous and powerful, as might be expected of a race which from early days has played an important part in the financial operations of the world.

The Rothschild Method

Jewish high finance first touched the United States through the Rothschilds. Indeed, it may be said that the United States founded the Rothschild fortunes. As so often occurs in the tale of Jewish riches, the fortune was founded in war. The first 20 million dollars the Rothschilds ever had to speculate with was the money paid for Hessian troops to fight against the American colonies.

Since that first indirect connection with American affairs, the Rothschilds have often invaded the money affairs of the country, though always by agents. None of the Rothschild sons thought it necessary to establish himself in the newly-founded United States. Anselm remained in Frankfort, Solomon chose Vienna, Nathan Meyer went to London, Charles established himself in Naples, and James represented the family in Paris. These were the five war-lords of Europe for more than a generation, and their dynasty was continued by their successors.

Rothschild power, as it was once known, has been so broadened by the entry of other banking families into governmental finance, that it must now be known not by the name of one family of Jews, but by the name of the race. Thus it is spoken of as International Jewish Finance, and its principal figures are described as International Jewish Financiers. Much of the veil of secrecy which contributed so greatly to the Rothschild power has been stripped away; war finance has been labeled for all time as "blood money," and the mysterious magic surrounding large transactions between governments and individuals, by which individual controllers of large wealth were made the real rulers of the people, has been largely solved and the plain facts disclosed.

The Rothschild method still holds good, however, in that Jewish institutions are affiliated with their racial institutions in all foreign countries. As a leading student of financial affairs puts it, the world of high finance is largely a Jewish world because of the Jewish financiers "absence from national or patriotic illusions." To the International Jewish Financier the ups and downs of war and peace between the nations are but the changes of the world's financial market; and, as frequently the movement of stocks is manipulated for purposes of market strategy, so sometimes international relations are affected for mere financial gain.

It is known that the first World War was postponed several times at the behest of international financiers. If it broke out too soon, it would not involve the states which the international financiers wished to involve. Therefore, the masters of gold, the international masters, were compelled several times to check the martial enthusiasm which their own propaganda had aroused. The Jewish Press alleges that there was discovered a Rothschild Letter dated 1911, and urging the Kaiser against war. The year 1911 was too early. There was no such insistence in 1914.

There is no question whatever of International Jewish Finance being deeply concerned in the matter of war and revolution - this is never denied as to the past; it is just as true of the present. The league against Napoleon, for example, was Jewish. Its headquarters were in Holland. When Napoleon invaded Holland, the headquarters were moved to Frankfort on-the-Main. It is remarkable how many of the International Jewish Financiers have come out of Frankfurt - the Rothschilds, the Schiffs, the Speyers, to name but a few. Jewish influence in German affairs came strongly to the front during the 1914-1918 war. It came with all the directness and attack of a flying wedge, as if previously prepared. There are no stronger contrasts in the world than the pure Germanic and pure Semitic races; therefore, there has been no harmony between the two in Germany, and though Jewish influence became strong in that country it was not gained without challenge, but Jewish power became paramount in the Revolution which followed the war. The Revolution would not have come if they had not brought it. The principal Jewish influences which brought down German order may be named under three heads: (a) the spirit of Bolshevism which masqueraded under the name of German Socialism; (b) Jewish ownership and control of the Press; (c) Jewish control of the food supply and the industrial machinery of the country. There was a fourth, "higher up," but these worked upon the German people directly. It will be recalled that the German collapse in that war was directly due to food starvation and material shortages, and to industrial unrest. As early as the second year of the war, German Jews were preaching that German defeat was necessary to the rise of the proletariat. Strovel declared: "I openly admit that a full victory of the country would not be in the interest of the Social Democrats." And also: "The exaltation of the proletariat after a won victory is an impossibility." Revolution is the expression of the Jews' will to power. Parties are but tools for the Jewish plan to power. The so-called "dictatorship of the proletariat" is really and practically the dictatorship of the Jews.

The 1914-1918 war brought about a condition which threw a new light on the internationalism of Jewish finance. During the years of American neutrality there was opportunity to observe the extent of the foreign affiliations of certain men, and also the extent to which ordinary national loyalty was subordinated to the business of international finance. That war really forced a coalition of Gentile capital on one side of the struggle, as against certain blocks of Jewish capital which were willing to play both sides. The old Rothschild maxim: "Do not put all your eggs in one basket," becomes perfectly plain when transposed into national and international terms. Jewish finance treats political parties the same - bets on them both, and so never loses. In the same way Jewish finance never loses a war. Being on both sides, it cannot miss the winning side, and its terms of peace are sufficient to cover all advances to the side that lost. This was the significance of the great swarming of Jews at the Versailles Peace Conference.

But a strange fatality seems to follow all forms of Jewish supremacy. Just as the capstone is ready to be placed on the edifice of Jewish triumphs, something occurs and the structure shrinks. It occurs so often in Jewish history that the Jews themselves have been exercised to find an explanation. In many cases "anti-Semitism" offers the readiest excuse, but not always. Just at the present time, when the light which was shed by the fires of war has revealed so many matters formerly hidden in shadow, the awakening of world attention is called "anti-Semitism," and the explanation is given that "after every war the Jew becomes the scapegoat" - a curious admission which would lead a less self-centered people to inquire, Why?

Scope Of Jewish Money Power

In the firm of Kuhn, Loeb and Company, Jewish finance in the United States reached its high-water mark. The head of this firm was the late Jacob Schiff, who was born in Frankfort-on-the-Main and whose father was one of the Rothschild brokers. One of Jacob Schiff's associates, Otto Kahn, was born in Mannheim, and was early associated with the Speyers, who also originated in Frankfort and who came to great power in England during the reign of Edward VII. Another associate, Felix Warburg, married into Jacob Schiff's family, and the Warburgs became some of the most influential members of America's diplomatic representatives.

Early flank movements of Jewish financiers in America sought out other objectives in foreign countries whose future influence on American affairs proved to be considerable. The first flank movement was toward Central and South America. The financial assistance, practical and advisory, offered to Mexico during the most unsatisfactory period of her relations with the United

States was given by Jewish groups. The political upheavals and the financial arrangements in the tiny but strategically placed countries of Central America are too notorious even to occasion comment.

It is known that Jacob Schiff gave material assistance to Japan in the 1905 war with Russia. This was explainable on the ground of good business and also of a desire to revenge Russia's treatment of the Jews. Schiff used the opportunity also to instill the principles, which have since grown up into Bolshevism, into the minds of the Russian prisoners in Japanese war camps. The attempt to gain influence in Japan, in those distant days, came off rather badly. The Japs kept the business deal strictly a business deal, and Mr. Jacob Schiff was displeased with Japan generally. The idea at the beginning of the century appears to have been to add the newly rising Japan to the string of financial conquests, but the Japanese were credited with knowing much more about the "Jewish peril" than did the United States. This is well worth recalling in view of the intensive propaganda which, for years before the 1914 war and again just before the 1939 war, constantly sought to create misunderstanding between the United States and the Empire of Japan.

Jewry emerged from the 1914-1918 war more strongly entrenched in power, even in the United States, than it was before. In the world at large the ascendancy of the Jew at the present time is even more marked. In those countries which can justly be called unfriendly to the Jew, now or in the recent past, the rule of the Jew is stronger than anywhere else. The more they are opposed the more they show their power. At a moment when, as all Jewish spokesmen inform us, there is a world-wave of "anti-Semitism," - which is their name for a new awakening of people to what has been going on - what should occur but that at the head of the Chief Magistracy of the World a Jew appears. Nobody seems to know why. Nobody can explain it.

"Disraeli of America" - A Jew of Super-Power

In the United States we had a term of Jewish rule almost as absolute as that which exists in Russia. This appears to be a very strong statement, but it is milder than the facts warrant. And the facts are not of hearsay origin, nor the product of a biased point of view; they are the fruits of an inquiry by the lawful officials of the United States who were set aside in favor of a ready-made Jewish Government, and they are forever spread upon the official records of the United States.

The Jews have proved that the control of Wall Street is not necessary to the control of the American people, and the person by whom they proved this was a Wall Street Jew!

This man has been called "the pro-consul of Judah in America." It is said that once, referring to himself, he exclaimed: "Behold the Disraeli of the United States!"

To a select committee of the Congress of the United States he said: "I probably had more power than perhaps any other man did to the war; doubtless that is true."

He did not overstate the case. He did have more power. It was not all legal power, this much he admitted. It reached into every home and store and factory and bank and railway and mine. It touched armies and governments. It touched recruiting boards. It made and unmade men without a word. It was power without responsibility and without limit. It was such a power as compelled the Gentile population to lay bare every secret before this man and his Jewish associates, giving them an advantage and knowledge that billions of gold could not buy.

Not one American in a million ever heard of this man before the entry of the United States into the war in 1917. He glided out of a certain obscurity unlighted by public service of fame, into the high rulership of the nation at war. The constituted government had little to do with him save vote the money and do his bidding. He said that men could have appealed over his head to the President of the United States but, knowing the situation, men never did.

Who was, who is, this figure, colossal in his way, and most instructive of the readiness of Judah to take the rule whenever he desires?

His name is Bernard M. Baruch. He was born in South Carolina in the 1870's, the son of a Jewish doctor, Dr. Simon Baruch. He was graduated at the College of the City of New York when he was just under 19 years of age. After going down to Wall Street as a clerk and a runner, and when he "was about 26 or 27," he became a member of the firm of A. A. Housman and Company. "In about 1900 or

1902" he left the firm, but he had meanwhile gained a seat on the Stock Exchange.

He then went into business himself, a statement which must be taken literally in view of his testimony that he "Did not do any business for anybody but myself. I made a study of the corporations engaged in the production and manufacture of different things, and a study of the men engaged in them."

Emerging from his evidence before Congress, Baruch's operations are seen to be in various fields; principally in the field of metals and the organization of various commercial enterprises. He was instrumental also in the purchase of tobacco companies, various copper, steel tungsten, rubber and smelting companies, and he was responsible for the building up of the great industries in rubber in Mexico. As a young man, he is found to be the master of large sums of money, and there is no indication that he inherited any. He is very wealthy. What change the war made in his wealth is not known, but certainly many of his friends and closest associates reaped great quantities of money from their activities during the war.

Dictator Baruch

Cross-examined by the Congress Inquiry it was amply proved that Baruch's influence over President Wilson made such changes in the Administration as to make Baruch the most powerful man in the war. The Council of National Defense eventually became the merest side show. It was not a Council of Americans that ran the war, it was an autocracy headed by a Jew, with Jews at every strategic point down the line. In his own evidence he describes one of his visits to the President in 1915.

Mr. Baruch: "I thought a war was coming long before it did . . . I explained to him as earnestly as I could that I was very deeply concerned about the necessity of the mobilization of the industries of the country. The President listened very attentively and graciously, as he always does . . . My attention was brought to the Council of National Defense . . . The Secretary of War asked me what I thought of it. I said I would like to have something different." A council is a council. Mr. Baruch wanted something different. He did get something different. He got the President to change matters so as to make Mr. Baruch the "most powerful man in the war." What Baruch did was very masterly, but it was not in the American manner. No one but a member of his race would have wanted to do it.

There is no discounting the testimony Baruch gave before Congress. The President of the United States did exactly what Baruch wanted in a thousand ways, and what Baruch apparently wanted was a ruling hand on productive America, and he got it. He got it in a larger way than even Lenin or his successors ever got in Russia; for here in the United States the people saw nothing but the patriotic element; they did not see the Jewish Government looming above them. Yet it was there.

So Baruch did things. Before he got through, he was head and center of a system of control such as the United States

Government never possessed and never will possess until it changes its character as a free government. As told by himself, his power consisted in the following authorities:

---

1. Authority over the use of capital in the private business of Americans. (This authority was nominally under the Capital Issues Committee, the controlling factor of which was another Jew, Eugene Meyer, Jr.)
2. Authority over all materials. This, of course, included everything. Mr. Baruch was an expert in many of the lines of materials involved, and had held interests in many of them. In lines where Mr. Baruch was not an expert he, of course, had other experts in charge; Jews. "The members of that committee were picked out by myself; the industries did not pick them out," he stated.
3. Authority over industries. He determined where coal might be shipped, where steel might be sold, where industries might be operated and where not. He said, it is in his recorded testimony, that there were 361 or 357 lines of industry under his control in the United States including "practically every raw material in the world. I had the final authority."
4. Authority over the cases of men to be called to military service. Baruch virtually pointed out to the Provost Marshall of the United States, the classes of men to be taken into the army. "We had to decide virtually the necessity of things," he said. "We had to decide that the less-essential industries would have to be curbed,

and it was from them that the man-power would have to be taken for the army. It was, of course, necessary that some ruling should be made, but why one man, why always this one man?

5. Authority over the personnel of labor in the country.

> "We decided upon a dilution of men with women labor, which was a thing that had always been fought by the labor unions." "We fixed the prices for the total production, not alone for the army and the navy, but for the Allies and the civilian population."

And now behold as complete an illustration of one part of the Protocols as ever could be found in any Gentile Government: "We will force up wages which, however, will be of no benefit to the workers, for we will at the same time cause a rise in the prices of necessities": the First Protocol.

It was not only during the war, but also after the Armistice, that tokens of signal choice were showered on Baruch. He went to the Versailles Peace Conference as a part of the President's entourage.

Mr. Baruch:

> "Whenever he asked my advice I gave it. I had something to do with the reparations clauses. I was the American Commissioner in charge of what they called the 'Economic Section.' I was a member of the Supreme Economic Council in

> charge of raw materials."

Baruch admitted in his evidence that he sat in council with the men who were negotiating the Peace Treaty and that he participated in the meeting of the "Big Five" Premiers. Jews were so conspicuous in the American Mission as to excite comment everywhere. Frenchmen called Versailles the "Kosher Conference." So numerous and ubiquitous were the International Jews, headed by Baruch, so firmly established in the inner councils, that the keen observer, Dr. E. J. Dillon, in his book, "The Inside Story of the Peace Conference" (Harpers), said this:

> "It may seem amazing to some readers, but it is none the less a fact, that a considerable number of delegates believed that the real influences behind the Anglo-Saxon peoples were Semitic." (p.496).
>
> ". . . the sequence of expedients framed and enforced in this direction were inspired by the Jews, assembled in Paris for the purpose of realizing their carefully thought-out program, which they succeeded in having substantially executed . . . The formula into which this policy was thrown by the members of the Conference, whose countries it affected, and who regarded it as fatal to the peace of Eastern Europe, was this: 'Henceforth the world will be governed by the Anglo-Saxon peoples, who in their turn, are swayed by their Jewish elements'." (p. 497).

This is not the whole story by any means.

Why was Baruch chosen to be the first Dictator of the United States? What had he been, what had he done, that he should have been chosen as head and front of governmental power in the first World War, the first major war in which the United States were involved, and which turned that country from a debtor nation into the most powerful of all time in military and financial power? And with a minimum of military sacrifice and comparatively trifling effort. His antecedents do not account for it. Neither his personal nor commercial attainments account for it. What does?

Men who can manipulate this political and money power in time of war can do so in time of peace. The United States is living under some of the peace-manipulation now. The operating groups, governments, are bankrupt. Only their power of confiscation keeps them up. The United States, commonly referred to as the richest country in the world, is just as poor as a government as is any other; it is in debt and borrowing. And its creditors are constantly discounting their obligations and putting it into worse hands than ever. The amount of our National Debt is the measure of our enslavement to Jewish World Finance. We live in a democracy, yet loans are contracted that always cost more than the amount of the loan, and no one has a word to say about it. We Americans do not know how much interest we pay every year, and we don't know to whom we pay it.

Chapter 15: The Battle for Press Control

The first instinctive answer which the Jew makes to any criticism of his race coming from a non-Jew is that of violence, threatened or inflicted. This statement will be confirmed by hundreds of thousands of citizens of the United States who have heard the evidence with their own ears, seen it with their own eyes.

If the candid investigator of the Jewish Question happens to be in business, the "boycott" is the first answer of which the Jews seem to think. Whether it be a newspaper, or a mercantile establishment, or a hotel, or a dramatic production; or any manufactured article whose maker has adopted the policy that "my goods are for sale, but not my principles" - if there is any manner of business connection with the student of the Jewish Question, the first "answer" is "boycott."

The technique of this: a "whispering drive" is first begun. Disquieting rumors begin to fly thick and fast. "Watch us get him, is the word that is passed along. Jews in charge of national ticker news services adopt the slogan of "a rumor a day." All leading news agencies in America are Jew-controlled. Jews in charge of newspapers adopt the policy of "a slurring headline a day." Jews in charge of the newsboys on the streets (all the street concerns are preempted by Jewish "padrones" who permit only their own boys to sell) give orders to emphasize certain news in their street cries - "a new yell against him every day. "The

whole campaign against the critic of Jewry, whoever he may be, is keyed to the threat, "Watch us get him."
"The whispering drive," "the boycott," these are the chief Jewish answers. They constitute the bone and the sinew of that state of mind in non-Jews which is known as "the fear of the Jews."

Bennett's Struggle

This is the story of a boycott which lasted over a number of years; it is only one of numerous stories of the same kind which can be told of America. There have been even more outstanding cases since this one, but it dates back to the dawn of Jewish ambitions and power in the United States, and it is the first of the great battles which Jewry waged, successfully, to snuff out the independent Press.
It concerns the long defunct "New York Herald," one newspaper to remain independent of Jewish influence in New York. The Herald enjoyed an existence of 90 years, which was terminated in 1920 by the inevitable amalgamation. It performed great feats in the world of news-gathering. It sent Henry M. Stanley to Africa to find Livingstone. It backed the Jeannette expedition to the Arctic regions. It was largely instrumental in having the first Atlantic cables laid. Its reputations among newspaper men was that neither its news nor its editorial columns could be bought or influenced. But perhaps its greatest feat was the maintenance during many years of its journalistic independence against the combined attack of New York Jewry. Its proprietor, the late James Gordon

Bennett, a great American citizen famed for many helpful activities, had always maintained a friendly attitude toward the Jews of his city. He apparently harbored no prejudices against them. Certainly he never deliberately antagonized them. But he was resolved upon preserving the honor of independent journalism. He never bent to the policy that the advertisers had something to say about the editorial policy of the paper, either as to influencing it for publication or suppression. In Bennett's time the American Press was in the majority free. Today it is entirely Jewish controlled. This control is variously exercised, sometimes resting only on the owners' sense of expediency. But the control is there, and for the moment it is absolute. Fifty years ago there were many more newspapers in New York than there are today, since then amalgamation has reduced the competition to a select few who do not compete. This development has been the same in other countries, particularly Great Britain.

Bennett's Herald, a three cent newspaper, enjoyed the highest prestige and was the most desirable advertising medium due to the class of its circulation. At that time the Jewish population of New York was less than one-third of what it is today, but there was much wealth represented in it.

Now, what every newspaper man knows is this: most Jewish leaders are always interested either in getting a story published or getting it suppressed. There is no class of people who read the public press with so careful an eye to their own affairs as do the Jews. The Herald simply adopted the policy from the beginning of this form of harassment that it was not to be permitted to sway the Herald from its duty as a public informant. And this policy had a reflex advantage for the other newspapers in the city.

When a scandal occurred in Jewish circles (and at the turn of the century growing Jewish influence in America produced many) influential Jews would swarm into the editorial offices to arrange for the suppression of the story. But the editors knew that the Herald would not suppress anything for anybody. What was the use of one paper suppressing if the others would not? So editors would say: We would be very glad to suppress this story, but the Herald will use it, so we'll have to do the same in self-protection. However, if you can get the Herald to suppress it, we will gladly do so, too.

But the Herald never succumbed, neither pressure of influence nor promise of business nor threats of loss availed. It printed the news.

There was a certain Jewish banker who periodically demanded that Bennett discharge the Herald's financial editor. The banker was in the business of disposing of Mexican bonds at a time when such bonds were least secure. Once when an unusually large number of bonds were to be unloaded on unsuspecting Americans, the Herald published the story of an impending Mexican revolution, which presently ensued. The banker frothed at the mouth and moved every influence he could to change the Herald's financial staff, but was not able to effect the change even of an office boy.

Once when a shocking scandal involved a member of a prominent family, Bennett refused to suppress it, arguing that if the episode had occurred in a family of any other race it would be published regardless of the prominence of the figures involved. The Jews of Philadelphia secured suppression there, but because of Bennett's unflinching stand there was no suppression in New York.

A newspaper is a business proposition. There are some matters it cannot touch without putting itself in peril of becoming a defunct concern. This is especially true since newspapers no longer receive their main support from the public but from the advertisers. The money the reader gives for the paper scarcely suffices to pay for the amount of white paper he receives. In this way, advertisers cannot be disregarded any more than the paper mills can be. As the most extensive advertisers in New York were, and are, the department stores, and as most department stores were, and are, owned by Jews, it comes logically that Jews often influence the news policies of the papers with whom they deal.

At this time, it had always been the burning ambition of the Jews to elect a Jewish Mayor of New York. They selected a time when the leading parties were disrupted to push forward their choice. The method they adopted was characteristic. They reasoned that the newspapers would not dare to refuse the dictum of the combined department store owners, so they drew up a "strictly confidential" letter which they sent to the owners of the New York newspapers, demanding support for the Jewish mayoralty candidate. The newspaper owners were in a quandary. For several days they debated how to act. All remained silent. The editors of the Herald cabled the news to Bennett who was abroad. Then it was that Bennett exhibited that boldness and directness of judgment which characterized him. He cabled back, "Print the letter." It was printed in the Herald, the arrogance of the Jewish advertisers was exposed, and non-Jewish New York breathed easier and applauded the action.

The Herald explained frankly that it could not support a candidate of private interests, because it was devoted to the interests of the public. But the Jewish leaders vowed vengeance against the Herald and against the man who dared to expose their game.

They had not liked Bennett for a long time, anyway. The Herald was the real "society paper" of New York, but Bennett had a rule that only the names of really prominent families should be printed. The stories of the efforts of newly-rich Jews to break into the Herald's society columns are some of the best that are told by old newspaper men.

The whole "war" culminated in a contention which arose between Bennett and Nathan Straus, a German-Jew whose business house was known under the name of "R. H. Macy and Company," Macy being the Scotsman who built up the business and from whose heirs Straus obtained it. Straus was something of a philanthropist in the ghetto, but the story goes that Bennett's failure to proclaim him as a philanthropist led to ill-feeling. A long newspaper-war ensued, the subject of which was the pasteurization of milk, a ingenuous discussion which no one took seriously, save Bennett and Straus.

The Jews, of course, took Straus' side. Jewish speakers made the welkin ring with laudation of Nathan Straus and maledictions upon James Bennett. Bennett was pictured in the vilest business of "persecuting" a noble Jew. It went so far that the Jews were able to put resolutions through the Board of Aldermen.

Long since, of course, Straus, a very heavy advertiser, had withdrawn every dollar's worth of his business from the Herald. And now the combined and powerful elements of New York Jewry gathered to deal a staggering blow at Bennett. The Jewish policy of "Dominate or Destroy" was at stake, and Jewry declared war.

As one man, the Jewish advertisers withdrew their advertisements. Their assigned reason was that the Herald was showing animosity against the Jews. The real purpose of their action was to crush an American newspaper owner who dared to be independent of them.

The blow they delivered was a staggering one. It meant the loss of 600,000 dollars a year. Any other newspaper in New York would have been put out of business by it. The Jews knew that and sat back, waiting for the downfall of the man they chose to consider their enemy.

But Bennett was a fighter. Besides, he knew the Jewish psychology probably better than any other non-Jew in

New York. He turned the tables on his opponents in a startling and unexpected fashion. The coveted positions in his papers had always been used by the Jews. These he immediately turned over to non-Jewish merchants under exclusive contracts. Merchants who had formerly been crowded into the back pages and obscure comers by the more opulent Jews, now blossomed forth full page in the most popular spaces. One of the non-Jewish merchants who took advantage of the new situation was John Wanamaker, whose large advertisements from that time forward were conspicuous in the Bennett newspapers. The Bennett papers came out with undiminished circulation and full advertising pages. The well-planned catastrophe did not, then occur. Instead, there was a rather comical surprise. Here were the non-Jewish merchants of America enjoying the choicest service of a valuable advertising medium, while the Jewish merchants were unrepresented. Unable to stand the spectacle of trade being diverted to non-Jewish merchants, the Jews came back to Bennett, requesting the use of his columns for advertising. The "boycott" had been hardest on the boycotters. Bennett received all who came, displaying no rancor. They wanted their old positions back, but Bennett said, No. They argued, but Bennett said, No. They offered more money, but Bennett said, No. The choice positions had been forfeited.

Bennett triumphed, but it proved a costly victory. All the time Bennett was resisting them, the Jews were growing more powerful in New York, and they were obsessed by the idea that to control journalism in New York meant to control the thought of the whole country.

The number of newspapers gradually diminished through combinations of publications. Adolph S. Ochs, a Philadelphia Jew, acquired the "New York Times." He soon made it into a great newspaper, but one whose bias is to serve the Jews. It is the quality of the Times as a newspaper that makes it so weighty as a Jewish organ. In this paper the Jews are persistently lauded, eulogized and defended, no such tenderness is granted other races.

Then Hearst came into the field, a dangerous agitator because he not only agitates the wrong things, but because he agitates the wrong class of people. He surrounded himself with a coterie of Jews, pandered to them, worked hand in glove with them, but never told the truth about them, never gave them away.

The trend toward Jewish control of the press set in strongly, and has continued that way ever since. The old names, made great by great editors and American policies, slowly dimmed.

A newspaper is founded either on a great editorial mind, in which event it becomes the expression of a powerful personality, or it becomes institutionalized as to policy and becomes a commercial establishment. In the latter event, its chances for continuing life beyond the lifetime of its founder are much stronger.

The Herald was Bennett, and with his passing it was inevitable that a certain force and virtue should depart out of it. Bennett, advancing in age, dreaded lest his newspaper, on his death should fall into the hands of the Jews. He knew that they regarded it with longing. He knew that they had pulled down, seized, and afterward built up many an agency that had dared to speak the truth about them, and boasted about it as a conquest for Jewry. Bennett loved the Herald as a man loves a child. He so arranged his will that the Herald should not fall into individual ownership, but that its revenues should flow into a fund for the benefit of the men who had worked to make the Herald what it was. He died in May, 1919. The Jewish enemies of the Herald, eagerly watchful, once more withdrew their advertising to force, if possible, the sale of the newspaper. They knew that if the Herald became a losing proposition, the trustees would have no course but to sell, notwithstanding Bennett's will.

But there were also interests in New York who were beginning to realize the peril of a Jewish press. These interests provided a sum of money for the Herald's purchase by Frank A. Munsey.

Then, to general astonishment, Munsey discontinued the gallant old paper, and bestowed its name as part of the name of the “New York Sun."

The newspaper managed by Bennett is extinct. The men who worked on it were scattered abroad in the newspaper field and, in the main, retired or dead.

Even though the Jews had not gained actual possession of the Herald, they at least succeeded in driving another non-Jewish newspaper from the field. They set about obtaining control of several newspapers, their victory is now complete. But the victory was a financial victory over a dead man. The moral victory, as well as the financial victory, remained with Bennett while he lived; the moral victory still remains with the Herald. It demonstrated what could be done by fearless, independent minds, supported by men who knew their work and loved it for its own sake. It demonstrated what could have been achieved had these men received the support of wide-awake, active, non-Jewish Americans. The Herald is immortalized as the last bulwark against Jewry in New York, in America. Today the Jews are more completely masters of the journalistic field in New York than they are in any capital in Europe. Indeed, in Europe there frequently emerges a newspaper that gives the real news of the Jews. There is none in New York.

And thus the situation will remain until Americans shake themselves from their long sleep, and look with steady eyes at the national situation. That look will be enough to show them all, and their very eyes will quail the oriental usurpers.

Chapter 16: The State of All-Judaan

Judaism is the most closely organized power on earth. It forms a State whose citizens are unconditionally loyal wherever they may be and whether rich or poor.

The name which is given to this State, which circulates among all the states, is “All-Judaan."

The means of power of the State of All-Judaan are capital and journalism, or money and propaganda.

All-Judaan is the only State that exercises world government; all the other States can and may exercise national government only.

The principal culture of All-Judaan is journalistic; the technical, scientific, literary performances of the modern Jew are throughout journalistic performances. They are due to the marvellous talent of the Jews for receptivity of others' ideas. Capital and Journalism are joined in the Press to create a political and spiritual medium of Jewish power.

The government of this State of All-Judaan is wonderfully organized. Paris was the first seat, but has now been moved to a lower place. Before 1914 London was its first, and New York its second capital. New York now supplants London.

All-Judaan is not in a position to have a standing army and navy, other states supply these for it. It was the British Fleet which guarded from hindrance the progress of all-Jewish world economy, or that part of it which depends on the sea. In return, All-Judaan assured Britain an undisturbed political and territorial rule.

Then New York supplanted London. The drift of the Jews in the 19th century, expedited into a great flood after World War I, made the United States the seat of Jewish power and influence. “America,” and her fleets, armies, citizens, takes the place of Britain as the "ruler of the world." It merely means that Jewry has moved from the British Empire to the American Continent.

All-Judaan is willing to entrust the government of various strips of the world to nationalistic governments; it only asks to control the governments. Judaism is passionately in favor of perpetuating nationalistic divisions for the Gentile world. For themselves, Jews never became assimilated with any nation. They are a separate people, always were and always will be.

All-Judaan's only quarrel with any nation occurs when that nation makes it impossible, or tries to make it so, for All-Judaan to control that nation's industrial and financial profits. It can make war, it can make peace; it can command anarchy in stubborn cases, it can restore order. It holds the sinews of world power in its hand and it apportions them among the nations in such ways as will best support All-Judaan's plan.

Controlling the world's source of news, All-Judaan can always prepare the minds of the people for its next move. The greatest exposure yet to be made is the way that news is manufactured and the way in which the mind of whole nations is molded for a purpose.

When the powerful Jew is at last traced and his hand revealed, then comes the ready cry of persecution and it echoes through the world press. The real cause of the persecution (which is the oppression of the people by the financial practices of the Jews) is never given publicity.

All-Judaan has its vice-governments in every capital. Having wreaked its vengeance on Germany, it will go forth to conquer other nations. Britain it already has. France and Russia it has long held. The United States, with its good-natured tolerance of all races, offered a promising field. All-Judaan is here. The scene of operations changes, but the Jew is the same throughout the centuries.

Signed:
Henry Ford Sr., founder of Ford Motor Company

A2.4 Henry Ford about Nilus in 1921

"The only statement I care to make about the Protocols is that they fit in with what is going on. They are sixteen years old, and they have fitted the world situation up to this time. They fit it now."
Indeed they do!
The word "Protocol" signifies a precis gummed on to the front of a document, a draft of a document, minutes of proceedings. In this instance, "Protocol" means minutes of the proceedings of the Meetings of the Learned Elders of Zion. These Protocols give the substance of addresses delivered to the innermost circle of the Rulers of Zion. They reveal the converted plan of action of the Jewish Nation developed through the ages and edited by the

Elders themselves up to date. Parts and summaries of the plan have been published from time to time during the centuries as the secrets of the Elders have leaked out. The claim of the Jews that the Protocols are forgeries is in itself an admission of their genuineness, for they never attempt to answer the facts corresponding to the threats which the Protocols contain, and, indeed, the correspondence between prophecy and fulfillment is too glaring to be set aside or obscured. This the Jews well know and therefore evade.

Captain A.H.M. Ramsay records in his classic, The Nameless War: "According to a letter published in "Plain English" (a weekly review published by the North British Publishing Co. and edited by the late Lord Alfred Douglas) on 3rd September, 1921:-

> "The Learned Elders have been in existence for a much longer period than they have perhaps suspected. My friend, Mr. L. D. van Valckert, of Amsterdam, has recently sent me a letter containing two extracts from the Synagogue at Mulheim. The volume in which they are contained was lost at some period during the Napoleonic Wars, and has recently come into Mr. van Valckert's possession. It is written in German, and contains extracts of letters sent and received by the authorities of the Mulheim Synagogue. The first entry he sends me is of a letter received:-

"In return for financial support will advocate admission of Jews to England: This however impossible while Charles living. Charles cannot be executed without trial, adequate grounds for which do not at present exist. Therefore advise that Charles be assassinated, but will have nothing to do with arrangements for procuring an assassin, though willing to help in his escape." 16th June, 1647. From O.C. (i.e. Oliver Cromwell), by Ebenezer Pratt.
In reply was dispatched the following:-
"Will grant financial aid as soon as Charles removed and Jews admitted. Assassination too dangerous. Charles shall be given opportunity to escape: His recapture will make trial and execution possible. The support will be liberal, but useless to discuss terms until trial commences." 12th July, 1647.To O.C. by E. Pratt.
Captain Ramsay quotes Isaac Disraeli, father of Benjamin, Earl of Beaconsfield, Britain's first Jewish Prime Minister, in his two volume "Life of Charles I", published in 1851:

> "The English Revolution under Charles I was unlike any preceding one . . . From that time and event we contemplate in our history the phases of revolution." There were many more to follow on similar lines, notably in France. In 1897 a further important clue to these mysterious happenings fell into Gentile hands in the shape of the Protocols of the Elders of Zion.

In that document we read this remarkable sentence: "Remember the French Revolution, the secrets of its preparation are well known to us for it was entirely the work of our hands." (See Protocol No. III, XIV).

In 1865 a certain Jewish Rabbi named Rzeichorn delivered a speech at Prague. It is a very accurate summary of many aspects of the Protocols which would come to light several decades later and was published eleven years later by Sir John Radcliff, who was assassinated shortly afterwards, giving testimony to the powers of the secret organisation of inner elite Jewry even then.

The presumption is strong that the Protocols were issued, or reissued, at the First Zionist Congress held at Basle in 1897 under the presidency of the Father of Modern Zionism, the late Theodore Herzl.

There has been recently published a volume of Herzl's "Diaries," a translation of some passages which appeared in the Jewish Chronicle of July 14, 1922. Herzl gives an account of his first visit to England in 1895, and his conversation with Colonel Goldsmid, a Jew brought up as a Christian, an officer in the English Army, and at heart a Jew Nationalist all the time. Goldsmid suggested to Herzl that the best way of expropriating the English aristocracy, and so destroying their power to protect the people of England against Jew domination, was to put excessive taxes on the land. Herzl thought this an excellent idea, and it is now to be found definitely embodied in Protocol VI!

The above extract from Herzl's diary is an extremely significant bit of evidence bearing on the existence of the

Jew World Plot and authenticity of the Protocols, but any reader of intelligence will be able from his own knowledge of recent history and from his own experience to confirm the genuineness of every line of them, and it is in the light of this living comment that all readers are invited to study Mr. Marsden's translation of this terribly inhuman document. Here is what Dr. Ehrenpreis, Chief Rabbi of Sweden, said in 1924, concerning the Protocols:

Long have I been well acquainted with the contents of the Protocols, indeed for many years before they were ever published in the Christian press. The Protocols of the Elders of Zion were in point of fact not the original Protocols at all, but a compressed extract of the same. Of the 70 Elders of Zion, in the matter of origin and of the existence of the original Protocols, there are only ten men in the entire world who know. I participated with Dr. Herzl in the first Zionist Congress which was held in Basle in 1897. Herzl was the most prominent figure at the Jewish World Congress. Herzl foresaw, twenty years before we experienced them, the revolution which brought the Great War, and he prepared us for that which was to happen. He foresaw the splitting up of Turkey, that England would obtain control of Palestine. We may expect important developments in the world.

And here is another very significant circumstance. The present successor of Herzl, as leader of the Zionist movement, Dr. Weizmann, quoted one of these sayings at the send-off banquet given to Chief Rabbi Hertz on October 6, 1920. The Chief Rabbi was on the point of leaving for HIS Empire tour of H.R.H., the Prince of Wales. And this is the "saying" of the Sages, which Dr. Weizmann quoted:

> "A beneficent protection which God has instituted in the life of the Jew is that He has dispersed him all over the world." (Jewish Guardian, Oct. 8, 1920.)

Now compare this with the last clause of but one of Protocol XI.

> "God has granted to us, His Chosen People, the gift of dispersion, and from this, which appears to all eyes to be our weakness, has come forth all our strength, which has now brought us to the threshold of sovereignty over all the world."

The remarkable correspondence between these passages proves several things. It proves that the Learned Elders exist. It proves that Dr. Weizmann knows all about them. It proves that the desire for a "National Home" in Palestine is only camouflage and an infinitesimal part of the Jew's real object. It proves that the Jews of the world have no intention of settling in Palestine or any separate country, and that their annual prayer that they may all meet "Next Year in Jerusalem" is merely a piece of their characteristic make-believe. It also demonstrates that the Jews are now a world menace, and that the Aryan races will have to domicile them permanently out of Europe.

www.ingramcontent.com/pod-product-compliance
Lightning Source LLC
Chambersburg PA
CBHW060305030426
42336CB00011B/946
* 9 7 8 1 6 4 5 5 0 4 9 8 6 *